Skymates

The Astrology of
Love, Sex and Intimacy

Skymates

Steven Forrest
Jodie Forrest

Grateful acknowledgment is made to the following:
From *Some Sort Of Epic Grandeur: The Life of F. Scott
Fitzgerald*, copyright © 1981 by Matthew J. Bruccoli, reprinted
by permission of Harcourt Brace Jovanovich, Inc. From *The
Theory of Celestial Influence* by Rodney Collin, used by
permission of Robinson Books Ltd. 1954/Shambala 1986.
Birth data for F. Scott Fitzgerald from *An Astrological Who's
Who*, copyright © 1972 by Mark Penfield, Arcane Publications,
York Harbor, Maine. Birth data for Dustin Hoffman from *The
Gauquelin Book of American Charts*, published in 1982.
Birth data for Zelda Fitzgerald from *Profiles of Women*
by Lois Rodden.

Cover designed by Maria Kay Simms

ISBN 0-917086-44-9

Printed in the United States of America

Published by ACS Publications
P.O. Box 34487
San Diego, CA 92163-4487

First Printing, February 1992
Second Printing, June 1992

Open eyes, open heart:
this book is dedicated to you.

The key to the understanding of sex is the knowledge that sexual energy is the finest and subtlest naturally produced by the human organism. This sexual energy can be turned to any purpose, can express itself on any level. It contains the potentiality of the highest forms of creation, and it also contains the possibility of destroying a man, and wrecking him, physically, morally, and emotionally. It can combine with his most bestial side, with criminal impulses of cruelty, hatred, and fear; or it can combine with his most refined aspirations and keenest sensibilities. And in either case it will immensely heighten the tendency to which it becomes attached...

By pure sex, the ordinary man may gain in a moment what the ascetic denies himself for years to achieve, what the saint prays a lifetime to feel. But this is only on the condition that he approaches it already free from fear, from violence, and from greed. And on condition also that he does not afterwards deny what he learns in sex, but on the contrary allows the understanding attained in sex to pass into all other sides of his life, mellowing, harmonizing, and enriching them also.

– Rodney Collin,
The Theory of Celestial Influence

Contents

Preface

Love is the wild card. That's true no matter how blessed or jinxed a partnership might seem from the astrological point of view.

Play that wild card and any partnership can be made to work. The fights may be glorious, the obstacles seemingly insurmountable. But with voluntary, intentional love binding the lovers together, the friction of personalities is no more life-threatening than a dose of poison ivy or a brush with a belligerent cat.

Without love no intimate relationship could survive a year–no matter how good the two birthcharts looked together. The two lovers would defend themselves against the shock of intimacy with an ice storm straight out of the arctic wastes of the human spirit.

Starry eyes and roses are not the point. Love, as we use the word here, is more than emotion, just as we human beings are more than emotion. Love is a commitment to honesty and caring, even when all the good feelings have vanished for a while. It is a commitment to shared growth, a commitment to forgiveness, to patience, and to humility.

This is a book about that kind of love. It is a book about *synastry*–the astrology of intimacy, sex, and partnership. The subject is an ancient one, but we will not make the ancient mistake of ignoring the awesome, life-shaping power of adult love. We will not slip into the fatal, demeaning error of assuming that human beings are robots, or that our relationship experiences are preprogrammed by Venus and Mars, Mercury and Saturn.

This freedom of which we write is no theory; it's as real as the earth and stars. How do we know that? Simply because Jodie and I have played the wild card in our own lives. We needed to.

My coauthor, Jodie Forrest, has Venus in Pisces. I have Venus in Sagittarius. The two planets make what astrologers call a square aspect, which is usually interpreted as a source of dreadful conflict. Since we're married and Venus is the traditional "Goddess of Love," any discord here is ominous. Theoretically we might as well pawn our wedding rings and start composing ads for the "Personals" column.

Why? What could be so unnerving about a ninety-degree angle between two planets? The (mis)fortune-teller would say, quite correctly, that with Venus in Sagittarius I am attracted to Sagittarian qualities in a woman–adventuresomeness, indepen-dence, a fiery spirit. Without that kind of rough-and-tumble playfulness, I could never sustain romantic feelings–at least not for any longer than it takes to flush the offending hormones out of my bloodstream. Jodie, on the other hand, experiences love in an utterly different way. With her Venus in Pisces, she's drawn to mystical, sensitive men. What sharing a hard beat to windward in a sailboat is to me, a candle-lit evening listening to music is to her. So our marriage is theoretically doomed.

The horror of that kind of astrology is that it is nearly true. The square aspect between our Venuses has been the source of some painful conflicts for Jodie and me. If a traditional astrologer had caught us on a bad day a few years ago and told us, "Frankly, you guys don't have a chance," we might have believed him.

Instead, we played the wild card. Driven by love and guided by astrology, we've worked on the issues that our Venus configura-tion represents. We won't turn this book into a comic strip by making giddy claims about how "astrology saved our marriage." That would be ridiculous. Love saved our marriage, and contin-ues to save it. But astrology helped us–and it can help you too.

How? By exorcising the demons of misunderstanding. Just being able to *talk* about Venus in Sagittarius and Venus in Pisces has been an enormous aid to Jodie and me. The words themselves are helpful, simply as a way of getting a handle on a lot of complex emotions. Without that knowledge, it's easy to slip into a narrow, contracted state in which each one of us perceives the other as making unreasonable demands or behaving in incomprehensible ways. With our basic needs unmet, rage and insecurity take over. Our positions become increasingly adversarial and polarized, and our love evaporates.

Enter astrology. Suddenly we have a wise counselor, an all-knowing third party who loves both of us with supernatural clarity, insight, and caring. "Steve, these are Jodie's needs. She's not trying to hurt you. She's not making pointless, melodramatic demands. She's begging for oxygen, that's how basic this Pisces stuff is to her."

Experience has taught me to trust astrology with the same confidence I feel for other physical laws–like gravity. So I listen to this wise counselor. I make adjustments in my behavior. No great Christ-like sacrifices: just adjustments. I ask Jodie to go for a walk with me. I put a tape in our stereo, dim the lights, and lie down with her for an hour. I override my Capricornish tendency toward solitude and make an effort to tell her of my fears and dreams. I feed her Piscean Venus, in other words. And like magic, the scales fall from my eyes; I see the woman I married.

Of course, love is a two-way street. Since our marriage Jodie has started swimming a mile every other day. She's enrolled in a sailing class. She bundles up at night to go out and help me track down distant galaxies with our telescope. Not all of that behavior comes automatically to her, but she wants our marriage to work, and she understands that I have Venus in Sagittarius– to share love, we must share adventurous experiences.

Committed love is never easy. Perhaps, in this age of changing sex roles and collapsing families, it's harder than ever before. Astrology is not the answer, any more than psychotherapy is the answer. It's only a support, an ally. But it has helped Jodie and me. Maybe it can help you too.

No relationship will be pigeonholed in this book. For far too long, astrology has been used mechanically, unimaginatively, as if people were not capable of changing. Jodie and I are astrologers, but more importantly, we're lovers. We've got front-row seats on a living example of love in the twentieth century. Sometimes we're horrible to each other, sometimes we're wonderfully caring and sensitive. Most of the time we're bouncing around between the extremes. Sound familiar? Probably. We're not unusual in any of this. If our story can't be put in a box labeled "good" or "bad," I doubt that yours can either.

Our purpose in writing is not to make judgments on anyone's relationships; it is only to share what astrology has taught us about love and how to help it along. In this book, partnerships are painted in colors of possibility and living change, never in tones of entrapment. Relationships are represented in the same way that the individual personality is portrayed in the first two volumes of this series, *The Inner Sky* and *The Changing Sky*: as unpredictable explorations into the miraculous, uncertain realm of life.

Although much of what follows is directed toward understanding and supporting committed sexual relationships, its logic applies just as effectively to any kind of human interaction: family, business, friendship, even old animosities. The principles are the same, although in sexual love everything runs at a higher voltage and that makes the principles stand out more clearly.

Much of what follows in these pages is Jodie's gift to me and perhaps mine to her. I appreciate her knowledge of astrology and her skill with language. This is her first book, but she's not simply following in my footsteps. Far from it. She's an independent-minded Aquarian, and she sees through her own eyes. Perhaps you've seen her work in the astrological journals, *Welcome to Planet Earth* or Dell's *Horoscope*.

Most of all, I appreciate Jodie's feminine experience and woman's voice: Without those, this book would inevitably be too deeply rooted in the male viewpoint–a limitation I'd have a hard time escaping on my own.

So join us now for another astrological journey, not into the individual psyche, but rather into that mysterious, luminous region that springs into being whenever two people dare to open their hearts and love.

– STEVEN FORREST
Chapel Hill, North Carolina

ACKNOWLEDGMENTS

Our gratitude to the following people. Some have shared their skills or their insights with us. Others have shared their lives. Either way, their gifts have enriched these pages.

Alison Acker, Melanie Jackson, Marc Penfield, Tom Kenyon, Carol Cole, Rosales Wynne-Roberts, Laurel Goldman, Merrily Neill, Rebecca Dalton, Malcolm Groome, Marian Starnes, Leslie Cheeseman, Barbara Alpert, and astrologers Linda Curtiss, Michael Thurman, Jenovefa Knoop, and Maritha Pottenger.

A special thanks to the following couples, our unsung coauthors, for their generosity, friendship, and honesty. Sinikka Laine and Cyril Beveridge, Ed and Sylvia Kohus, Phyllis Smith-Hansen and Paul Hansen, Mary Pope Osborne and Will Osborne, Jeff Hamilton and Maryska Bigos, Dave and Donna Gulick, Olivia and Bob Giddings, Michael Rank and Sara Romweber, Ruth and John Rocchio, Bill and Eileen Chambers, Simcha Weinstein and Sara Gresko, Sue and Tommy Field, Dick and Bunny Forrest, Elmo and Barbara Jensen, Bernie Ashman and Beth Green, Carolyn and Richard Max, Tom and Jan McCall, Tom and Pam Kenyon, and Ben and Sandy Dyer.

Our gratitude as well to the other members of the Alpha Lyra Astrological Guild: Bernie Ashman, Lee Glenn, Carolyn Kane Max, Randy Wasserstrom, and Simcha Weinstein.

Finally, our profound thanks to the thousands of people who have shared their lives, their loves, and their birthcharts with us over the years. Without them, nothing.

Part One

THE BIG PICTURE

CHAPTER ONE

MAGIC OR MURDEROUS MYTHOLOGY?

Nothing strips us so naked. Nothing is quicker to reveal the angel we hide behind our eyes, and nothing is so quick to unmask our private madnesses. Who has not been lifted high by love? Who has not felt the world change in a moment of secret tenderness? And who has not been ripped open by love and left bleeding and alone, wide-eyed at four in the morning?

People speak of "fear of intimacy" as if it were some kind of modern disease. That's lunacy. I've never met anyone with enough brains to fill a teaspoon who didn't fear intimacy. It's dangerous. It's an awesome force. Once we've been around the mulberry bush a few times, we learn that and usually have scars to prove it. Kids don't know it, and maybe they serve to remind us of some innocent state of grace. But for most of us, in matters of love, it's "once burned, twice smart," and maybe that's not so bad. Maybe that hesitation has something to do with wisdom. Certainly it has to do with experience.

Yet most of us come back. Love draws us like a magnet, and only those whom love has battered into hopelessness see that return as a kind of madness. We return to love for the same reasons we hesitate: wisdom and experience. Once we've allowed ourselves to love, whatever the outcome, we're hooked. We have realized that little else can give us even half the joy. And perhaps if we're reflective, we've also learned that no force can so radically accelerate our long march toward sanity and inner peace.

On rare occasions, when love goes bad, the fault lies squarely on the shoulders of one person. One lover might simply be too irresponsible, too selfish, too damaged, or too confused about sex to make that kind of leap right then, and the other lover is left hanging. But that's rare. Most of the time, when love goes bad, we find two sets of fingerprints on the murder weapon.

Why? Part of the answer comes when we take a minute to contemplate a simple fact: most of us spend time with a lot more people than we marry. Chew on that, and it's not long before we realize that the vast majority of our relationships are "doomed to fail"–although "doomed to fail" is perhaps an overly grim prognosis. Certainly we learn from most of our courtship experiences. But the critical idea is that not every man or woman is right for us. We learn quickly enough to turn away from the ones with "poison" written in neon letters across their foreheads. But that still leaves a lot of possibilities, and sometimes we're halfway to the altar before we realize that the magic is falling victim to the craziness. Sometimes we're a few years beyond the altar.

Another part of the answer–and the part that forms the soul of this book–is that no matter how good our intentions and no matter how inspired our choice of partners, relationships are still perhaps the greatest challenge life will ever offer us. They push us right to the limits of our growth. They even make nuclear physics seem simple by comparison, as I suspect many a loving nuclear physicist will attest.

To make love work in our lives, we need help. In fact, we need all the help we can get. Astrology cannot create love. What astrology can do is serve as an ally in the process of loving.

The gift astrology offers is simply one of clear seeing. It serves as a wise third party, mirroring each lover's viewpoint with neutrality and evolutionary insight. Used sensitively, it does not pontificate and judge. If any astrologer ever exhorts you to "flee this man before he destroys you," then find another astrologer. That's not how the astrological ally operates. Instead, it seeks only to promote mutual understanding.

Where there are irresolvable dilemmas, astrology can often suggest adult compromises. Where there are basic harmonies, astrology can help you fan those flames with concrete strategies for joy and play. Where your dictionaries contain the same words with different definitions, astrology can often straighten out the tangled lines of communication.

If you are single, astrology can help you understand what kinds of people best suit your needs in the long haul, and it can warn you about fantasies that leave you with nothing but empty hurt. If you are currently in love, astrology can help you nurture those feelings, counseling gentleness here, force there, self-scrutiny in this area, hard questions for your partner in that one, slowly guiding you as you mold that love into a treasure.

All that, astrology can do. Loving, you must do for yourself.

Half the Truth

Romance is dangerous. That's a fact most of us can affirm from our own experience. But there are those who take an even darker view. Many think that romantic feelings are a kind of mental disorder. They point out that that kind of love often takes an otherwise sane individual and turns the person into a psychopath: jealous, insecure, possessive, and monomaniacally consumed with one other person, as if that single individual held the key to all the happiness and meaning in the universe.

Sound familiar? Well, if it's any comfort to you, I've been there too. What makes us act that way?

The Jungian analyst Robert Johnson, in his book, *We: Understanding the Psychology of Romantic Love* (Harper and Row, NY, 1984), offers some convincing arguments on the subject. His thesis, which he develops through insightful analysis of a twelfth century chivalric myth, is that romantic love is a relatively new invention, unique to Western civilization, and that, so far as healthiness goes, it's generally up there with PCBs and spent nuclear fuel. His notion, in a nutshell, is that with the collapse of the absolute authority of the church, our ancestors took a lot of emotional needs that had always been satisfied through religion and attempted to satisfy them through "courtly love"–the endless pining of a knight for an unattainable lady, usually married to someone else. Johnson implies that the "unattainable lady" was a pretty fair psychological substitute for God–until the knight got sick of pining for her and managed to get himself invited into her bed. Then the trouble began. The "perfect woman" soon proved to be a monkey like the rest of us.

Think about it: when you imagine the ideal sexual relationship for yourself, what kinds of experiences strike you? Ecstasy, mystical communion, psychic or extrasensory understandings, a sense of ultimate meaning–spiritual experiences, in other words. The stuff we used to expect from God, not from a man or woman. And that's a lot to ask of a monkey.

Johnson suggests that these unrealistic expectations, fueled by the Hollywood myth-machines, have led inevitably to pain and disillusionment for everyone–but that these expectations have become so much a part of our world view that they persist and continue to damage people. He compares our Western notions of marriage unfavorably with those current in India and Japan. He describes marriages in these cultures as often more loving and caring than what we see here, but without the mythology. He then points out how we, with our spiraling divorce rate and our soap operatic lives, arrogantly dismiss those kinds of marriages as "unromantic."

We is a powerful book, and to me at least its key insights have the ring of truth. We expect love to work wonders in our lives, and by the time we reach our thirtieth birthdays, most of us have been disastrously disappointed more than once.

How does all this relate to astrology? Very directly. Through the birthchart, you can often glimpse the silhouette of your soulmate in clear and explicit terms. Getting the message is easy. What's hard is knowing what to do with your soulmate once you've found each other.

Soulmate! The very word lies at the core of all the romantic mythology that has ever existed. The one true love with whom you are destined to be united! The one who fits you like a key fits a lock! Robert Johnson, and anyone who understands his work, must cringe when they hear the word. Let them cringe. The word "soulmate" is too beautiful and too elemental a part of our sanity to dismiss. Without it, one more psychologically essential piece of magic goes down the drain. The problem with the word is that for far too long we've let teenagers and Gothic novelists define it.

The Other Half of the Truth

There's a wise woman from northern Idaho who was kind enough to befriend me some years ago. Once I heard a tape of a psychic reading she had done for a couple I know. In it, she said, "You two are soulmates." After a dramatic pause she continued, "And soulmates often kill each other."

Just what does it mean to keep company with a soulmate? The first step is to forget the idea that time spent with a soulmate is some kind of blissful, orgasmic dream. That may be part of the process, but the core of the idea is that in a soulmate we meet someone who is capable of helping us alter our fundamental nature–helping us alter our **soul**, in other words. And that can make a ride on a roller coaster look like teatime with your maiden aunt.

Johnny plays lead guitar in a rock band. He's a natural musician but has never really pushed himself to explore the limits of his talent. He's been on the road for ten years and is increasingly reliant on alcohol, drugs, and cynicism to get him through the day.

Into Johnny's life comes Terry, his soulmate. As is often the case with such meetings, they react to each other quickly, moving into a sexual relationship. The honeymoon is short-lived. Terry sees what Johnny is doing to himself. As his soulmate, she also sees what he could be. She keys into his nature in such a way that his "decadent rock star" game suddenly seems awkward to both of them, little more than a thin defensive posture. Terry's very being seems to confront Johnny, challenging him–is this the best of what you are? Is this the highest truth you know?

In the Hollywood version of the story, Johnny obediently cleans up his act, marries Terry, hailing her as his savior, and they blissfully drive off to the suburbs in their late-model Chevy, living happily ever after.

In real life, they have one hell of a fight.

In real life, that fight brings up such defensiveness in both of them that Johnny and Terry very likely break up–at least for a while. Something deep inside Johnny senses that if he stays with Terry, the life he knows will be irremediably changed. Profound fears, locked behind elaborate defense mechanisms, loom large and demand battle. Brittle, comforting lies come crashing down.

Psychological "devil's bargains" he made back in childhood suddenly come up for review.

Why should Johnny vex himself with all this trauma? Is this woman really worth the trouble she's causing? Those are good questions, and ones he no doubt asks. Lena conveniently appears on the scene, and Johnny finds her overwhelmingly attractive. He has a cup of coffee with Terry and solemnly tells her that her nature is just "too intense" for him, and besides, Lena accepts him as he is. They both agree that their affair was a "learning experience," but that it's finished.

Why is Terry so quick to agree with Johnny's analysis? For the same reason he was so quick to produce it–she's terrified too. Just as with him, half of what she is has never been revealed. A soulmate relationship is never a one-way street. In this kind of human love, saviors always come in pairs.

Terry is a poet, and a fine one. She writes grown-up love poetry–poems of love and hate, passion and fear. But no one knows that about her. Her poetry is a dark secret. The few poems she's published appeared under a pseudonym. Long ago Terry learned to keep her feelings hidden. She has always been the one who takes care of other people, and that pattern goes right back to her childhood, where circumstances forced her to play the role of parent to her younger siblings. Being the rescuer is comfortable; equality and emotional nakedness are experiences she's never known, and they frighten her. Johnny, her soulmate, sees right through that mask.   When his eyes lock on to hers, something deep inside her gets profoundly uncomfortable. "Here's a man who could flush me out of hiding. Here's one who already seems to know about my secrets–not only my poetry, but also my hunger, my possessiveness, my need to remain in control. I'm getting out of here!"

What happens? No way to know. People write their own scripts. Maybe Johnny and Terry part ways, the potential of their soul-bond left untapped.   Maybe they stay together–and still leave the potential of their soul-bond untapped. How? Perhaps Johnny remains the perennial child, playing "bad boy" to Terry's "martyred mommy." Together they methodically build a marriage in which eyes never meet, sex occurs only in the dark, and a private joke is made out of what they mockingly describe as other couples' "growth experiences."

Those are sad choices, but they are available. How often have you seen love blow up in an explosion that was more smoke than fire? How many zombie marriages have you seen?

The alternative, for Terry and Johnny and the rest of us, is to recognize that if love is going to heal us, it must sometimes take us to the limits of our endurance first. Honesty, courage, humility, trust, forgiveness–the best of what we are–must hurl explosions of light into the darkest, most painful, most embarrassing corners of our psyches.

There's joy too, of course. This is not a pessimistic book you're holding in your hands. Quite the opposite. But couples often part nowadays, and it's rarely because of excessive joy. When soul touches soul, we experience perhaps the deepest happiness we'll ever know. We also experience growth, and it's there that we encounter those far limits of our potential as men and women.

Johnny and Terry, you and me–we're all free to do as we please. Astrology is no panacea for the hurt that love sometimes gives us. The panacea, if there is one, lies in the radical development of those virtues–honesty, courage, forgiveness, patience–that make ongoing love a possibility for us.

What if Johnny and Terry, after their breakup, find themselves drifting back together again? What if they realize that some invisible cord of love links their spirits–but that their fearful games are gnawing at it like a rabid dog?

Perhaps in their confusion, and with their hearts and minds open, they approach a modern humanistic astrologer. What happens? Johnny might learn that he is a fourth house Pisces with Sagittarius rising. Translated, he would learn that his entire identity is locked into a magical, mystical realm of imagination and creativity, but that as a result, his ego never quite crystallized. He would learn that people such as himself can serve as precious oracles for the rest of us–if they don't ruin that potential with dissipation, posturing, and escapism. He would learn that his Sagittarian Ascendant gives him a breezy, colorful "gypsy mask" to hide behind, which is just fine, as long as he doesn't start believing his own press releases.

Terry would hear that she's a Cancer with Capricorn on the Ascendant and the Moon in Virgo. To use the formula we introduced in *The Inner Sky*, she's the Mother (Cancer Sun) with the soul of the Servant (Virgo Moon) wearing the mask of the

Prime Minister–hence her urge to protect herself from true intimacy with Johnny by hiding behind the role of his guru, mother, or psychotherapist.

With Johnny and Terry sitting there looking into each other's eyes, that astrologer would lay the cards on the table. They could read their scripts like automatons in the ancient melodrama, Johnny playing the tragic rogue, Terry the doomed angel who loves him come what may. Or they could drop those games, face each other like three-dimensional adults, and help each other grow.

That astrologer could go a lot further. Wisdom and sensitivity artificially boosted by the two birthcharts, he or she could x-ray the bond that joins Terry and Johnny, checking it for any kind of interactive weakness, and in many cases offering practical solutions and supportive, positive interpretations of their dilemmas. Johnny, for example, has a fourth house Piscean need for occasional periods of absolute, uncontested privacy, in order to cultivate his creativity and spiritual life. If he doesn't get those periods alone, then he's likely to become withdrawn and moody, inclined toward staring at the television. Terry needs to learn that when Johnny asks for some space, it has nothing to do with her character or with their relationship, and she doesn't need to feel threatened.

 Terry, on the other hand, needs a bit more orderliness, predictability, and emotional support in her life than Johnny might be instinctively inclined to provide. That goes with the territory of Cancer, Virgo, and Capricorn–the signs that figure so prominently in her psychological makeup. Situations that would seem merely adventuresome and interesting to Johnny feel dangerously out of control to Terry. One taste, and she clams up, hiding behind one of her many parental masks. If she is going to feel safe enough to reveal the best of what is–the poet inside her– then she's going to need a lot of reassurance first.

Johnny is Johnny, and it would be wrong to ask him to mold his life around Terry's insecurities. But with the astrologer's assistance, he could perhaps recognize those insecurities for the first time and treat his soulmate with more sensitivity. For her sake? Yes, of course; that's in the nature of love. But also for his own sake: life is simply more pleasant with a sane woman than with a mad one.

Going further into the charts, taking in planets, houses, and other technical details that we'll be developing later on in the book, the astrologer might strike a vein of gold: Terry and Johnny might love to garden together, for example. That shared work might forge a powerful link in the chain of pleasures that binds them together–and without those pleasures, nobody but a masochist is going to last long in a relationship with a soulmate. Figuring out ways to emphasize and support the natural joys of the partnership is just as essential as negotiating solutions to the inevitable conflicts.   In some ways, it might even be more important, since for most of us, it's joy that keeps us working on a relationship, not the abstract promise of growth.

This then is the territory of synastry–the astrology of partnership. As you can see, our aim is an active, dynamic one. In this book you will learn more than how to issue postmortems on failed relationships or come up with astrological reasons for why a particular bond is working. Far more excitingly, you will learn how to use astrology to actively intervene in the process of loving, helping yourself and your loved ones experience improved communication, deeper happiness, personal growth, better sex, and clean, fair fights that tear walls down rather than build them up.

Technically, you will probably not find this book terribly demanding.   The procedures we introduce here are far less complex, for example, than those described in the previous volume of this series, *The Changing Sky* But the personal questions this book raises will very likely push you into emotionally explosive territory.

Fortunately astrology can also help guide you through those explosive places. It can calm you, counsel you, lift you above the hormonal fog. If astrology seems a bit technical or abstract at first, stick with it. There is nothing mysterious about it. Astrology is just life, translated into a kind of symbolic shorthand. It's just a craft, with clear-cut procedures and techniques. To use it, you don't need anything that you don't already have between your ears. In a few hours you'll learn enough to help yourself. With a few weeks of effort you'll acquire enough skill to begin helping others.

If you've read either of the first two books in this series, I think you'll find this one a breeze by comparison.   You've already learned the language. In that case you might want to skip the

next chapter, which is a crash course for beginners. If you've never paid any attention to astrology before, please pay close attention to the next few pages. You'll need that knowledge to make sense of the material that follows.

CHAPTER TWO

INSTANT ASTROLOGY

Never explored astrology before? Then this chapter is for you. A grand tour of all the basic symbolism–squeezed into a few pages–is all you'll need to follow the rest of this book.

That's one of the beauties of astrology–its simplicity. But don't let that simplicity fool you. Even though all the essentials can be expressed in a handful of elementary ideas, a lifetime of endless fascination can pass as you discover all their nuances and subtleties. Isaac Newton never got to the bottom of the astrological well. Neither did Pythagoras or Plato or Galileo or Carl Jung. Yet all started with the same raw material: Thirty-four basic astrological symbols and some connective tissue. Here we briefly survey that territory. If you'd like a deeper understanding of these ideas, try *The Inner Sky* or *The Changing Sky*, or any of the fine basic books included in the reading list at the end of this volume.

Signs, Planets, and Houses

Astrology is not one single system of symbols. It is three: signs, planets, and houses. Each set of symbols is separate and distinct. Each serves a unique purpose. Learning to keep them untangled is the first step in any orderly, effective approach to astrological interpretation.

Briefly, signs represent a set of twelve psychological processes, each with a clear goal, appropriate resources–and a few classic pitfalls. Aries, for example, represents the process of **seeking courage**. Its central resources are enthusiasm and **love of adventure**. But if the process goes sour, then instead of courage, we observe pointless explosiveness and temper.

Planets, quite distinct from signs, represent a map of the mind. Every one of us, for example, has the capacity for reason. Every has the capacity for feeling. Many times we find it useful to divide those two categories of experience. "On one hand, I think I should do this; on the other hand, my feelings tell me to do that." Planets work exactly the same way, except that they divide the mind into ten pieces of mental circuitry, not two. There's a planet for reason (Mercury) and one for feeling (the Moon), but there   are also planets for many other functions, such as self-discipline, assertiveness, and individuation. Everybody's got all ten; they just work differently in each of us.

Houses represent life's basic arenas. There are twelve of them, and each symbolizes a territory we can enter and explore. There's a "house of marriage," for example. There's also a "house of career." Some of the houses represent internal rather than external territories–there's a "house of the unconscious," for example.

Put signs, planets, and houses together, and they give us humanity's oldest and most evocative map of the mind. Here's a very simple way of keeping them straight: planets answer the question "What?" What part of the mind are we talking about? Ego development? Rational thought? Mate selection? Signs take us a step farther by answering the questions "Why?" and "How?' What is that planet's goal? What is its hidden agenda? How can that goal be realized? Houses complete the picture by asking us the final question, "Where?" In what part of life will we observe the most characteristic release of that planet-sign dynamic? Will it be in creativity, in love affairs, in the professional life?

Here's an example of how all this works in practice. Dustin Hoffman was born in Los Angeles on August 8, 1937, at 5:07 PM PST. That gives him the planet Mars in the sign Sagittarius late in his tenth house. What can that mean? Think like this: Mars is the what. In this case, we are talking about assertiveness. Everyone has assertiveness issues in his or her birthchart–what makes Dustin Hoffman unique? His assertiveness is motivated by the logic of the sign Sagittarius–that sign supplies the why and the how. In this case we see that his Mars is developmentally motivated by an urge to seek new horizons or to break up the familiar routines (Sagittarian goals). Where will we see the most characteristic expression of this desire? In his tenth house–the traditional "house of career."

Dustin Hoffman has apparently made a strong, self-aware response to his Mars configuration . He has shown eagerness to explore new, controversial, unfamiliar territories in his career. As an actor he has resisted Hollywood's tendency to typecast its stars–as anyone who has seen his hilarious portrayal of a woman in *Tootsie* will affirm.

Did Dustin Hoffman have any choice in the matter, or was he simply "programmed" by astrological forces? That is perhaps the single most important question any student of astrology could ask. Astrologers are divided: traditionally, one's "fate" could be read in the stars. Many astrologers still think that way. We disagree. To us, an individual's willpower and imagination play a huge role in determining how the astrological forces actually manifest. A modern astrologer rarely speaks of "destiny" in rigid terms. Dustin Hoffman–and everybody else–has a choice. He's apparently risen to the evolutionary challenge and done well with his tenth-house Sagittarian Mars. He could have done otherwise. His freedom includes the right to "chicken out" (Mars failure), abandon his expansive principles (Sagittarian failure), and wind up in some kind of boring, irritating work that has nothing to do with him (tenth-house failure). We should credit Dustin Hoffman's courage, not his birthchart, that he has accomplished so much.

For easy reference as you progress through this book, we are including an overview of the signs, planets, and houses in tabular form. This is shorthand, to put it mildly. People have literally written books about each one of these symbols. Ultimately they are all sufficiently multidimensional to deserve that kind of in-depth treatment. But if you're a beginner, these tables will get you started. As you read on and watch the symbols put to practical use, you'll learn much more.

Once again, these tables are not meant to be exhaustive. You can think of them as a kind of Berlitz phrase book in a foreign language. They'll give you a convenient framework; as you read

TABLE 1: THE PLANETS

Planet	Glyph	Function	Dysfunction
Sun	☉	Identity Formation Vitality	Selfishness Laziness
Moon	☽	Subjectivity Emotion	Moodiness
Mercury	☿	Intelligence Communication	Nervousness Worry
Venus	♀	Relaxation Relationship Formation	Vanity Manipulativeness Dissipation
Mars	♂	Assertiveness Territoriality	Rage (Self) Destruction
Jupiter	♃	Faith Enthusiasm	Overextension Pomposity
Saturn	♄	Self-discipline Reality-testing	Depression Unresponsiveness
Uranus	♅	Individualization	Eccentricity Rebelliousness
Neptune	♆	Self-transcendence Imagination	Confusion Escapism
Pluto	♀ ♇	Altruism Truthfulness	Cynicism Meaninglessness

TABLE 2: THE SIGNS

Sign	Glyph	Aim	Strategy	Shadow
Aries	♈	Courage	Adventure	Rage
Taurus	♉	Serenity	Silence Simplicity	Laziness
Gemini	♊	Openness	Experience	Chaos
Cancer	♋	Caring	Nurturance	Invisibility "Mothering"
Leo	♌	Joy	Creativity Play	Melodrama Self-importance
Virgo	♍	Perfection	Analysis Precision	Fussiness Self-doubt
Libra	♎	Balance	Aesthetics Courtesy	Indecision Inauthenticity
Scorpio	♏	Depth	Introspection Honesty	Moodiness
Sagittarius	♐	Understanding	Expansion Risk	Foolishness
Capricorn	♑	Accomplishment	Self-discipline Integrity	Mechanization
Aquarius	♒	Individuality	Questioning Authority	Alienation
Pisces	♓	Self-transcendence	Compassion Meditation	Confusion

TABLE 3: THE HOUSES

House	Traditional Name	Territory
1	House of Personality	Personal Style; "the Mask"
2	House of Money	Resources (material and psychological)
3	House of Communication	Exchange of Information
4	House of Home	Personal Roots; the deep self
5	House of Children	Self-expression; play
6	House of Servants	Responsibilities; craftsmanship
7	House of Marriage	Intimacy; commitment
8	House of Death	Instincts: Sexuality, Morality, the "Occult"
9	House of Journeys	Expansion; breaking routines
10	House of Honor	Profession; mission; social status
11	House of Friends	Personal goals; people who support them
12	House of Troubles	Self-transcendence; release

further, your familiarity with the symbols will grow rapidly.
There's a good reason for that–you already know all this material.
It's just life, translated into a kind of supercondensed code. You
don't have to learn the ideas; those you know right now. All you
need to learn is the code itself, and that's not so hard once you
practice for a little while.

Aspects

There's another link in the astrological chain: aspects. These
are simply geometric angles formed between planets. Long ago,
astrologers realized that certain particular angles were critical,
suggesting powerful interactions between planets, interactions
in which one planet flavored the meaning of the other. These
interactions can take many forms. Sometimes two planets
appear to be "best friends," helping each other and sharing
common goals.   Other times, the relationship between two
planets can be more problematic. They seem to be "natural
enemies."

We still read about "good" aspects and "bad" aspects, but those
ideas are silly ones and are gradually fading from the astrologer's
vocabulary. The so-called good aspects are better described as
"harmonious"–and that doesn't always mean "good." Two wild
teenagers can be in perfect harmony with each other about
"borrowing" that shiny red Corvette for an hour or two. Their
accord still doesn't make stealing that car a good idea. Maybe a
third friend introduces a "bad aspect," pointing out to them that

TABLE 4: ASPECTS

Aspect	Glyph	Separation	Orb	Interactive Process
Conjunction	☌	0°	7°	Fusion; synthesis
Sextile	✶	60°	5°	Stimulation; excitation
Square	☐	90°	7°	Friction; clashing
Trine	△	120°	7°	Harmonization; enhancement
Opposition	☍	180°	7°	Tension; polarization

another word for their proposed joyride is "Grand Theft Auto" and mentioning that he saw a police officer climb out of that very Corvette just an hour ago. These so-called bad aspects are disharmonious; but they often breed caution and sound judgment.

One more idea: although aspects are technically very precise angles, they tolerate a certain amount of slushiness. We call that slushiness the "orbs of the aspect." For example, a "square" is technically an angle of ninety degrees. In practice, a pair of planets separated by ninety-five degrees still interact the same way. In the table on page 19, we give our suggestions for these orbs, but please don't take them rigidly. Aspects never simply "turn on" or "turn off." They build gradually in intensity, then slowly fade out. The orbs we suggest are no more than rules of thumb to help get you off to a sound start.

Table 4 summarizes the action of the major aspects. If you'd like deeper understanding, you might want to read Chapter Nine of *The Inner Sky*.

Here's an example of how aspects work in practice. We've already looked at Dustin Hoffman's tenth-house Sagittarian Mars. He also has Saturn in early Aries in his second house. It makes a trine aspect to his Mars. How do we analyze this interaction?

Start by grasping the significance of each planet. We got a handle on Mars a few paragraphs back, so that leaves Saturn. What part of Dustin Hoffman's mental circuitry are we discussing? Saturn–his capacity for self-discipline and for adjustment to living in the real world. What motivates his Saturn? What is Saturn's hidden agenda, and what are its resources? The sign, Aries, provides our answer. At the highest level, he is using self-discipline (Saturn) to learn courage (Aries's aim). His resources in that process are a sense of adventure and a taste for risk (Aries material). Where will we see the most characteristic behavioral expression of this Saturn-in-Aries energy? In the second house: that is, in Hoffman's efforts to gain self-confidence, to prove himself to himself (second-house terrain). In plain English, if Dustin Hoffman is to feel good about himself (second-house), he must work in a self-disciplined, perfectionistic way (Saturn) and be willing to take risks there (Aries).

Now this Saturn function is in a supportive, harmonious **trine** aspect with his exploratory Mars in the "house of career"–and the two planets clearly share common ground and common goals. As one prospers, so does the other–but since each is inclined to mammoth outlays of energy, we also see the potential danger of emotional or physical burnout. He might, for example, be working near his limits, determined to take a much-needed break as soon as possible. On the eve of that vacation he's offered an exciting, challenging acting opportunity–starting tomorrow. His tenth-house Sagittarian Mars might find that offer irresistible, and his second-house Arian Saturn might give him the discipline and drive he needs to complete the project. But what happened to that vacation? And how long can his mind and body endure that kind of stress?

The Birthchart

Figure 1 shows Dustin Hoffman's complete birthchart. While detailed analysis of the chart would carry us too far afield, a guided tour of its layout will help you relate the ideas we've covered in this chapter to all those seemingly incomprehensible squiggles.

The first point to grasp is that a birthchart is simply a stylized map of the sky as it looked on the date of a person's birth, at the instant of his or her first breath, from the point of view of the birthplace.

The horizontal axis of the birthchart represents the horizon. Everything above that line was in the visible half of the sky at the instant Dustin Hoffman was born. Everything beneath the line was invisible, beneath the earth. The prominent "pie-slices" are the twelve houses. Here's the tricky part: east is on the **left,** not on the right where we customarily find it. This break with convention has more behind it than simple perversity, but since we're trying to cover a lot of ground quickly here, we won't waste time with explanations. If you're curious, look at Chapter Three of *The Inner Sky.*

Planets are scattered in what appears to be a random way through the houses. The Sun (☉) is in Hoffman's seventh house– find it on the right side of the chart above Pluto (♀) which lies above the horizon line. (Remember, west is on the right.) What

FIGURE 1

Dustin Hoffman
August 8, 1937
5:07 PM PST

Los Angeles, Calif.
34°N04' - 118°W15'

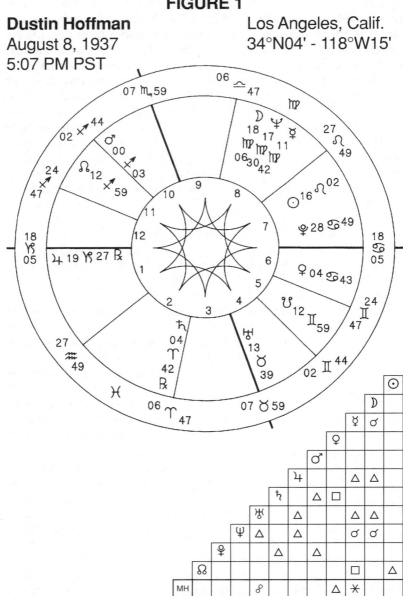

you are looking at is a setting Sun, low in the western sky, and that makes sense for a birth that occurred a 5:07 PM. If we found the Sun anywhere else, we'd know immediately that a mathematical error had been made. The birthchart, in other words, is a kind of clock. Learn how to read it, and you can do a rough check on the accuracy of the astrologer's computations. How? Simply by remembering that the Sun sets in the west in the afternoon, rises in the east at dawn, and so on.

Next to the glyph for Dustin Hoffman's Sun you see the notation 16♌02. This tells us where his Sun is in terms of the twelve signs. It lies in sixteen degrees, two minutes, of Leo. (A "minute" is one-sixtieth of a degree.) Each sign is thirty degrees wide, and a planet can be anywhere in the sign. Its meaning is not affected directly by the degree it occupies; just knowing the sign is enough for that. Why do we bother with degrees then? They become important when we start thinking about aspects, and they are also necessary to help us see exactly which house a planet occupies.

What about all those numbers around the outer rim of the wheel? Those notations show us where the wheel of signs has "stopped" in relation to Dustin Hoffman's houses; they establish the all-important relationship between the two wheels.

Think about it like this: earlier on the day of his birth the Sun was still in Leo–it spends a month there each year–but of course it was higher in the sky. If Hoffman had been born just before noon, for example, that Leo Sun would have been in the tenth house, not the seventh. We can easily see the apparent motion of the Sun around the Earth every day. Now just take that observation a step further and recognize that the signs do exactly the same thing. Like the Sun, they rise and set.

Look toward the eastern horizon of the birthchart. There, on the left, you see the notation 18♑05. This tells us that eighteen degrees, five minutes, of the sign Capricorn was rising at the instant Dustin Hoffman took his first breath. If he had waited an hour or so before being born, then the next sign, Aquarius, would have been rising. Even though we can't readily see it, the wheel of signs is spinning around the wheel of houses. In twenty-four hours each sign will rise once.

The "rising sign," along with the Sun and the Moon, is one of the three most significant factors in astrology. Together, they form the **primal triad**. Symbolically, the rising sign (or Ascendant, as it's often called) represents the social personality. It is the "mask" the psyche must adopt if it is to relate to the realities of social interaction. Insincerity is not the point; you don't, for example, necessarily tell the traffic cop how you feel about his giving you a speeding ticket. That's a superficial relationship, and it's best to keep it that way.

With Capricorn rising, Dustin Hoffman wears the "mask of the hermit." He would be hard to read at first, but he would radiate the Capricorn qualities of competence and responsibility. Jupiter was almost exactly on the eastern horizon when he was born, so his Ascendant is more complex than most. The clownish expansiveness of Jupiter mitigates some of Capricorn's typical reserve. Hoffman's mask might include some good-humored playfulness–but behind that surface we would certainly sense qualities of solitude and caution.

Numbers appear around the entire rim of the birthchart. They all work pretty much like the Ascendant. Each one shows where the **cusp** (that is, the beginning) of a house intersects the wheel of signs. Look, for example, at the cusp of his second house. There you will see the notation 27≈49, telling us that twenty-seven degrees, forty-nine minutes of the sign Aquarius lies at the beginning of that house. The top of Hoffman's birthchart shows 07♏59–he has seven degrees, fifty-nine minutes of Scorpio on his **Midheaven**, or tenth-house cusp–the part of the birthchart that refers to his relationship to the community: his "job" in the largest sense.

Aspects are shown in the triangular grid in the lower right corner of the chart. We've discussed the trine formed between Mars and Saturn. Where do we see it? Find the glyphs for Mars and Saturn in the aspect grid. Look down the Mars column until it intersects the Saturn row. In that box you see a little triangle–the glyph for the trine. Similarly, there's a sextile between Hoffman's Mercury and his Midheaven, a conjunction of the Moon and Neptune, and so on.

Two more symbols appear on the birthchart: the north (☊) and south (☋) **nodes of the Moon**. These are subtle symbols, subject to differing interpretations. Here's the best way we know to think about them: a baby is born. He or she is only thirty seconds old. Look into that baby's eyes. There's already someone in there!

One infant looks wise, another jolly; a third one seems kind of vacant. How did a personality get in there so quickly? The Hindu or the old Druid would speak of previous lifetimes. The scientist would tell us of heredity. The Pope might speak of some disembodied prebirth state "in the mind of God." Who knows? Pick the model that works for you personally. They all refer to "past lives" in some sense of the word. Whichever viewpoint you choose, look to the south node of the Moon to show you "what was in this baby's eyes at birth." The north node, always opposite the south, refers to the individual's evolutionary future. It represents the most challenging–and most spiritually rewarding–activity available to the person.

And that's the birthchart. Hopefully, if you're a beginner, this ancient wheel of hieroglyphics is not as cryptic as it was a few minutes ago.

A Helpful Shortcut

A birthchart can be almost as complex as a human being, and figuring one out is one of those endless, impossible tasks that can fascinate us for a lifetime. What's likely to be somewhat less obvious to you now is that a birthchart can also be extremely simple.

There's a trick, first introduced in *The Inner Sky*, that allows us to convert the essential message of any given birthchart into a single sentence. Naturally, in employing this shortcut, we lose sight of a lot of juicy details. But we gain that most precious of interpretive qualities: perspective. In all astrological work, and most especially in synastry, our great bugaboo is the threat of losing track of the big picture. The following technique, while utterly simple, is more than a free ticket down the path of least resistance. It's a strategy that supplies a framework to help you keep perspective as you move into more subtle levels of analysis.

The shortcut is based upon the three most critical factors in any birthchart: the Sun, the Moon, and the Ascendant. The Sun is taken to represent who the person is–his or her identity. The Moon, with its emotional, magical dimensions, represents the individual's soul. Finally, the Ascendant–our social personality– plays the role of our mask.

These three factors–Sun, Moon, and Ascendant–are then expressed as **archetypes**, according to the sign they occupy in each individual case. Archetypes are simple mythic images, like the "wise old man" or the "impetuous youth." A less charitable word for archetype is "cliche." That translation is accurate enough, but to call an archetype a cliche is to risk missing its real power, which is the capacity to convey a lot of information in a single image.

Here's a Table of Archetypes in which the spirit of each one of the twelve signs is expressed as a simple human image. There is nothing rigid about this table; these archetypes are merely suggestions. As your own experience with the sign deepens, we encourage you to add to the lists.

TABLE OF ARCHETYPES

Aries ♈
The Warrior
The Pioneer
The Daredevil
The Survivor

Taurus ♉
The Earth-Spirit
The Silent One
The Musician
The Solid Citizen

Gemini ♊
The Witness
The Teacher
The Storyteller
The Journalist
The Networker

Cancer ♋
The Mother
The Healer
The Sensitive
The Invisible Man/Woman
The Psychotherapist

Leo ♌
The King/Queen
The Performer
The Clown
The Child
The Movie Star
The Aristocrat

Virgo ♍
The Servant
The Martyr
The Perfectionist
The Analyst
The Critic

Libra ♎
The Lover
The Artist
The Peacemaker
The Diplomat
The Host/Hostess

Scorpio ♏
The Detective
The Hypnotist
The Sorcerer
The Psychologist

Sagittarius ♐
The Gypsy
The Student
The Explorer
The Anthropologist
The Philosopher

Capricorn ♑
The Hermit
The Father
The Prime Minister
The Authority
The Strategist

Aquarius ♒
The Genius
The Revolutionary
The Exile
The Scientist
The Truth Sayer

Pisces ♓
The Mystic
The Dreamer
The Poet
The Seer
The Romantic

Dustin Hoffman is a Sun sign Leo, with the Moon in Virgo and Capricorn rising. Unless you've been studying astrology for a while, that sentence might not mean a great deal to you. But now let's apply our formula. We might say that Dustin Hoffman is the "Performer" (Leo Sun) with the soul of the "Perfectionist" (Virgo Moon) wearing the mask of the "Hermit" (Capricorn Ascendant). Or that he is the "Clown" with the soul of the "Martyr" wearing the mask of the "Prime Minister." We can mix the images in any way we please; however they are assembled, they can illuminate in a few words one more facet of any complex human character.

Try the technique yourself. It's powerful. You've heard of number-crunchers. This is a symbol-cruncher. Within its limitations, the Table of Archetypes works wonders. Practice a few minutes, and you'll be able to glance at any birthchart and almost instantly say something intelligent about it.

If you don't feel that you remember everything you've just read, don't worry. The archetypes won't let you down, and for more detailed information you can always refer to the other tables. The main point to recall is that astrology is composed of three symbol systems: the **planets**, which describe the structure of the mind; the **signs**, which describe its motivations and needs; and the **houses**, which describe the world within which that mind explores and makes decisions. If you can remember that much, you are doing fine. The details will become clearer in the following pages as you watch the astrological drama of love and intimacy unfold. As you'll discover, nothing reveals the inner logic and illogic of a birthchart faster than putting it in the pressure cooker with another birthchart.

CHAPTER THREE

THREE STEPS

You've seen how signs, planets, and houses work in an individual birthchart. Now we'll examine what happens when two charts interact: the branch of astrology called **synastry.**

Your faithful friends Walter and Desdemona have eagerly offered to let you practice your astrological skills with them. Twenty minutes ago they showed up at your door, excited and laughing, and the three of you are installed in your living room with their birthcharts. The last nervous giggle has died away, and you're facing two pairs of expectant eyes–and ten pairs of planets that suddenly make as much sense as a crossword puzzle in ancient Chinese.

Desdemona's Neptune in twenty-nine degrees of Libra makes a square aspect to Walter's Moon in twenty-nine degrees of Cancer. Don't squares indicate friction? Would that aspect mean that Walter's emotional needs (Moon) clash with Desdemona's imagination and sense of self-transcendence (Neptune)? But Walter's Moon makes a harmonious trine aspect to Desdemona's Mercury (intelligence and communication) in late Pisces, so you're not sure he would put a damper on her imagination. And what should you say about Walter's Venus in Gemini squaring Desdemona's Mercury? Charts spinning like pinwheels before your eyes, you propose opening a bottle of champagne in honor of their relationship–and watch your synastry offer evaporate with the bubbles.

You avoid the preceding scene by using a systematic approach. Of course synastry is confusing sometimes. So is love! Trying to analyze even one relationship makes you feel like a distance swimmer contemplating the ocean.

Synastry will not make you an expert on relationships, any more than life will, but synastric and living skills can prepare you to approach the subject with more confidence. You wouldn't dive into the ocean with no clear destination, no idea how long you could swim, and no backup team pacing you in a boat: without a method. Neither should you dive into a synastry interpretation without the vital support of the following three steps. They're essential.   Learn them, and you won't turn into a dolphin overnight, but you won't drown, either.

Step One:
Understand the Individual

Woody Allen's classic romantic comedy, *Annie Hall*, contains a scene where the couple's therapists ask each of them, in separate sessions, how often they have sex.   Diane Keaton's character grimaces and says, "All the time! Three times a week." Woody Allen's character looks injured and says, "Practically never! Three times a week."

Relationships mean different things to different people, and individual needs and expectations vary widely.   You won't discover those separate perspectives from worrying about how Walter's north node makes a sextile aspect to Desdemona's Ascendant.   Your first step is to focus on each individual birthchart.

Look at each chart and ask yourself: Who is this person? What does she want? What does he need? What attracts her? What does he fear? How much privacy does she want? How passionate is he? Try to understand this individual as if he or she were operating in an emotional vacuum, with no reference to anyone else. Fail at this first step and your interpretations might make wonderful sense, but not to your clients.

Desdemona has a fifth-house Aries Sun conjunct Mars, with Scorpio rising and an eighth-house Leo Moon conjunct Uranus. To use the formula introduced in the previous chapter, she's the Warrior (Aries Sun) with the soul of the Performer (Leo Moon) and the mask of the Hypnotist (Scorpio Ascendant). Desdemona, in other words, is a firebrand, full of dramatic intensity about life in general and relationships in particular. How do we know that relationships are so important to her? Through her houses. They show us where her life happens. Desdemona's Sun is in the fifth house (self-expression and play), traditionally the house of "love affairs." Emphasizing the centrality of intimacy in her life, her Moon is in the eighth house (sexuality, with the eighth sign, Scorpio, rising to repeat this theme). She needs passion, honesty, and directness in relationships; Desdemona does not want a mild, "best friend" partner who stops short of gut-level intimacy.

Walter, on the other hand, is a fourth-house Taurus, with Capricorn ascending and a sixth-house Cancer Moon. He wants serenity, quiet, and security. He needs a sense of rootedness in a familiar environment, a concrete framework where he can nurture his inner world (earthy Taurus Sun in the house of the deep Self, with Moon in Cancer) and something approaching the "Protestant work ethic" (Moon in the house of responsibilities and craftsmanship, with goal-oriented Capricorn rising). He is reserved about expressing his feelings; Walter is a very private person (fourth-house Sun, self-disciplined Capricorn rising). Relationships are probably part of his life; they are part of the lives of most people, but they are not so central to him as they are to Desdemona. Walter needs a partner who provides stability and calm, one who does not rock the boat with invasive psychological demands.

Walter is the Silent One, or the Musician (Taurus Sun) with the soul of the Sensitive (Cancer Moon) and the mask of the Prime Minister (Capricorn). How do you think he'll react to the Warrior with the soul of the Performer and the mask of the Hypnotist? Are you starting to grasp the different feeling of these two charts?

But Desdemona has Venus (the Goddess of Love) in Gemini (curiosity), and Walter has Venus in Aries (gunpowder), and your synastry "cookbook" informs you that she therefore needs conversation, objectivity, and a primarily mental relationship (Gemini), while he needs fireworks and excitement (Aries)! What happened to Walter's reserve and Desdemona's flamboyance? This leads us to a primary insight in synastry: If you ignore the wholeness of the two charts and head straight for a planet-by-planet interpretation, you'll lose perspective. You can make an astrological pronouncement and be met with a polite stare from Walter or a shocked one from Desdemona. Consider each birth map as a whole! In Walter's reflective, security-oriented chart, the Arian Venus might translate into "liking people who challenge me to do my best at work." In Desdemona's passionate, relationship-oriented chart, the Geminian Venus might create a penchant for "people who never bore me, who always bring something new and different into our relationship."

Step Two:
Understand How the Birthcharts Interact

Once you've absorbed each chart's message, it's time to compare them. How would Walter meet Desdemona's needs? How would his life change if she moved in?

Step two really consists of several "giant steps," whose technical procedures form the bulk of this book. Right now, we're only surveying the territory. Later we'll analyze each of these steps in detail. For the purposes of this chapter, we can divide step two into three phases.

First, analyze the aspects between Desdemona's planets and Walter's planets, paying special attention to aspects involving the Sun, the Moon, and the Ascendant, plus two relationship-sensitive planets, Venus and Mars. For example, Walter's Taurus Sun opposes Desdemona's Scorpio Ascendant, and his Venus in Aries sextiles her Venus in Gemini. These "interaspects" (a term coined by astrologers Ken and Joan Negus) reveal much about how two people get along, where the relationship flows smoothly, where points of tension lie. We'll analyze this technique in detail in chapters Seven and Nine.

Second, note where Walter's planets fall within Desdemona's house structure, and vice versa. This technique shows what areas of one person's life (houses) are most affected by the other. For example, if her seventh house begins at thirteen degrees Taurus, and his Sun lies at fifteen degrees Taurus, we would say that Walter's Sun falls in Desdemona's seventh house, "lighting up" this area of marriage, intimacy, and commitment. We'll explore this process in Chapter Eight.

Finally, compare the overall feeling of Desdemona's chart with Walter's. How do they complement each other? Where do they clash? What we're looking for now is the "big picture." Search for basic strengths and harmonies between the two charts. How can the couple emphasize them? Where can they maximize what they have in common? There are many specific techniques for answering these questions; mostly, however, it's a matter of using imagination and common sense.

Suppose, for example, that Walter and Desdemona met because he's directing a play in which she has the starring role. His job as director capitalizes on his ability to bring an inner vision (the playwright's) into concrete reality (earthy Taurus Sun in the house of symbolism and the deep Self; efficient Capricorn Ascendant). He must also encourage imaginative, sensitive performances from the cast (emotional, nurturing Cancer Moon in the house of craftsmanship). Desdemona is a born actress (fiery Aries Sun in the house of self-expression; dramatic, performing Leo Moon; intense, moody Scorpio Ascendant). The play gives them a shared goal with deep meaning for each person, one that lets Walter's more withdrawn nature work literally "behind the scenes," and puts Desdemona at center stage.

Is theater the only salvation for Walter and Desdemona? Of course not. There are many places where these two could find common ground, and the only limits are your imagination and theirs. For example, Walter and Desdemona might enjoy working with children together; she has a playful, childlike Leo Moon, and he has a tender, caring Cancer Moon. Desdemona has a taste for adventure (Aries Sun), and Walter has a fondness for the outdoors (Taurus Sun); camping expeditions could be a shared activity. As you become more familiar with the basic meanings of signs, planets, and houses, it will become easier for you to spot the harmonies between two charts.

Be alert also for fundamental tensions between the couple. Your goal is not always to resolve them. That's often an impossible task, unless each person distorts his or her basic nature. Walter can't become a passionflower, and Desdemona will never be a still, calm pool. Your goal is to raise the consciousness of each person regarding the other, helping both parties to minimize misinterpretations and distortions of each other's behavior, and to reach rational compromises about those conflicting needs.

Step Three:
Understand the Couple

When Walter and Desdemona meet and fall in love, their friends secretly take bets on how long it will last. They predict that Walter will spend even more time than usual reading in the theater library to get away from Desdemona's histrionics, and that Desdemona will starve for intensity and connectedness. After six months Walter and Desdemona mystify their friends by opening an acting school together. He drew up the curriculum; she's thrown herself into teaching. They're delighted with the project, and their friends forget about those bets.

What happened? One plus one doesn't always equal two! Two (or more) birthcharts can be combined to construct a chart for the relationship itself. Such a chart reveals the internal logic and dynamics of the couple. Just as we can describe the happiest life available to an individual from his or her birthchart, we can use this composite chart to help us understand how to keep this couple alive and vibrant. These composite charts work exactly like normal birthcharts. All we need to do is remember that we are speaking of the relationship in and of itself.

A glance at Walter and Desdemona's composite chart reveals that together they have a third-house Taurus Sun with a sixth-house Leo Moon. The relationship itself demands shared third-house experiences of a Taurean nature if they are to grow as a couple. What might those experiences be? Let's look at the nature of Taurus and the third house for some ideas. Taurus is ruled by the planet of relationship formation, Venus, and these relationships can be creative as well as emotional. Taurus people, like Libra people, are frequently drawn to the arts as a means of establishing inner harmony, but with Taurus the arts are likely to be concrete and three-dimensional: mime, sculpture, dance, acting. The third house is the house of teaching, communication, and shared information, so Walter and Desdemona's acting school is one possible expression of their Sun's presence in the third house (teaching) and in Taurus (three-dimensional arts). Together they also have an emotional need (Moon) for shared responsibilities (sixth house) involving creativity, performance, and flair (Leo).

In Walter and Desdemona's case, the composite chart resembles both of them: He is a Taurus, and she has a Leo Moon. Some composites resemble one partner much more than the other, while some resemble neither partner. Both of these cases require different kinds of adjustments from the people involved. Regardless of the appearance of the composite chart, it creates a third force in the relationship that must be taken into account. In a sense it symbolizes the couple's "chemistry," an overriding "mood" of the relationship that can enhance or suppress each person's individuality. Composite charts are a tricky but penetrating technique. No approach to synastry would be complete without them. We'll devote chapters Ten and Eleven to an in-depth exploration of this powerful strategy.

So those are the three steps in synastry: understand each chart individually; look at the interaspects while watching for the harmonies and conflicts that they symbolize; finally, examine the composite chart. Most of the text of this book is devoted to a detailed explanation of these steps. Master them, and you are well on your way to the rewarding experience of performing an effective synastry interpretation. Let's move on to a close examination of the individual birthchart from a relationship perspective, in Part Two.

Part Two

LOVE AND INDIVIDUALITY

CHAPTER FOUR

WHOM DO YOU LOVE–AND HOW?

A man and a woman sit together in silence. Each is engrossed in reading. An evening passes. Not a word is spoken. At eleven o'clock the man arises, walks across the room, bends over, and plants a kiss on the woman's forehead. She look up warmly and whispers, "I love you." He smiles and his eyes linger on hers for a moment. Then he walks off to brush his teeth, grateful that she's part of his life.

Down the block, another couple sits in silence. He's reading. She's playing solitaire. An hour passes. Suddenly the woman explodes, "If you don't start talking to me, we'll both go crazy! I feel like I'm living with a stranger!" She storms out of the room, slamming the door. He mutters and goes back to his book.

Every partnership needs communication. Every partnership needs silence too. That much is universal and can safely be applied to everybody. Beyond that, we enter the gray zones. For the first couple, long periods of shared silence are a source of renewed closeness and connectedness. For the second couple– at least for the woman–that same silence is a painful problem. What nourishes the first marriage poisons the second one; what might seem like pointless banter in the happier relationship could be a source of joy and healing for the strained one.

Two marriages. That means four people. Four unique human beings, each with his or her own separate hungers, tolerances, and prickly places.

The woman in the traumatized marriage charges out of the house angry and drops in on a friend. She complains that her husband's "obsession" with reading is his way of avoiding meaningful contact with her. She expresses the opinion that he is an "emotional basket case," and that if he had any sensitivity, he'd recognize his problem and make an appointment with a psychotherapist, as she has suggested on countless occasions.

Her husband, meanwhile, finds himself unable to concentrate on his book after the tiff with his wife. He strolls down to the corner and meets a friend. They settle down to talk. Now we hear the husband's side of the argument. Unsurprisingly, the situation looks very different to him than it does to his wife. "What can I do? I sit down for an hour to read and she goes off like Mount Vesuvius. She's like a child. She needs constant attention. To hear her talk, the minute I stop gazing into her eyes, I'm a psychopath! The instant I get interested in anything, I'm avoiding her. I can't win."

Who's right? That, of course, is a silly question. They are both right. That is, both are expressing perfectly legitimate needs. The problem is that the woman needs more active, intensive interaction than does her husband. He, on the other hand, is not quite as "psychological" as she is. For him, feelings of personal fulfillment arise more from an exploration of ideas than from an exploration of feelings. Perhaps he has been longing for the day when she would read a book herself and share an intelligent discussion with him.

Should they be married? That's a legitimate question. One might read a few too many self-help books and get the notion that any two people chosen at random will spontaneously experience marital bliss if only they maintain the right attitudes. Perhaps there is some ultimate truth in that assertion, but for practical purposes, half the battle in creating a satisfying bond with another person lies in choosing the right partner. Maybe the man and the woman in this story are ill-suited to each other. Maybe meeting each other's needs would involve such a fundamental betrayal of each one's own nature that they would be better off apart.

These questions are not for the astrologer to answer. They belong strictly to the two individuals. The astrologer's task is to help the man and the woman understand each other and to provide them with practical support and suggestions. Beyond that, their course is for them to decide. No matter how impossible a relationship might appear astrologically, the astrologer's central responsibility is to describe ways in which the bond might be made to work. This is especially true when, as in our example, the couple has already made a commitment.

Everyone wants love. That is one of the few unqualified statements we can make on the subject of intimacy. Beyond that, we enter the infinitely complex world of human differences. One needs silence; another needs talk. One needs adventure and stimulation; the other craves security. Placid harmony versus growth and challenge. Total sharing versus radical individuality. A love of family versus an appreciation of childlessness. How much intellectual input do you need from your partner? How much playfulness? How much seriousness? How much sexual contact? The list of variables goes on and on. There is no "generic" experience of human love. For each of us the experience of love is unique, utterly special, and totally unprecedented.

Our first step as astrologers is to come to grips with that uniqueness. Before we consider any kind of interaction between people, our first requirement is to acquire a thorough understanding of the individuals. And that process starts with a long, hard look at the two birthcharts separately.

Sun Signs: Blessing or Curse?

Practically everyone knows his or her Sun sign. Even among people who laugh at astrology most know enough to say "I'm a Taurus" or "I'm a Virgo." Astrology, at least at that level, is woven into the fabric of our culture as tightly as the tales of Mickey Mouse or Conan the Barbarian.

The parallels between that kind of astrology and Mickey Mouse or Conan run deep. Sun signs and comic book characters both serve essentially the same purpose: They provide evocative, mythic images of fundamental human principles. Conan the Barbarian represents Brute Force. Mickey Mouse represents Irrepressible Pluck. In much the same way, Aries represents

Courage while Pisces represents Sensitivity. And just as it might shock the pants off you to find Conan the Barbarian standing in line behind you in the grocery store, you'd likely be quite surprised ever to meet the pure unadulterated principles astrologers call Aries or Pisces. They're comic book material too.

Unlike a Sun sign, a birthchart is no two-dimensional illusion. It is a multidimensional entity, full of ambiguities and shadowy corners. Comparing the insights we get from Sun sign astrology with those available from an accurate birthchart is like comparing *Indiana Jones and the Temple of Doom* with the works of Ernest Hemingway or Hermann Hesse.

Still, Sun signs survive. There are two reasons for that. First, they are simple and accessible. "What's your birthday? OH– you're a Gemini." It's that easy. No calculations. No daunting columns of figures. No gap between question and answer.

The second reason why Sun signs survive is a better one: they work. Despite their limitations, they serve a practical purpose. Astrology's critics often object to the way it "puts people into neat little boxes." Sun sign astrology is certainly guilty of that–but those same critics often categorize people with even simpler typologies. "She's such an introvert!"

As typologies go, Sun signs are actually fairly sophisticated– despite the protests of astrology's detractors. There are twelve sign categories, enough to allow for some subtleties. But it is essential to remember that no human being actually is a category. We're all vastly more complex than that.

Are Sun signs a blessing or a curse? That's a very difficult question to answer honestly. Many astrologers develop a knee-jerk reaction against them. We feel like poets who are writing for an audience that recognizes only twelve words. That's the dark side of the coin: Sun signs, with their easy temptations, have trivialized astrology, converting it from the repository of ancient humanity's psychological wisdom into a commodity that can be sold in the grocery store alongside pulp newspapers and glamor magazines.

The blessing? Because of the effortlessness of Sun signs, almost everyone in this society has some exposure to astrology, and that has undoubtedly helped to keep the system alive. Without Sun signs, astrology might have faded from the popular

imagination along with alchemy, herbalism, and divination by
rune stones.

Perhaps the brightest course is not to condemn Sun signs, but
rather to make an effort to resurrect them from triviality and
understand them in the context of the larger astrological framework.

Sun, Moon, and Ascendant

Everyone knows his or her Sun sign–but how many people are
aware of their Moon signs? One in a hundred? A pop-astrologer
might defend that lapse by claiming that the Sun is more
important than the Moon. Don't be deceived! To imply that the
Sun is more important than the Moon is to imply that ego is more
important than imagination or that logic is more important than
emotion.

Both the Sun and the Moon–and every other planet for that
matter–operate as distinct functions in the psyche. One of the
most critical skills in astrology is learning to keep straight in our
own minds which of these functions we are discussing. Traditionally the Sun has been associated with so-called "masculine"
qualities such as reason, leadership, and individuality, while the
Moon has been viewed as "feminine"–nurturing, emotional, and
unstable. But every birthchart contains both! Any human being
who lacks a fully developed solar function and a fully developed
lunar function is at best half-mad. And the idea that "the Sun is
more important than the Moon" flows from the same spring of
"wisdom" that once convinced us it was better to have a son than
a daughter.

The Sun helps us build an identity and to support that identity
with concrete accomplishments. The Moon helps us feel pleasure
and pain, joy and sorrow. As we learned in Chapter Two, the Sun
tells us who we are, while the Moon describes our soul–that is, the
Moon reflects the "soulful," affective side of life. Each function is
shaped by a sign, and that sign serves to describe a specific goal
toward which our solar ego or our lunar soul is journeying. The
sign also offers a road map to that goal; that is, it describes a set
of experiences we can gather and digest that move us rapidly
toward that goal. Finally, all that material can be fouled up by

laziness or fear, and can turn into an unpleasant syndrome of attitudes and behaviors we dub the sign's "shadow."

Toward the end of this chapter we'll go over each one of the twelve signs in detail. For now, it's enough to remember that each sign is a psychological process with a distinct goal, specific strategies for attaining it–and absolutely no guarantees except for a few fundamental resources. Beyond that, we're on our own, free to experience the heights of creativity and joy or the depths of depravity, all based on decisions we make.

How does this relate to intimacy?

A Sun sign astrology book might inform us that all Arians require stimulation and adventure, and that therefore they should dutifully marry other fire signs–Sagittarius and Leo. But what if one particular Arian has her Moon in Virgo? Then we have a much more complicated situation–and a much more human one! Her solar Arian function–her everyday "personality," that is–does require more intensity and variety of experience than average. But her lunar "soul" has a Virgoan spirit: at the level of instinct (Moon) she's a bit more cautious and conservative. She could enjoy a rewarding casual friendship with a man who embodied all the pyrotechnics and color of fire–but it is doubtful whether he could ever touch her very deeply. Her Virgo Moon simply wouldn't trust him enough! For anyone to get through to her on that inner level, he would have to first convince her that he could satisfy the needs of Virgo. In other words, he would need to demonstrate responsibility and competence and prove to her that he can keep his promises.

She might, in her youth, fall madly in love with a free-spirited Sagittarian musician, only to have her heart broken when she realizes that he might never feel ready to make a commitment to her. His energetic charisma feeds her Sun, but leaves her Moon starving. She might rebound out of that situation and fall in love with a solid Taurean accountant–who soon threatens to bore her to death with his predictability. He might be as faithful as Rin Tin Tin, and therefore a delight to her Virgo Moon. But then her Sun is left hungry.

Through an accumulation of experiences like these, our heroine eventually comes to realize that her intimacy needs are more subtly shaded than the "Thou shalt marry a Leo" injunctions she received in the Sun sign book. And eventually, as she matures,

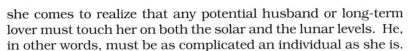

she comes to realize that any potential husband or long-term lover must touch her on both the solar and the lunar levels. He, in other words, must be as complicated an individual as she is.

So far we have limited our considerations to the Sun and the Moon. With the Sun alone, we divide humanity into a simple pattern of twelve "types." When we add the Moon sign, the number of possible combinations leaps to 144–and as we have just seen in our example, the power of the astrological symbols to describe our intimacy needs increases proportionately.

Eventually we need to add the rest of the planets, as well as aspects and houses. By the time we get to that point, we'll be light years beyond any schematic "typologies." We'll be talking about real people, with all their subtleties of character. But that's tricky business and it's best to approach it one step at a time.

For now let's suffice to add one more vegetable to the astrological stew: the Ascendant.

Like the Sun and the Moon, the Ascendant serves a psychological purpose that is separate and unique. It helps us organize an outward, social personality. In a word, the Ascendant represents a person's style. The word "style" is accurate, but unfortunately it also conveys an air of insignificance or ultimate dismissability– and that's very misleading.

The proverbial farm boy is attempting to ask a girl for a date. He's had his eye on her for months. Finally he's gotten up the courage to approach her. Now that he's standing in front of her, he discovers that his courage is gone. Beads of sweat form on his forehead. He shuffles his feet. He glares at his shoes. "There's a dance on Saturday...uh...I might go fishing though." He winds up walking away from the girl without popping the question. It's a thoroughly agonizing experience for both of them.

This little tale is a cliche, of course. We've seen it on the screen many times. And most of us have lived it out once or twice as well. But if we take a closer look, it can teach us something about the Ascendant. At the deepest motivational levels there is really nothing at all wrong with that farm boy. He likes the girl. That's a good thing. They could perhaps share some experiences that would be important to both of them. His problem is purely one of style. He is unable to translate his inward psychological reality into the outward terms of his actual behavioral surface. And very technically then, that's a superficial problem–that is, it's on the surface. It's also an emotional disaster.

The Ascendant interlocks all the complexities of our inner world with the requirements of external reality. If we make a strong response to it, we feel "centered" and at ease, readily feeding our deep psyche with a set of meaningful external experiences. If we make a weak response, then the opposite happens: we feel "goofy" and disconnected, and usually painfully self-conscious.

The woman in our example is a solar Arian with her Moon in Virgo. Now let's carry our astrological analysis a step further. When she took her first breath, the sign Taurus was rising in the east. With that Ascendant, her social personality–for better or worse–radiates on a Taurean wavelength. We say "for better or worse" because she has a lot of freedom in determining how she's going to respond to those potentials. At best she'll present herself unpretentiously, in a spirit of naturalness and an earthy tranquillity. As she matures, she'll increasingly develop a mask (Ascendant) of quiet efficacy and easy warmth. On the down side, we could imagine her slipping into a posture of stolidness, stubbornness, and predictability.

In intimacy she'll respond to a man whose style complements her own. That suggests that she might have difficulty in the long run with an "airy-fairy" or a self-appointed wizard full of long-winded abstractions. That kind of man would be just too abstruse for her more concrete personality. Virgo, like Taurus, is an earth sign, so despite her Fiery Sun, we see that here we have a woman in whom the earthy ideals of patience, realism, and the practical "long view" predominate–but who still draws her basic solar vitality from the Arian process of courage-seeking.

Adding the color of the Ascendant to our astrological palette radically expands the subtlety of our typology. As we have seen, there are twelve Sun sign categories and 144 possible Sun-Moon combinations. With the rising sign we leap to 1,728 different patterns–and we are still only scratching the surface. Anyone who ever finds himself or herself using the twofold typology of introversion and extroversion (or "good guys" and "bad guys") should think twice before accusing astrology of "cubbyholing" anyone!

One more point regarding the Ascendant: if one sign is rising, then the sign directly opposite must be setting in the west at the same instant. This sign, called the individual's Descendant, is also the cusp of the seventh house, the traditional "house of marriage." In synastry, the descending sign takes on extra significance. It represents a quality that compliments or balances the tone of our Ascendant. Since the Descendant opposes the Ascendant, the essential quality of the interaction involves tension as well as attraction.

Think of the Descendant like this: the Ascendant, representing our "style," is by its very nature a superficial symbol, as we have seen. This is not to diminish the significance of its role in the birthchart, only to indicate that its field of action is the surface of the personality. Such "streamlining" of the psyche is essential if we are to meet the practical requirements of daily life. But it comes at a cost. Much of what we are is left out. A risk exists that we might become too identified with our Ascendants and therefore shallow and rigid. All style and no substance. Human consciousness, as reflected in astrological symbolism, seems to recognize this problem and make an effort to compensate for it. We are drawn to people whose natures are opposite our own–people, in other words, who have qualities like those symbolized by our descending sign. Typically we experience an emotional "tug-of-war" with them as our characters seek to come into equilibrium. But that tug-of-war insures that neither one of us becomes a two-dimensional caricature of our ascending sign, cocksure and empty.

The woman in our example has Taurus rising. A look at any birthchart shows us that the sign opposite Taurus is Scorpio. That sign, then, is her Descendant, and here is how it works for her: With her Taurean Ascendant, there is a danger that she could become too simple in her outer expression, that some of the more complex and shadowy dimensions of life could be denied, which of course only gives them more power in the long run. Put very simply, she could become too quiet for her own good while tricky psychological ambiguities and hungers slowly inched toward the boiling point.

Enter the Descendant. Or perhaps we could say "enter her soulmates."

With Scorpio on her seventh-house cusp, our protagonist is drawn to individuals in love and friendship whose natures emphasize Scorpio qualities: that is, they are people who like to delve into the murky areas of human consciousness, asking hard questions and breaking conventional social "taboos" in their interactions with her. These people may upset her at times, but she needs them, lest her life become too prosaic. Similarly, she might in turn help them by giving them perspective on themselves, assisting their own efforts to achieve balance. How: By offering them her more down-to-earth visions of the sometimes disconcerting Scorpio territory, helping them laugh, relax, and perhaps take themselves a bit less seriously.

One of the more miraculous dimensions of the Descendant is that despite the delicacy of the purpose it serves, its operation is largely unconscious and automatic. We simply like people who resonate with our seventh-house cusps. We are drawn to them. We experience–initially at least–an easy comradeship with them, often spiced with romantic or sexual feelings. Only once the bonds have formed does the more subtle "combat" of balancing, deepening, and healing begin.

These then are the primary features of our astrological individuality: the "primal triad" of Sun, Moon, and Ascendant–and for purposes of synastry, the Descendant. A thorough grasp of all four functions guarantees a solid foundation in our understanding of how one person approaches the labyrinths of human love.

Before we consider the twelve signs in detail, let's recapitulate what we've covered so far.

- The Sun represents identity, self-image, and the more conscious or intentional dimensions of the personality.
- The Moon represents instinct, emotion, and the more unconscious and subjective dimensions of experience.
- The Ascendant symbolizes our outward "style" and the most ideal "interlock" between our psychological selves and outer reality.
- The Descendant represents a kind of person to whom we are drawn in an unconscious effort to balance our most characteristic blind spots or limitations.

These four functions are universal. They exist in everyone. But in each person they operate differently depending on which of the twelve signs are shaping them. In the pages that follow, we'll introduce the signs in detail, emphasizing their particular approach to questions of intimacy and love.

If you're a beginning astrologer, it's fine to think of these twelve descriptions in relation to Sun signs, but we hope that by now you're convinced that there's more to the picture than the solar ego! Always remember that while a given sign can shape one's individuality (Sun), it can just as readily modify one's "style" (Ascendant) or cast its light over the private landscape of our intimate inner life (Moon).

Real skill in astrology arises when we learn to keep these Sun-Moon-Ascendant distinctions clear.   Conversely, the surest course to astrological chaos lies in putting all the key concepts you've memorized about Aries, Virgo, and Taurus into the mental Cuisinart, closing your eyes, and pressing the button.

The Twelve Signs

Knowing one's Sun sign is as simple as knowing one's birthday–almost. If you are born on February twenty-fifth, then any pop-astrology book will tell you that "you're a Pisces." But if you're born on February twentieth, then you'll get mixed messages. One book says "Pisces" while another one tells you "Aquarius." There's a simple reason for that. The Sun does not enter a new sign on exactly the same day each year. No need for a complex explanation of that problem here. It's enough to point out that astrology is based on the true solar year, and that year is not precisely 365 days long. As a result, astrological events can't be lined up exactly with our calendars.

In the pages that follow, we explore each one of the twelve signs. For convenience, we also give the approximate date marking the entry of the Sun into each sign. If you don't know your Sun sign, you can find out below–unless you happen to be born right on any one of the specific dates we mention or on the day before or the day after. In that case, don't trust us! To learn your true Sun sign, you'll need to have an accurate birthchart. (See the Appendices.)

In any case, no matter what your birthday, to learn your Ascendant or your Moon sign, you definitely need a birthchart. If you know the date, time, and location of your birth, then there's nothing stopping you. No need to face any complex calculations.

For less than the cost of this book, you can send away and have a computer set up your chart (again, see the Appendices). Then you'll have the complete astrological picture–Sun, Moon, Ascendant, all the planets, houses, and aspects. If you don't already have your birthchart, we strongly recommend that you get one. No sense flying on one engine.

Once again, nothing that follows is limited to Sun signs. Our descriptions of the twelve basic astrological processes apply just as readily to the Moon and the Ascendant. In later chapters we also apply them to the planets. No matter what your Sun sign, we encourage you to read about all twelve signs. As you'll discover later in the book, each one plays some kind of role in your birthchart.

Aries the Ram
(March 21 through April 20)

ARCHETYPES
The Warrior
The Pioneer
The Daredevil
The Survivor

DEVELOPMENTAL AIM
Consciously or unconsciously, any Arian astrological feature is striving toward **courage**. To reach the full flower of its potential, that feature must sharpen its willpower, especially in the face of stress and obstacles. Fearlessness is not the point–that's just a schizophrenic state in which we are out of touch with natural emotions. For Aries, the motto must be "feel the fear and do it anyway."

STRATEGIES AND RESOURCES
To learn courage we must intentionally expose ourselves to stress. For Aries, that means accepting risk and seeking adventure. Swallow your fear and take that scuba diving class! You will learn more than how to dive. In facing your fear of deep water, you teach your unconscious self a lesson about its own strength–and the next time you have to walk across a dark parking lot at two o'clock in the morning, the unconscious self remembers that lesson and feels less fearful.

The Ram's resource, rather paradoxically, is courage. All that Arian bravery already exists in the person, but it must be invoked by a set of scary circumstances before the individual becomes fully conscious of it. "Until I actually had the experience of keeping my cool when I met that hammerhead shark forty feet down, I had no idea I had that kind of courage!"

The Arian courage-gathering process doesn't always involve swimming in shark-infested waters. The process is not always so physical. The "shark" we must face might well be a human one: an obnoxious boss, a critical parent, a lover who won't acknowledge the truth. The "shark" might even be cigarettes if we're trying to quit smoking, or a bowl of Breyer's Mint Chocolate Chip ice cream if we're trying to lose a few pounds.

Whatever the nature of the shark, the Arian principle is the same: face enough sharks without flinching, and you've become a lot more courageous than you were.

SHADOW

The dark side of the Ram lies in the misdirection of that fiery power. Perhaps a woman commits the Arian "cardinal sin" and allows fear to prevent her from fulfilling a dream. "I'd **love** to take that scuba class with you, Jane, but I just don't have the money right now." Then the energy that should have gone into conquering her fear of deep water dissipates itself pointlessly and destructively in bursts of temper, silly arguments, and random passions.

ARIES IN LOVE

Aries is an intense, experience-oriented sign. In relationships, it needs robust contact and a certain amount of psychological "arm wrestling" with its partner. If a relationship shows symptoms of going to sleep, the Ram instinctively rocks the boat. Remember that in love, as in every other part of life, Aries is learning courage–and its lover better be ready to hold up his or her end of that bargain.

With the Sun in Aries, the individual's entire identity (Sun) is Arian. In matters of intimacy there is likely to be a pronounced love of directness. Negatively, the possibility arises of pointless fireworks and purely symbolic arguments that needlessly damage both partners, often creating a caustic atmosphere of mistrust.

With the Moon in Aries, the intimacy logic remains the same except that it is buried more deeply. The individual is learning emotional courage. The ideal is a willingness to share needs and fears with the partner no matter how impolitic that might seem. On the dark side, we can sometimes observe a distinctly irrational (lunar!) quality of touchiness or combativeness as the Arian wildfires burn out of control.

The Arian Ascendant suggests a developmental emphasis upon building a more direct and confrontive personal style. The shadows remain the same–misdirected temper and symbolic warfare–but now the process is closer to the surface. Many people with Aries rising come to learn, often much to their shock, that their Arian "vibrations" frighten people, and that they must make an effort to reassure their partners that they are not as dangerous as they seem.

Taurus the Bull
(April 21 through May 21)

ARCHETYPES
The Earth-Spirit
The Silent One
The Musician
The Solid Citizen

DEVELOPMENTAL AIM
What does Taurus seek? Peace. Security. Gentleness. Ease. Naturalness. Simplicity. Silence. If you roll all those virtues into one fuzzy, sweet-smelling ball, you've grasped the developmental aim of the Bull. Any Taurean astrological feature, whether the person understands it or not, is embarked on a course with that mellow, timeless feeling at its logical end.

STRATEGIES AND RESOURCES
Taurus is instinctively attracted to anything (or anyone!) that offers steadiness, reliability, and peace. The security the Bull seeks is an internal condition, not so much an outward one. Taurus might reach its goal a thousand times faster sitting in the woods on a June morning than it ever would guzzling Pepto-Bismol on the New York Stock Exchange, however lucrative that course might be.

Music soothes Taurus. So do reliable tools, tried-and-true friends, familiar landscapes. Planting a garden is a Taurean joy. Painting too. And building a bookcase out of fine oak. Or feeling the texture of a fine old violin.

The Taurean strategy is one of endless simplification. No existential melodramas. No exhausting "heavy personal changes" that don't really change anything. Just a gradual paring away of life until we are left with its essence–health, truth, love, and silence...and a reverence for them.

SHADOW

The Bull's shadow lies in confusing inward peace with external security. Taurus can become obsessed with stability at every outward level: financial, interpersonal, experiential. As a result, this sign can bore itself to death, becoming stubborn, materialistic, and fearful of breaking up routines. The Bull needs to be reminded that motion and change are two of the most characteristic qualities of life–and that one of the most universal features of death is stability.

TAURUS IN LOVE

In affairs of the heart, Taurus seeks the same ends it pursues elsewhere: stability, solidness, reliability. There is a sensual quality to the Bull, and even a romantic one. It would be misleading to get the idea that Taurus seeks a lover with the same attitudes and methods one might associate with buying a used car. The key astrological insight is to recognize that the Bull is concerned with the long haul. Rarely will this sign be taken in by mere glamor or the flimflam of glittery fantasy. The Moon, being emotional, will emphasize the Bull's sensuality and its instinct for stability. The Sun, being more rational, focalizes the Taurean quality of down-to-earth reasonableness–and dogged persistence–in emotional situations. The Ascendant, being more external, gives an air of naturalness and honesty, conducive to planting relationships on the solid ground of realism.

Gemini the Twins
(May 22 through June 21)

ARCHETYPES
The Witness
The Teacher
The Storyteller
The Journalist
The Networker

DEVELOPMENTAL AIM

Gemini's ultimate evolutionary goal is the attainment of a sense of wonder. The Twins must learn to give the universe "permission" to be amazing, full of surprises, thick with miracles. **Confusion**–that's their aim, provided we think carefully about the word. "Confusion," in this sense, as a psychological condition in which what we have allowed ourselves to experience, is a giant step ahead of what we have already figured out.

STRATEGIES AND RESOURCES

The central Geminian strategy is experience–and lots of it. Curiosity, restlessness, a distaste for repetition and predictability: all these are the Twin's resources. So is a love of conversation. Pop-astrology generally emphasizes the talkativeness of this sign. That quality is usually there, but more central to Gemini's work is its love of listening. Why? Simply because we usually learn more with our mouths closed than with them open.

Gemini is often described as a "youthful" sign. It's a pity to use that word since we then imply that open-mindedness, freshness of thought, and a willingness to be surprised are adolescent qualities. Those qualities shouldn't be limited to anyone's early years–especially if his or her Sun, Moon, or Ascendant lies in the sign of the Twins.

SHADOW

The sheer rapidity of the Geminian process can be its downfall. Slickness and superficiality can result. So can overextension, nervousness, and a blithering, dithering lifestyle in which everything is in perpetual crisis. Working with this energy is like driving a Porsche Turbo Carrera down a mountain road at ninety miles an hour–you can probably do it, but only if your concentration is absolute. At that speed life is not very forgiving. Stop, take a breath, and read the fine print: that's good advice for the Twins.

GEMINI IN LOVE

As always, once we understand the basic developmental aims of a sign, an understanding of its relationship dynamics follows rather logically. Gemini seeks wonder. It is driven by curiosity. It responds to stimulation. It turns away from the routine and the predictable. Any lover capable of holding the Twins' attention must certainly offer more than solid middle-class virtues. Those virtues might be part of the package, but he or she had better offer the spice of exciting ideas, surprise, and wide-ranging interests as well.

Pop-astrology suggests that Gemini is fickle. Certainly that's a possibility. But we must recognize this "fickleness" for what it is: the Twins' insatiable appetite for experience. One way of fulfilling that appetite is to maintain contact, sexual or otherwise, with a variety of fascinating people. But don't let that mislead you: happy commitment in monogamous love is a Geminian option–with two provisos. First, the Twins must have access to many lively friends, all with the mate's blessing. The second proviso is even more central: the lover must be willing and eager to contribute equally to a shared life of surprise and variety. The ideal marriage for Gemini would revolve around one rambling till-death-do-us-part conversation, funny, profound, and endless.

Cancer the Crab
(June 22 through July 23)

ARCHETYPES

The Mother
The Healer
The Sensitive
The Invisible Man/Woman
The Psychotherapist

DEVELOPMENTAL AIM

Perfect sensitivity to the inner realms of feeling and imagination–that's the Crab's goal. To understand that aim accurately, we must recognize that this sensitivity ultimately applies not only to the Cancerian individual's own psyche, but also to his sensitivity toward other people as well. First: a healing of the Crab's own heart, an opening of the imagination, of the ability to

feel. Then: an extension of that process out into the world, as Cancer adopts a loving role of nurturance and support.

STRATEGIES AND RESOURCES

Like his saltwater counterpart, the astrological Crab requires a shell. He is born fluent in the language of the deep Self: the language of feeling. In Cancer, the volume is turned all the way up on subjectivity and emotion. If this world were the Garden of Eden, that kind of vulnerability wouldn't present any problems. But the world isn't quite that gentle. The Crab must protect his inner processes, often hiding inside a shell of shyness or withdrawal while he gathers strength.

Radical self-protection is fine at first, but after a while Cancer must take courage and dare to shed the shell–dare to love, that is. If he is brave enough to take that step, then, just like the saltwater crab, Cancer grows a second shell, a larger one, more suited to his more evolved dimensions. He now relates actively to the world, protecting himself within his new, more formidable shell: the role of the healer and the helper, the comforter–extending outwardly the very processes of delicate nurturance he first employed inwardly to explore the misty terrains of his own spirit.

SHADOW

Both the Crab's shells present evolutionary dangers. If Cancer gets caught in the first shell–shyness–then typically he adopts a fearful, conservative posture in life, enduring a dull job, a silent marriage, a spirit bound and gagged.

In the second shell–that of the nurturer–there lurks another shadow: the trap of continually being cast in the role of the forgiver, the protector, the psychotherapist. These roles are natural and healthy ones for the crab, until they become so automatic and so addictive that the multidimensional wholeness of the Cancer person becomes invisible, lost behind the shell of "mothering."

CANCER IN LOVE

"Defensiveness" is a word we must use with great caution when discussing Cancer. The scurrying ghost crab on an Atlantic beach–is she defensive? Or would it be plain foolhardiness for her to shed her shell beneath the hovering eyes of the sea gull? Sensitivity must defend itself. The alternative is self-destruction.

In romantic situations, if Cancer seems a bit guarded, it's only because she is playing for high stakes: once someone is allowed inside her shell, she's utterly vulnerable. So the Crab is cautious, extending her "feelers" into the other spirit, sounding him for dangers. One who would court the Crab must first convince her of his gentleness, his honesty, his capacity for tenderness and commitment, his willingness to "nest" with her. Until then, he'll see only shell: maybe ice, maybe aloof wisdom, maybe even wit. But never the Crab's soul.

With the Sun in Cancer, the trajectory of intimacy tends to follow rather closely the patterns we've just described–unless the Crab's shadow side dominates the scenario. Then the shell is never shed.

With the Moon in Cancer, the situation is trickier. Much then depends upon the Sun sign. The Cancer Moon seeks a safe shell to lurk behind, and the Sun often provides an excellent one. It might be quite a while before the lover is allowed to penetrate the extraordinarily tender base of emotion that arises when the planetary symbol of feeling (the Moon) interacts with the sign symbol of subjectivity (Cancer). Until then, he or she experiences only the other, more outward features of the person's birthchart.

Cancer on the Ascendant suggests that the individual's style is Cancerian: just "getting through the door" is the hard part with such a person. With great reserve and patient circumspection he or she will at first study us as if we were a distasteful and perhaps dangerous zoological specimen. Then, if we pass scrutiny, the floodgates of caring and tenderness will be opened–but only if we pass scrutiny.

Leo the Lion
(July 24 through August 23)

ARCHETYPES
The King/Queen
The Performer
The Clown
The Child
The Movie Star
The Aristocrat

DEVELOPMENTAL AIM
The lion's developmental aim is a warm, confident, self-expressive sense of **belonging** in the world. It is a sense of safety–but not of caution. The Lion's safety is based on a feeling of being totally accepted, spontaneously and uncritically, by everyone.

The Leonine ideal is one of blissful, unpremeditated abandon. "Life–I love you! I celebrate you!" And once we have a few miles on our existential odometers, we might add one more clause: "Life, I forgive you!" In a word, the evolutionary goal of the Lion is joy.

STRATEGIES AND RESOURCES
Feeling good–it's easy to talk about, not always so easy to accomplish. For Leo, joy and spontaneity do not arise automatically. They must be attained through the use of certain very specific strategies. The fact that these strategies often arise unconsciously does not diminish their power.

Leo is a woman who has been lonely for a while, maybe hurt too. Now she's two weeks into a new relationship–and scared. She writes a poem about it, straight from her heart. Passionate. And revealing–maybe too revealing, considering the usual politics of an embryonic sexual bond. Should she show the poem to her lover? She takes the risk...and he responds. As he looks up from the poem, a tear runs down his cheek. They hug. For the rest of the evening she feels more relaxed and spontaneous with that man than ever before.

That little tale contains in microcosmic form a clear description of Leo's evolutionary strategy: learning to take the risk of self-expression. If we reveal ourselves that way–and earn applause for it–then we instantly feel better, safer, more positive about our place in the world.   Life feels friendlier to us–and that, in a nutshell, is the Lion's goal.

Leo's resources?   Creativity, a sense of drama, verve: all the elements of an endearing, praise-gathering performance.

SHADOW

What if the poem falls flat? "Leo, I've got some advice for you: Don't write poetry."   Maybe the Lion clams up, never taking another risk.   Maybe she whips herself into a frenzy of "people-pleasing" and performance, desperately pursuing her lover's affirmation, even at the price of falsifying herself.   Down either road lies Leo's shadow.   The first course–clamming up–usually leads eventually to haughtiness and egomania.   Those Leo fires just can't be bottled up that way.   The second course–"people-pleasing"–inevitably produces a noisy brand of superficiality, the kind of brainless "good vibes" you expect in a Pepsi commercial. The Lion is simply trying too hard.

So what's the answer?   It's deceptively simple: find a more appreciative audience.   To evolve, the Lion must leave some tangible evidence of her internal process in the hands of the world and that evidence must be appreciated.   For the Leo's strategy to work, she must see to it that both conditions are satisfied: honest, creative, uncalculated self-expression and a positive reception for that self-expression.   If either condition is unmet, then her strategy is mere bluster, accomplishing nothing.

LEO IN LOVE

Courtship is a natural activity for the Lion.   Self-expression– telling one's personal story–is one of the essential processes of sexual bonding.   So are the giving and receiving of praise.   So is playfulness.   And all of them are right up the Lion's alley.   Roses, poetry, heartfelt talks, candlelight: these are the coin of the realm for Leo in love.

Falling in love comes easily for Leo.   What about staying in love? That's a possibility too, but only if the Lion continues to receive affirmation, attention, and appreciation from her lover.   Nobody likes the numbness of love gone stale.   For Leo that numbness is fatal–unless it's cured immediately with a hefty dose of joy and renewed courtship behavior.

The Leo Moon still needs the same applause, but that need might remain invisible: an unexpressed emotion.   Clap your hands for the Leo Moon, and you'll see a smile that can't help but remind you of sunrise on the open road. This one has the soul of a performer. It just might not show.

The Leo Ascendant can be misleading. Wearing the "mask of the King (or Queen)," the Leo rising individual might not look as if he or she needs any praise. Don't be fooled–there's hunger behind that aristocratic bearing. Feed it, and you'll pass the outer perimeters of that person's defenses. Starve it, and you'll go no further.

Virgo the Virgin
(August 24 through September 23)

ARCHETYPES
The Servant
The Martyr
The Perfectionist
The Analyst
The Critic

DEVELOPMENTAL AIM
Purity–that's the Virgin's goal. But don't be fooled by the word "Virgin" into thinking that Virgo's purity has anything to do with sexual inexperience, or with any other kind of inexperience for that matter. It doesn't. Virgo's aim is to attain the highest, most refined levels of her potential. Her "purity" is a style of living and a quality of thought uncontaminated by anything less than the best truth she knows. In a word, the Virgin's aim is **perfection.**

STRATEGIES AND RESOURCES
Virgo's fundamental resource is a sense of the ideal. A sense of what could be.   She is also blessed with a meticulous, scrupulously honest sense of what is. In the tension between those two–the ideal and the real–Virgo's growth is accelerated and directed. She has a restless insurance policy against laziness and complacency. No matter what she attains, she wants more, knows that more is possible.   Relentlessly, and often with cunningly effective tactics, she transforms her personal reality into ever more perfect patterns.

To the medievals, Virgo was the sign of the Servant. Take heart: Working as a stock clerk or a chambermaid is not the point. The point is a very specific evolutionary strategy. Virgo looks inward, finding some aspect of herself that can be polished brightly and offered to the world. She finds, in other words, the most nearly perfectible part of herself. Then she becomes radically identified with that virtue. In a sense she becomes a servant of that particular virtue. How? Simply by logging a lot of hours practicing it.

Perhaps a particular Virgo is a writer, for example. When she's writing, she feels that she is living out her "best self." So she writes and writes, refining her style, always seeking to weave her words more economically and eloquently today than yesterday.

Perhaps our Virgo writer is also inclined to gossip; definitely not the part of her character that she'd call her "best self."

Here's the crux of her strategy: when she's writing, she doesn't have time to gossip. That part of her character is starved. The better part is fed. Don't be deceived by the apparent simplemindedness of this Virgoan strategy. It works. Given a lifetime, it can utterly transform a character, move it toward perfection. And perfection, as we've seen, is the Virgin's goal.

SHADOW

"There's my ideal. That's what my life could look like...if I weren't crazy. Here, on the other hand, is what I am...God help me." Perfection is a harsh mistress, and the shadow she casts is crippling, destructive self-criticism. Virgo must learn self-acceptance and self-forgiveness. Otherwise, she falls into a bleak pattern of doubt and self-limitation. And if she succumbs to that poison, she quickly falls prey to a second shadow: criticism, cynicism, and negativity regarding anything and everything around her.

VIRGO IN LOVE

In intimacy Virgo values two qualities: realism and commitment to growth. She might not use those words, but let either quality disappear in her lover–and Virgo soon disappears along with it.

Under realism, we would include virtues such as logic, clearheadedness, patience, competence, perhaps ambition. All the qualities that help us live in reality, in other words.

A commitment to growth: under this Virgoan requirement, we find honesty, a capacity to receive criticism gracefully and appreciatively, and a willingness to make concrete efforts to alter our bad habits.

For the Virgin's love to survive, the love itself must be constantly changing and growing. She responds to a lover who offers shared projects, new ideas to be explored in detail, plans for the future. She might fall for empty glamor once in her life, but it won't last long. With some experience behind her, she simply won't trust enough to love someone until the object of her affections has proven himself trustworthy.

On the dark side, Virgo's love of perfection can lead to nagging criticisms of the partner–criticisms that eventually erode the trust and shared joy upon which love thrives. Similarly, the Virgo shadow of self-doubt can lead one into a self-destructive liaison with an insensitive, selfish, or authoritarian partner.

Libra the Scales
(September 24 through October 23)

ARCHETYPES
The Lover
The Artist
The Peacemaker
The Diplomat
The Host/Hostess

DEVELOPMENTAL AIM
Serenity–that's Libra's aim. The Scales symbolize balance. Equilibrium. Underlying every healthy Libran action is the effort–conscious or unconscious–simply to calm down. Releasing tension, finding the middle ground, smoothing ruffled feathers, the Scales move step-by-step toward their goal: the attainment of unflappable peace.

STRATEGIES AND RESOURCES
A cynic has a rigid view of the world: everyone is looking out for himself, no matter what kind of philosophical masks that person might use to disguise his selfishness. Faced with an act of pure altruistic charity, that cynic is first confused, then struggles to force that perception into his bitter view of life. So hooked is he on his dark picture of human motivation that charity makes him nervous and pushes him into a frenzy of rationalization.

Another person is determined that every event, however agonizing, has a purpose and is ultimately a lesson. Faced with the
brutal murder of a friend's daughter, this more "spiritual" person
feels a sense of strain very similar to what the cynic felt in the first
instance. The effort to squeeze the murder into the more prosaic
model of life doesn't work very well either. Once again, the
muscles of the face become tense. The mind whirs into high-gear
rationalization. And a feeling of struggle overwhelms the psyche.

Truth is always complex, always paradoxical. Any effort to cling
to simplifications or to defend them against reality always results
in stress. And stress is the antithesis of Libra's developmental
aim. As a result, Libra is given a powerful resource: a high
tolerance for paradox and ambiguity. The Scales weigh both
sides of every issue. They seek the middle ground and find their
balance there.

Beauty soothes us too. We are surprised by a lovely sunset. We
sigh. We release tension. Cultivating the aesthetic side of life is
therefore a Libran strategy, either passively as an appreciator or
actively as a creator of art.

Interpersonal tensions–fights with our mate, for example–are
extraordinarily stressful. Libra has a strategy in this area as well:
it is courtesy. That can be a pale word, but as we use it here, we
don't mean the "courteous" ability to discern which fork is the
salad fork. Courtesy is the ability to gauge our actions partly by
a sense of how they impact upon another person–and Libra has
that ability in abundance.

SHADOW

The Libran shadow, as is the case with dark sides of all the
signs, is nothing but a distortion of the Scales' normal strategies
and resources. Libra's tolerance for ambiguity can be corrupted
into mere wishy-washiness and indecision. The sign's aesthetic
sensitivity can descend into glossy tackiness. Courtesy can
collapse into shallow slickness and an inability to face real
conflicts squarely. Paradoxically, all these perversions of the
Libran nature lead directly to increased levels of tension. In other
words, they do worse than merely subvert the healthy strategies;
they work actively in the opposite direction.

LIBRA IN LOVE

To medieval astrologers, Libra was "the sign of marriage." In a symbolic sense that's still true today. In Libra we find the principle of balance, of two very different entities coming into a state of equilibrium with each other: an effective symbol for the spirit of healthy marriage and commitment in general. Each one of the twelve signs functions in relationship and is drawn to some extent into a relationship. But for no sign is intimacy such a fundamental evolutionary proving ground. Libra needs the challenges and pitfalls of love; as nothing else does, they accelerate this sign's growth.

In intimacy Libra requires courtesy and emotional delicacy from the partner. There is a refined sensibility here; coarse jokes and pats on the fanny just won't fly in Libran airspace. For Libra, intimacy is an art. It must be approached with grace, with the senses open, with awareness of every move. A clean shirt is a great help. So is a thorough grasp of the spirit behind the collected works of Miss Manners. Don't misunderstand this penchant for grace: Libra is no social drill sergeant. Stiff, formulaic "correctness" is not the point; rather, it is courtesy in the true, deep sense. That is, the art of gracefully minimizing the inevitable frictions that arise whenever two human egos are put in the same small box.

The Scales must beware of going too far in the direction of smoothing out life's inevitable social wrinkles. The risk here lies in so thoroughly understanding and internalizing another person's viewpoint that the Libran individual loses track of his or her own needs. Libra can create the appearance of blissful harmony in a relationship, only to realize his or her true individuality has been completely submerged behind a false mask of sweetness, patience, and acquiescence.

Scorpio the Scorpion
(October 24 through November 22)

ARCHETYPES
The Detective
The Hypnotist
The Sorcerer
The Psychologist

DEVELOPMENTAL AIM
Sigmund Freud was once asked for a brief definition of psychoanalysis. His response: "Psychoanalysis is the process of making the unconscious conscious." In those words he unwittingly produced a succinct definition of the process astrologers call Scorpio.

Each one of us sits on a volcano; each one of us is motivated by unconscious–or unconsidered–psychological forces we understand only vaguely. Sex is an example of one of these forces. Ask a fifteen-year-old boy to explain exactly why he likes girls. First, he looks at you as though you were crazy. Then he mumbles, "I dunno...it's something about the way they look, I guess." For most of us, that's enough. We simply accept those unconscious "givens" in our lives. For Scorpio, that's only the beginning.

STRATEGIES AND RESOURCES
Penetrating self-analysis is the fundamental Scorpionic evolutionary tactic. No sign peers with such unremitting intensity into the depths of the human psyche. Instinctively Scorpio is suspicious–"whatever I see, the truth is more than that." Probing, feeling, sensing the inner terrain, Scorpio grows wiser and deeper, more aware of the dimly illuminated core of the human spirit, unless in the course of that inward journey it slips into the snares of the shadow.

To make that passage into the depths of the psyche safely, Scorpio must support this strategy of emotional self-analysis with two essential resources. Neither of them arise automatically. Both must be cultivated intentionally. The first resource is the ability to stand back from oneself and gain perspective. This strategy involves swallowing a bitter pill: Scorpio must sacrifice some of its self-seriousness. It must learn to laugh at itself, to see the humorous side of its tendency toward extreme self-analysis.

The second Scorpionic resource? In a word, it is friends. But a better word might be "allies" or perhaps "partners in growth." These are people who help the Scorpion maintain perspective. They help it laugh. They support a healthy, active interest in the outer world. How? Partly by offering Scorpio fascinating external alternatives to its instinctive self-preoccupation: "Let's go to the beach this weekend!" Other times, these allies dive right into the heart of the psyche with Scorpio but offer those resources that the Scorpion might lack: humor and a sense of the larger picture.

SHADOW

The Scorpion's shadow is morbid introspection. Brooding. Moodiness. Heaviness. Those are the traps. That "defective repressive mechanism" gives Scorpio wonderful access to the unconscious. But it's a two-way street: the unconscious also has wonderful access to Scorpio. Without the critical resources–perspective and friends–all the painful, confusing material in the deep psyche eventually erodes the Scorpionic spirit, dragging it downward into a swampy morass of dark emotions. A Scorpio person who follows that low road eventually hurts not only himself or herself; in the grips of the shadow the Scorpion begins to sting others as well, pointlessly forcing them to "face them-selves," insisting that they deal with all manner of painful psychological realities. Gentleness is sacrificed on the altar of truth. Pandora's box is opened...but no one knows how to close it or what to do with the demons that have been released.

SCORPIO IN LOVE

Pop-astrology suggests that Scorpio is the sexy sign. We've run a little survey on the subject and discovered that sex is actually rather popular with the other eleven signs as well. This is one area where no sign has cornered the market. The idea that "Scorpio is sexy" is a distorted perception of a more fundamental astrological idea: Scorpio is the sign of cathartic emotional intensity. The fact that our culture tends to associate those kinds of feelings with sexuality doesn't mean that they can't be found through other avenues–or that sexuality cannot exist without them. There are plenty of people for whom sex is essentially "fun" and no complex psychological depths need to be invoked. But none of those people are healthy Scorpios.

My nose is two inches from your nose. We're not just looking at each other; rather, my pupils are focused on your pupils. Suddenly we're both covered with goose bumps. I blurt out, "My God...you're a soul inside a body!"

That's Scorpio. Whether or not we're lovers is immaterial.

In intimacy Scorpio requires a sense of encounter. A touching of spirits. A willingness always to cut deeper. For this sign the word "nakedness" has little to do with clothing. The "nakedness" the Scorpion requires is a nakedness of the soul. If the Scorpion's lover is not a "partner in growth," then all feelings, sexual ones included, quickly fade. With the Moon in Scorpio, the logic remains the same, except that the Scorpionic hungers might be more buried, less immediately visible, less rational. Such a person must get in tune with the Scorpion's way, or all his or her relationships will feel unsatisfying, often for vague reasons or contrived ones. There will be silent, simmering moodiness punctuated with horrific outbursts.

Scorpio rising puts the Scorpionic process on the surface, in the person's "mask." Here we might find an intimidating intensity. A penetrating gaze. But what's behind it? That depends upon the deeper structures of the birthchart. Easily we can find one who has a knack for getting into incredibly intense intimacies with extremely intense individuals–but doesn't know what to do with them now that they've begun. The Ascendant relates to the surface of the character. In questions of ongoing love and sexuality, it plays an important role, but not nearly as important as the role played by the Moon or the Sun.

Sagittarius the Archer
(November 23 through December 21)

ARCHETYPES
The Gypsy
The Student
The Explorer
The Anthropologist
The Philosopher

DEVELOPMENTAL AIM
Life, to Sagittarius, is above all else a **quest.** The Archer is a seeker. Restless and relentless, a sense of endless searching

motivates the inner logic of this sign. What does the Archer pursue? Ultimately, the goal is a sense of life's quintessential meaning. As always in astrology, this goal is not necessarily one of which the individual is fully aware. Many times, in fact, quite the opposite is true, and that's true of all twelve signs. But conscious or not, the developmental aim of the sign still drives the person and accounts for much of his or her behavior–behavior that otherwise might seem utterly incomprehensible and pointless.

STRATEGIES AND RESOURCES

To find the meaning of life! Is that goal completely quixotic? For Sagittarius, that is not the question. The question is what life means, not whether it means anything. This is a primary Sagittarian resource: a feeling of confidence in the idea that behind all the seeming randomness of our lives there exists a great Pattern.

How to find the key to that Pattern? Experience. Exploration. A willingness to break up the mind-deadening routines of daily existence. These are the Archer's strategies.

Without freedom, no quest is possible. As a result, no sign is so chary of compromising its right to expand into new experiences. Critics of Sagittarius might interpret this love of freedom as a fear of commitment. In individual cases that analysis might be quite accurate. But more broadly we must recognize that without freedom, the Archer withers. And it is a sad but seemingly inescapable fact that love is often very hard on freedom.

SHADOW

But there is another side to love: it can enhance one's freedom and vastly enrich one's experience of the human condition. The meaning of life? Who knows?-but most of humanity's great teachers have agreed that whatever life means, that meaning has something to do with love. The Archer's shadow lies in his possible avoidance of real caring, the kind of caring that only arises when we have truly thrown in our lot with another person come what may. Sagittarius can skitter across the surface of life like a stone bouncing and careening across a frozen pond...and learn just about as much.

The principles at stake here are broader than questions of intimacy and sexuality. They expand to include the notion that

Sagittarius can often learn more about the great Pattern from poring over one excellent book in minute detail than he ever would by skimming page one of every volume in the Library of Congress. Breadth is a virtue, but no one needs to remind the Archer of that. More necessary might be the reminder that intensity and focus are virtues too–whether in love or in the library!

SAGITTARIUS IN LOVE

In affairs of the heart Sagittarius has a reputation for eloquent theorizing and poor performance. This need not be the case, but to avoid unpleasant Sagittarian scenarios such as divorce or compulsive infidelities–or a lonely pattern of superficial emotional contacts–the Archer needs to take a series of intentional steps. The first is the development of a philosophical commitment to the idea that under certain circumstances ongoing love can be a healthy, exciting journey. Ideas are powerful motivators for Sagittarius–but they must be convincing. No empty-headed romantic Mooning is going to hook the Archer for long, at least not long after that experience has been sampled and digested.

The second step is especially critical: Sagittarius must choose his or her potential lovers extremely carefully. Our culture attempts to stabilize marriage by engendering an essentially false interdependence between the partners. Women, for example, are socialized into crippling incapacity in the face of malfunctioning mechanical objects. Men, on the other hand, are socialized into ignorance and helplessness in the face of their own nutritional needs. With the Archer's love of independence, it cannot allow itself to be caught in these snares. It must maintain its ability to be free, even in the light of love's temptations. Furthermore, Sagittarius must choose a partner who values freedom too, one who has his or her own separate interests and separate friends, one who is open to endless change, one who is free of infantile jealousies. If all these requirements are fulfilled, then the Archer grasps an elemental Sagittarian secret: the quest is far richer and far deeper if it is shared.

Capricorn the Sea-Goat
(December 22 through January 20)

ARCHETYPES
The Hermit
The Father
The Prime Minister
The Authority
The Strategist

DEVELOPMENTAL AIM
Among modern men and women, at least among those who would be drawn to astrology or psychology, there exists one certifiably non-controversial remark: "It's good to be in touch with your feelings." But what if we were all simply in touch with our feelings, and nothing arose to balance them? Think of the mayhem: absenteeism, the rampant running of red lights, homicide...

Capricorn represents the other side of the coin. Not being "out of touch with feelings." But rather the radical development of those virtues that balance emotion: integrity, patience, character, persistence, the ability to delay gratification, the capacity to resist temptation.

STRATEGIES AND RESOURCES
To grow, Capricorn must take on some great work, some endeavor that pushes him to the limits of his potential. He must struggle and persist, wrestling with the inner demons, not just in principle, but it can be a misleading truth. The Sea-Goat's "great work" might very well unfold in the forum of the professional world. But other possibilities exist. Capricorn might take a small sailboat across a wide ocean. He or she might raise a healthy, happy family in a ghetto. A novel might be written. A homestead might be established in the Montana outback.

The point with Capricorn is always to make one's actions reflect one's intentions rather than one's feelings–especially in circumstances where those emotions are full of trepidation, surrender, and frustration.

SHADOW
To fulfill Capricorn's developmental aim, natural emotions must be controlled and directed. The horror is that they can be

suppressed entirely. When he is subjected to stress, the last of the Sea-Goat's functions to collapse is behavior. The surface. Even with the spark of life flickering out, Capricorn sticks to his course. Is that good or bad? A foolish question. Life is more complicated than those categories. The danger is not so centrally that Capricorn might "get out of touch with its feelings." It's more that everyone else might get out of touch with Capricorn's feelings. He can find himself locked into the role of the Authority, the Rock of Gibraltar, flawlessly running the show–and meanwhile withering in self-imposed solitary confinement.

CAPRICORN IN LOVE

Commitment might come relatively easily to the Sea-Goat. It's what to do once that commitment is made that baffles him. Capricorn must learn the discipline of emotional self-expression if love is to be viable and satisfying. Otherwise he (or she, of course) tends to get caught in a mechanically efficient, ritualized pattern of relating, often stoically enduring all the necessary disciplines of love without reaping any of the benefits.

Choosing the right partner is critical for Capricorn. Quite instinctively he or she is drawn to a man or woman who embodies solid virtues: dependability, a sense of responsibility, self-sufficiency, a level head. Less obvious is the need to find a partner who also fills in some of the gaps in the Sea-Goat's own behavioral repertoire: someone with an easy emotional expressiveness, a certain "sparkle."

Sun sign Capricorn people, unless there is much in their birthcharts to suggest the contrary, follow closely the pattern we've just described.

With the Moon in this sign, there is a mood (Moon!) of solitude about the individual. He or she must often learn a set of alien skills–sharing skills–if his or her love is to survive. Such a man or woman also requires a partner who won't be too profoundly shocked to discover that while he or she may be well loved, he is ultimately not needed.

On the Ascendant, Capricorn can denote a hard shell, businesslike and cautious. Such a shell is typically not as shy as one might expect based on the "reserve" that is usually attributed to Capricorn. The shell is just efficient. Socially and otherwise. The goatish mask usually develops an instinctive understanding of the ways of the world. It can be urbane, even expansive. But there's probably a full house pressed close to the Sea-Goat's vest, and a poker player's eyes gauging the hands of everyone else around the table.

The Capricornian mask may be easy to like, but it's hard to love. For real love to evolve, this Ascendant–and all others for that matter–must sooner or later be dropped to reveal the deeper material behind it. For some individuals that dropping will occur quickly, almost without effort, as soon as trust develops. For others it might never happen. What's behind the Capricorn Ascendant? Only one way to find out: look at the rest of the birthchart.

Aquarius the Water-Bearer
(January 21 through February 19)

ARCHETYPES
The Genius
The Revolutionary
The Exile
The Scientist
The Truth Sayer

DEVELOPMENTAL AIM
A woman appears on the nightly news: she is the first person to have climbed Mount Everest single-handedly in Nike sneakers. We marvel, quite rightly, at her courage. What we might not be so quick to realize is that ninety-eight percent of the courage it took to get her to the top of that mountain was already expended by the time she reached the foothills. Simply becoming the kind of person who would choose to climb Mount Everest–that's the heart of her accomplishment.

Her parents wanted her to marry the boy next door. Her peers pressured her into conventional styles of living: career, family, children, Society, in other words, put many "mountains" between her and her Everest. Each one had to be scaled.

Not all of us have come into the world to climb mountains. Most of us, in fact, have deep, poignant, spiritually valid experiences while leading relatively conventional lives. Normalcy is no sin! But for some of us the experiences that feed our hearts are not the experiences Ann Landers has in mind for us. These people are typically the ones whose birthcharts are touched in some central way by the sign Aquarius. Their developmental aim? In a word, it is the attainment of **individuality.**

STRATEGIES AND RESOURCES

Aquarius must learn to break the rules. Throwing bricks through windows is not the point; that's closer to the Aquarian shadow, as we'll soon see. The point is closer to the idea of constantly questioning authority. Sometimes that strategy is behavioral: "Father, I'll not be joining the firm after all. I'm planning to become an astrologer." Sometimes the strategy is more internal, as we learn to recognize that society got us when we were very young and programmed us with a set of values and assumptions that might have little to do with our real needs or our true purpose in the world. We must sort out our identity from all that mythology.

We speak of "free spirits"–but the truth is that most of the real human free spirits were eaten by saber-toothed tigers aeons ago. As a species, our survival has always depended upon our ability to band together. Now, this far down the evolutionary road, our species is gregarious and tribal. Instinctively we seek membership in the group and are usually willing to dance to any tune to gain that membership. The tribe might not always be the great American middle class. Many times people prefer membership in some subculture. Don't be fooled–that's still the tribal instinct.

The Aquarian strategy is to override the tribal instinct. "I am what I am. If you like me, that's delightful. If you think I'm crazy...that's interesting." That's the Water-Bearer's way.

Aquarius has resources to support its developmental strategy. The Water-Bearer is born with an instinctive distrust of paternalistic hierarchies. It tends to be a "divergent thinker," drawn magnetically into areas of thought that arise outside the mainstream. It has an "outsider's" mentality, the kind of clear, cold vision we expect of exiles in a new land, men and women who expect surprise–and don't expect understanding.

SHADOW

Symbolic rebellion–that's the Aquarian shadow. The woman who was supposed to climb Mount Everest instead succumbs to social pressure, marries conventionally, pursues a conventional career. What happens? All those rebellious, independent Aquarian instincts are vented on irrelevant targets. She insists upon her God-given right to wear purple stockings to work. She refuses adamantly ever to speak to her grandfather again. Instead of defending her individuality and her right to have some unique Aquarian human experiences, she wastes that energy defending pointless quirks. With her true individuality left undeveloped, she increasingly hides behind those eccentricities. People sense that she's "not there" somehow, despite her superficial self-assurance. They describe her as "aloof" or perhaps "cold," mistaking the hand of the shadow for her real individuality, now absent.

AQUARIUS IN LOVE

Love can be hard on individuality–or it can support and enhance it. For Aquarius, everything depends upon making sure that coin lands heads up. How? First, the Aquarian man or woman must have a solid start on becoming aware of his or her uniqueness. For this reason, although marriage can be healthy and happy for Aquarians, early marriage is usually stultifying and often short-lived.

A partner must be selected who is willing to give the Aquarian a lot of room to maneuver. Claustrophobic intimacy may be fine for Scorpio or Cancer, but never for the Water-Bearer–unless the rest of his or her birthchart bends over backward to say the opposite. For Aquarians, periods of separation are times of healing in a committed bond, not merely times of stress.

If the world were full of Aquarians, we might still have marriage, but it would look different from the patterns to which we are accustomed. For one thing, many happily married couples might choose not to live together! And that arrangement would be seen as perfectly normal and in tune with psychological reality.

Perhaps the most critical insight about Aquarius and intimacy is this: Sexuality is an exceedingly complex subject, and society often comes to our rescue in that department by providing us with prefabricated "scripts" about how to handle it. Promiscuity is discouraged, or carefully directed into prescribed courtship rituals. Monogamy is generally supported–and where it's not supported, "safe" outlets are provided. Women are encouraged to "nest." Men are encouraged to develop an unreasoning compulsion to earn money. All these themes have the effect of channeling sexuality in socially acceptable ways. We can criticize that channeling, but we might also observe that it represents the accumulated wisdom of humanity regarding a very tricky subject. Flawed wisdom, certainly. But the best we've got.

For most of us it's helpful to plug into those patterns to some extent, if only to help us keep our balance. Not for the Water-Bearer. For Aquarius, everything must be questioned. "Let's get married–and not live together!"

Pisces the Fishes
(February 20 through March 20)

ARCHETYPES
The Mystic
The Dreamer
The Poet
The Seer
The Romantic

DEVELOPMENTAL AIM
Pisces is the last sign of the zodiac. In a sense it's the highest sign–although a far more practical way of expressing it is to say that in Pisces the stakes are the highest. We win big or lose big. This is the sign of the "great escape." Not an escape from the world so much as from the tyranny of our own self-aggrandizing egos. In the Fishes we become aware of the fact that ultimately we are the consciousness that observes the personality and expresses itself through it. We stand back. We experience ourselves as players in a vast drama. And from that perspective our "normal" preoccupations with success and failure, gain and loss, pride and humiliation, all become unspeakably, inexpressibly funny.

This distinctly Piscean humor is not biting or cynical. There is not a drop of sarcasm in it. If anything, it fills the heart with compassion as well as giggles. Ultimately it is difficult to describe the Piscean developmental aim without drifting into mystical, religious language. That is simply the file in the great human card catalog where we've traditionally stored our information about the Fishes' experience.

The Piscean aim? In a word, it's **self-transcendence**.

STRATEGIES AND RESOURCES

To attain the Piscean goal, we must experience ourselves as something more than our name, rank and serial number. We must go beyond the part of ourselves that has a role to play in the human melodrama. We can call this process "meditation." That's a perfectly good word, except that society has put a lot of salad dressing on it. Here, when we speak of meditation, we do not mean to imply any particular system of beliefs. We certainly don't mean to suggest any particular "spiritual" lifestyle. No metaphysics. No sociology. Just the raw, uninterpreted process of consciousness becoming aware of itself. That's meditation–and that's also the central Piscean evolutionary strategy.

How does it work? Anyone can meditate. You don't even have to be "a Pisces." Just close your eyes, breathe deeply and slowly, and watch for the silent spaces in between your thoughts. Pop!– meditation. Nothing to it. The trick lies in learning to string those silent spaces together until they form long, unbroken chains of pure awareness. If Pisces succeeds in accomplishing that, then the individual begins to actually experience himself or herself as consciousness–just as if one plays basketball constantly, one soon learns to experience himself as a set of physical reflexes.

SHADOW

Pisces can misread this inner urge for self-transcendence or misunderstand how to go about it. The sign then descends into mere escapism. Old-fashioned astrology books are full of injunctions about the dangers of drink. Nowadays we must add the abuse of drugs, television, food, sex, sleep, novels, work, music, money, art, foreign travel, shopping, hobbies, education, social activism, and religion. Virtually anything we enjoy can be used in an escapist way. The point is not to avoid pleasure, but rather to avoid the Piscean tendency to disappear into it.

PISCES IN LOVE

There is profound tenderness in Pisces. For no other sign does the romantic ideal of "merging with one's partner" seem so palpably real. The only kind of relationship that is likely to survive for the Fishes is one with a "spiritual" basis. We put the word "spiritual" in quotation marks not to indicate any dubious feeling about those traditions, but rather to indicate that we must look carefully at the word. Like most cliches, it can slip from our tongues without really passing through our brains.

Two Piscean Presbyterians might sit together in church, have profoundly Presbyterian experiences, and still not have a spiritual relationship. Why? Simply because their spirits are not relating! On the other hand, two atheists might sit together in silence before a campfire and drift off into a meditational state– "dreaming the fire," as the Swahili people put it. They are dimly aware of each other's presence, and appreciative that they can share this magical space without comment and without the threat of any intrusive idiot humor: "Earth to Jane! Come in please! We've lost your signal!" That's a spiritual relationship. Those spirits are touching. They have entered an "altered state of consciousness" and still feel a sense of contact: Piscean paradise.

In intimacy Pisceans need to choose partners who are receptive to entering these transcendent states of mind. Whether or not their belief systems are in harmony is quite irrelevant. One can be a Presbyterian and the other one a Zen Buddhist. That doesn't matter. What counts is the shared experience, not the shared interpretation of the experience. Once they have found each other, then their bond must be fed with the kinds of input that induce these high touchings: silent time together, candlelight, quiet walks on the beach or in the forest, perhaps experiences in churches, temples, or formal meditation groups. Given all that, then the two lovers, connected on the Piscean wavelength, share something only the Fishes know: a sense of loving, dancing hilarity, a sense of the cosmic joke.

CHAPTER FIVE

LOVE AND WAR

You've learned something about the Sun, the Moon, and the Ascendant as the primal triad of the personality. But mature love exists between two human totalities, and all planets can be relevant to questions of intimacy, just as the entire person is involved in a relationship. Two planets, however, are particularly effective at revealing our intimate behavior. It's time to meet Venus and Mars–the Goddess of Love and the God of War.

Since antiquity, traditional astrologers have equated Mars with "masculinity," courage, initiative, assertiveness, and will. Venus has been associated with "femininity," gentleness, relatedness, receptivity, and beauty. But this chapter does not have a Venus section for women and a Mars section for men. In the twentieth century both principles of relationship are increasingly active in and accessible to both sexes. Mars does not represent testosterone, but rather drive, determination, and the impulse to seek what we desire. Venus is not estrogen; it symbolizes the capacity to form relationships, to create, to attract. Mars pursues and Venus attracts. Aren't you capable of both, regardless of your gender?

Sometimes we actively try to establish a relationship, and other times we play a more passive role, letting someone else take the initiative. Mars shows how we reach out to the person who catches our eye. Venus reveals how we make ourselves attractive and hope to capture attention. An important point to remember is that Venus also indicates what we find appealing in others. Astrologer Stephen Arroyo advises learning someone's Venus sign when trying to please him or her! When it comes to Venus, all of us act on the principle that "like attracts like." Someone who embodies the qualities of our Venus attracts us, and we demonstrate our Venusian qualities when trying to attract others. Mars goes after that Venusian bait. Venus is the siren and Mars is the suitor. Venus is the lure and Mars is the hunter. Venus is strategy and Mars is tactics

Let's examine these ideas in more detail and start by noting the four major orientations from which these archetypical winds blow, the elements.

The Four Elements

Fire, earth, air, and water are the astrological names for four states of consciousness active in all of us to varying degrees. Fire's principles of dynamic energy, adventure, play, and the intuitive leap toward the unknown animate the signs Aries, Leo, and Sagittarius. Earth represents matter: concrete reality, practicality, resourcefulness, and mastery of the tangible, measurable world. Earth's incarnations are the signs Taurus, Virgo, and Capricorn. Air symbolizes the mental functions of perception, reason, detachment, clarity, and curiosity. Air questions the world through the signs Gemini, Libra, and Aquarius. Water's realm is the emotions, subjectivity, sensitivity, imagination, and nurturing. Water's feelings flow through the signs Cancer, Scorpio, and Pisces.

Your Venus or your Mars is conditioned by its element, and that conditioning is fine-tuned by the sign within that element. As you read the following descriptions of Mars and Venus in each element and sign, please keep in mind that each planet represents only one feature of a chart, and no feature should be considered separately from the rest. No one relates only from Venus or from Mars. Remember work-oriented Walter from Chapter Three, whose Venus in Aries translated into liking people who challenged him to do his best on the job. Think of these descriptive paragraphs as guidelines to trigger your own interpretive process, and you won't lose sight of the chart as a whole.

Where Are Your Venus and Mars?

If you don't know, or if you want to locate these planets in someone else's chart, please turn to the mini-ephemeris for Venus and Mars in the Appendices.

VENUS IN FIRE

Venus in Fire people attract by showing us how much fun they are, how colorful, plucky, adventurous, and noble-spirited–by displaying the qualities of Fire, in other words. Their relationship advertising says that we'll really be missing out on something special if we ignore them. How can we resist such derring-do and slapdash gallantry?

Venus in Aries bills itself as the Warrior or the Amazon, charging through life with a pioneering spirit that survives all blows, even thrives on them. "Look how gutsy I am. I'm not just a date; I'm an adventure. I am Elemental Passion." Venus in Aries is quite willing to be swept off his or her feet by your mad impulsive desire. They may get into–and out of–relationships rather quickly. Venus in Aries throws out a romantic challenge, daring you to win his or her hand. "Hit me with your best shot." Venus in Aries appreciates independence, spunkiness, and directness. These people are risk-takers. They have a taste for healthy competition, especially if they get to win. Marilyn Monroe and Elizabeth Taylor, two of the most courted, pursued women of all time, have Venus in Aries. So does Jack Nicholson, whose longtime companion Anjelica Houston says, "He makes my blood boil."

Venus in Leo people either clown their way into your heart or try to impress you by their regal, aristocratic ways. "If you're a connoisseur, you'll like me." They will make grand plays and sweeping gestures for your attention. An admiring audience doesn't hurt either, and they make sure you have the front row seat. "Out of all my fans, you're number one. All the world's a stage, and you and I have top billing. Let's enjoy the show." Venus in Leo demonstrates how dramatic or noble he or she is, how generous, how creative, how entertaining, how worthy of respect, and what a feather in your cap he or she would be. If you're very eligible yourself, so much the better: may your kingdoms unite. These people can act like Richard the Lion-hearted or a petty tyrant, depending on how much their self-respect has been supported or punctured. Circus owner P. T. Barnum had Venus in Leo, and so does conductor Leonard Bernstein.

Venus in Sagittarius has a complex approach to the art of attraction, alternating among its archetypes: the Gypsy, the Scholar, the Philosopher, the Explorer, and the Anthropologist. The Gypsy or the Explorer says, "Look how adventurous and carefree I am. Kick over your traces and go to Europe with me." The Scholar tantalizes you with glimpses of the accumulated wisdom of the ages. The Philosopher convinces you that your spiritual path leads directly to him or her. The Anthropologist waltzes you through a spellbinding collection of human types, a dowry of fascinating friends and acquaintances. Sagittarius is ruled by Jupiter, the king of the gods, lawgiver–and philanderer. These traits are certainly not present in everyone with Venus in Sagittarius, but they illustrate the enormous appetite these people have for experience, adventure, and variety, and their sometimes conflicting attachment to ideals and principles. Never bore them, never belittle their beliefs, and enjoy the safari. Guitarist extraordinaire Jimi Hendrix, who called his group "Band of Gypsies," had Venus in Sagittarius, as do political activists Jane Fonda and Joan Baez. "Anthropologists" of the human comedy Lenny Bruce and Federico Fellini share this Venus sign.

MARS IN FIRE

The saying "Faint heart never won fair maid" exemplifies Mars in Fire. These people favor direct, active pursuit; they burn hot. They find it easy to take the initiative. Mars in Fire is the Irresistible Force.

Mars in Aries comes on saying "I won't take no for an answer." Rocker Pete Townshend has Mars in Aries, and his song titles show it: "Gonna Get Ya," "Rough Boys," and "I Am an Animal." Ardent and impetuous, the Warrior-archetype Mars person battles to win your heart. Passion and directness are tactics here, unless the rest of the birthchart is very mild. Competition sparks Mars in Aries; it likes the thrill of the chase. Clint Eastwood ("Go ahead–make my day") has Mars in Aries. If you want to be the object of this single-minded attention, it's wonderful. Don't give in too soon, and it will be even more wonderful when you do. If the feelings aren't mutual, prepare for a siege and don't give any quarter, which will be interpreted as a sign of capitulation. If you can convince your suitor that the battle is hopeless, Mars in Aries will eventually follow an impulsive attraction to a more receptive target.

Mars in Leo woos by "the divine right of kings." Excelling at "courtly love," this person plays the knight in shining armor, ready to carry you away, especially before witnesses. Mars in Leo understands the dramatic effects of courtship better than any other sign. They pay attention to stage settings and props. Kings shower gifts on their intended ones. So do Mars-in-Leo people, whether or not they can afford it, which might upset you if you're more attuned to practical Earth. Mars in Leo sends roses–to your office. Mars in Leo proposes in a crowded elevator. How can you spoil the tableau by refusing? These people can be truly noble, warm, honest, loyal, and affectionate. Be truthful in return and don't hurt their pride, or the Lion might roar. Some very well-loved entertainers have Mars in Leo: Robert Redford, Bruce Springsteen, and Frank Sinatra. Robert Graves, famous for his love poetry and studies of the archetypal Great Goddess, had Mars in Leo.

Mars in Sagittarius pursues through the archetypes of this sign. The Scholar asks you to a poetry reading. The Philosopher or Anthropologist makes your world more comprehensible, less confusing, by offering their perspectives. They take you to a political demonstration. The Gypsy and the Explorer promise adventures: experiential, romantic, or sexual. Mars in Sagittarius impresses you with its love of freedom, inquiring mind, idealism, and visionary qualities. This Mars sign is more frank and blunt than Aries or Leo, preferring to get right to the point rather than waste time in pursuit or show. If you're direct too, you'll appreciate that quality. If you're more sensitive and prefer gentler courtship, you might be bruised. This sign can be painfully honest and unsubtle about its attractions, to you or others, whether or not it acts on them. Outspoken rock star Janis Joplin had Mars in Sagittarius. French poet Arthur Rimbaud, who claimed that a poet had to make himself a seer by overwhelming all his senses with experience, had Mars in Sagittarius. Active sportsman Prince Charles has Mars in Sagittarius.

VENUS IN EARTH

Those of us with Venus in Earth seek to make ourselves attractive by displaying this element's qualities of realism, practicality, mastery of the three-dimensional, concrete world. These people have an earthy, physical orientation. Venus in Earth shows us how sensual, patient, reliable, and efficient it is, how mature, how grounded.

Venus in Taurus attracts through emphasizing the physical, body-centered nature of Earth. They radiate touchability; they're cuddly. "Look how natural and easy it is to be with me," they say. "Look how soothing my company could be for you. Put your feet up and put on the headphones. I am the Earth Father/Mother. I make everything simple." Venus in Taurus appreciates comfort and luxury; they appeal to your senses or your pocketbook. They may not tell you they like you in words, but seek to draw you in by showing you how right it feels to be together, how much they have to offer physically or in material wealth. John Wayne, hero of many back-to-the-land Westerns, had Venus in Taurus. Actors Ryan O'Neal and Marlon Brando both exemplify the earthy attractiveness of Venus in Taurus.

Venus in Virgo looks appealing by informing you how perfect life could be if you were together. Venus in Virgo shows us how much attention he or she pays to every detail of a relationship, how willing he or she is to make improvements. "See how honest I am; see how eager I am to make this relationship all it could be." These people also demonstrate their Mercurial wit and critical abilities, their discrimination. They make themselves indispensable to you in as many ways as possible. Two extremes of behavior can occur with this configuration: sometimes Venus in Virgo becomes too critical and thinks no one is good enough for him or her, and sometimes Venus in Virgo thinks he or she isn't good enough to deserve a relationship and bends over backward to serve or be worthy of the partner. Obviously either extreme should be avoided! Eleanor Roosevelt, indispensable to her husband Franklin Delano Roosevelt, had Venus in Virgo. Poet and mythological historian Robert Graves had Venus in Virgo, showing the verbal abilities of this placement. Rolling Stone vocalist Mick Jagger has Venus in Virgo; note his titles, from "Under My Thumb" to "She's the Boss."

Venus in Capricorn people arouse your interest with Capricornian strategy and efficiency. They project an aura of reserve, fascinating you with still waters that run deep. "I may be a lone wolf, but I like **you**; somehow you have found a way into this Hermit's heart." Then they offer a further enticement. "But I'll never be clingy and suffocating." They stress their sense of responsibility, efficiency, and integrity. "I'm reliable. I'm not some empty-headed bit of fluff. I'm not a phony. You can count on me." They impress you with their mastery of the material world, perhaps with their status, their reputation, or their personal fiefdom. "I may not be flashy, but I'm like a classic blue-chip stock. I'm a good investment, and I'll improve with age." These people are usually not horrified at the idea of commitment, regardless of whether current fashion supports that concept, and quietly they'll let you know it.   James Dean and Katherine Hepburn have Venus in Capricorn, showing the "lone wolf" and "classic" sides of this Venus placement.

MARS IN EARTH

In this methodical element, Mars uses practicality, patience, and strategy to pursue its intended. Mars in Earth doesn't talk or wish about it; Mars in Earth carries out a concrete plan. If waiting is part of the plan, that's not a problem. Like a general on maneuvers, these people keep track of your habits, movement patterns, likes and dislikes, and adjust their tactics accordingly. They believe that persistence pays off.

Mars in Taurus comes on as the "good provider," not only financially but sensually, and that means all five senses. Mars in Taurus looks out for your physical comfort, whether it's helping balance your checkbook, putting your preferred meals on the table and your preferred music on the turntable, rubbing your back, or wearing your favorite cologne. They want to lull you and relax you. They'll enlist Mother Nature on their side, taking you to the zoo in the spring or walking you through the honeysuckle on a summer's evening.   This is a very physical, hedonistic placement for Mars, and a determined one, bordering on stubborn or possessive. If they want you, they want you a lot, and they'll want you for a long time. Dancing partners Rudolf Nureyev and Margot Fonteyn both have Mars in Taurus; so do Sidney Poitier and Mick Jagger.

Mars in Virgo says "Look how much you and I could help each other. A relationship with me is like being an amoeba in a zoologist's 'growth medium'; you're guaranteed to go through some changes. Don't you want to be all you can be?" Mars in Virgo challenges you to perfect your interpersonal skills as you would perfect your artistic or musical skills, with attention to technique and detail. These people minutely scrutinize you and your life and offer suggestions for improvement. They are always ready to help; they know a better way. They impress you with their intelligence and analytical streak. If they seem overly critical of themselves or of you, remember that their aim is to convince you that this could be a perfect relationship, and they use analysis and criticism as means to that end. Dedicated dancer Mikhail Baryshnikov, and Jacqueline Kennedy Onassis, who refurbished the White House, have Mars in Virgo,

Mars in Capricorn is the master strategist, putting the savvy and cool-headed efficiency of the Prime Minister or Executive archetypes to work to get you to "join the company." They play their cards close to the vest until they're sure you're interested, sizing you up before they make a move. They plan a conquest like scaling the Matterhorn; when they pursue you, their methods are well organized and carefully orchestrated. They want results and tend not to chase unattainable targets. They will give you practical, demonstrable, often tangible reasons to convince you that your best interests are with them. These people may not be gushing wells of emotion, although much depends on the rest of the birthchart. Don't be fooled by a seeming lack of warm, easy demonstrativeness. You can feel assured they genuinely care by noting their responsible actions toward you–more important in the long run than hearts and flowers. David Bowie, who has lasted a long time in the music world through changing styles, has Mars in Capricorn. Marlon Brando drew on his Capricorn Mars for his portrayal of the Godfather.

VENUS IN AIR

People with Venus in the mental element attract through the power of personifying some concept. They use intellect and logic to make themselves interesting. They promise a fascinating life of the mind, well spent with them. They're brilliant; they're witty; they sparkle. They draw you in with ideas.

Venus in Gemini people believe that the way to your heart is through your brain. This person is the original Good Conversationalist, a raconteur who will keep you enthralled with stories about the lectures attended, authors read, events experienced. They make wonderful correspondents. They'll impress you with their library. "I'm intelligent, but I'm not a pedant. I'll never be boring; we'll always have something to discuss." They like verbal byplay; they flirt well. The eighteenth century institution of the salon, where great minds of the day could meet over coffee at the home of an intelligent hostess, was probably created by someone with Venus in Gemini. These people are observant and friendly, interested in almost everything and disposed to talk to almost anyone, unless the rest of the birthchart suggests a taste for solitary vigils and Tibetan caves. If you have a wide variety of interests, you will appeal to Venus in Gemini all the more. They are not so much deliberately fickle as endlessly curious. Keep them entertained, and they'll keep you entertained. Bill Cosby and Cher have Venus in Gemini, as do poet-songwriter Bob Dylan and William Shakespeare.

Venus in Libra people attempt to charm you with their social graces, their love of peace, harmony, beauty, and their aesthetic sensitivity. They show you how refined, delicate, artistic, warm and other-centered they are. "I am a gentle Romantic with a capital R." Venus-in-Libra people demonstrate how fair and ethical they are, how much they love justice and hate wrangling and bigotry–and therefore how sweet life could be with them. Remember the Libran archetypes; they give Venus in Libra people several options when trying to attract others. The Artist impresses you with creativity, the Lover with sensitivity, the Counselor with empathy, the Diplomat with tact, and the Peacemaker with fairness and balance. The mental quality of Air tends toward idealism and romanticism in Libra, and sometimes to an attachment to verbal harmony at all costs, if the rest of the chart isn't that of a scrapper. The Diplomat and the Peacemaker may make too many concessions for their own good, or demand too many of you. When you have a bone to pick with them, pick it gently but firmly, and don't be bamboozled by their silver tongues. Oscar Wilde, a playwright who wrote polished high-society comedies, had Venus in Libra. Stunningly beautiful actress Vivien Leigh, best known for her role in *Gone With the Wind* and very serious about her career as a performing artist, had Venus in Libra.

Venus in Aquarius broadcasts its originality, independence, and open-mindedness in order to attract others. "I have revolutionary ideas and insight that can liberate you." Venus in Aquarius people point out their clarity of thought, their attachment to speaking the truth as they see it, their quality of "genius," however it manifests in them. "I am a citizen of the future. I'm a visionary who's ahead of my time, and I'm so glad you can see that." These people make themselves worthy of attention by being different, by not fitting in, by questioning what they see around them. "I'm independent. You can be completely yourself around me, and I'll like you even more for it." These people both need and will give you a lot of space, to the point of seeming overly detached. Unless the rest of the birthchart indicates otherwise, Venus in Aquarius wants to be as open, free, and non-possessive as possible, and chides itself and you for falling too short of that goal. These people not only break the existing rules, they like to throw the rules out completely and substitute their own, or none at all. Feminists Simone de Beauvoir, Gloria Steinem, and Erica Jong have Venus in Aquarius, along with existentialist playwright Edward Albee.

MARS IN AIR

Mars in Air pursues you with the power of persuasion. These people use verbal ability, eloquence, or rationalization to woo you, and they can be very convincing. They talk a good game. They write letters, poetry, cards, and explanations. They make torrid phone calls and declarations. Using the mental agility of Air, they muster all the arguments possible to win you.

Mars in Gemini will dazzle you with wit, brilliance, and precocity. They write sonnets for you, or copy someone else's and send them instead. Mars in Gemini will ask to read your poetry and take you to every rare-book store in town. They read your favorite book so that you can discuss it together. Mars in Gemini will talk to you and listen to you, making every attempt to refine and deepen the level of communication. These people like to surprise you with tickets for your favorite author, or for that play you've been dying to see. Mars in this experience-hungry sign might suggest a trip to the state fair, the circus, or the Third World. They tell you stories; they make you laugh; they pin an original limerick to your door, starring you. The aim of all this mental thrust and parry is to establish an intimate dialogue with you and persuade you to continue it. Writers F. Scott Fitzgerald, Ram Dass, Richard Bach, and Erica Jong all have Mars in Gemini.

Mars in Libra, sounds like a contradiction in terms at first: the God of War in the sign of the Lover? Think about Libra methods (understanding and empathy) employed by Mars (the pursuer), and you'll grasp this configuration. Mars in Libra will make its move by insisting how well it understands you (the Counselor), and how peaceful and harmonious (the Peacemaker) your life could be if only you would surrender to this relationship (the Lover). "I tell you, I **know** you; I know everything about you; you're an open book to me." Mars in Libra people expend energy to create intimacy with you (the Diplomat). The Artist wants to take your picture or put you on stage or buy you clothing that becomes you. The Lover uses romanticism, being tender and sensitive. The Counselor listens to you and advises you. All of these archetypes want to get along well with your friends, to enlist their support. Romantic poet Percy Bysshe Shelley and the founder of psychotherapy Sigmund Freud had Mars in Libra. In the biographical movie *Lenny*, Lenny Bruce filled his wife Honey's dressing room with wall-to-wall flowers. Whether or not this incident actually occurred, it's a good example of Mars in Libra, which Bruce had.

Mars in Aquarius, like Mars in Gemini, comes across as an intellectual, but in Aquarius the tone is different. "I am a genius, and you should recognize that. Everyone else will eventually. Stay with me and you'll get the truth, and freedom to be yourself. Now, what are you going to do with it?" They intrigue you by their unique viewpoint on the world, their originality. They offer you a nonrestrictive, individuality-enhancing lifestyle. "I'm not like everybody else. I may exasperate you, but I'll never bore you." Mars in Aquarius can come on like the Rebel Without a Cause, the Mad Scientist, the Misunderstood Genius, or the Harbinger of Social Progress. Civil rights activist W. E. B. Du Bois, botanist Luther Burbank, and writer J. D. Salinger have Mars in Aquarius.

VENUS IN WATER

People with Venus in Water are conditioned by the elemental symbol of emotions and subjectivity. They appeal to us through our feelings. They let us know that they're the sensitive kind, that they see into our hearts and will be gentle with what they find there. They invite us into the enchanted, subjective world of the imagination.

Venus in Cancer attracts by showing how protective, tender, and healing it can be. "Come to me, you who are weary and heavy laden, and I will give you rest." Astrological tradition labels those with Venus in Cancer as mothering or smothering types, domestic, clingy, and full of maudlin sentimentality. The shadow side of this and every planetary position carries drawbacks, but that "smothering mother" description shortchanges Venus in Cancer. These people offer to help you find your roots and to nourish those roots, whether they are domestic, psychological, or archetypal. "See how understanding I am, how tuned into the real you. I recognize Superman under your mild-mannered Clark Kent exterior. I'll supply the telephone booth." They offer you a "home base" where you can feel secure. Venus in Cancer appeals to you by demonstrating how fanciful and imaginative it is, and what a good copilot it would be in your own flights of imagination. Judy Garland had Venus in Cancer and drew on it in her characterization of home-loving Dorothy wandering through the fantastic Land of Oz. Carl Jung had Venus in Cancer, assisting him in the exploration of his clients' personal myths.

Venus in Scorpio people exude mystery, power, and sexuality when they want to be noticed. They radiate magnetism; the archetype of the Hypnotist operates in this Venus placement. "You cannot escape me. Look into my eyes, deeper, deeper." Through the Sorcerer archetype they invite you to explore the psychic dimensions of relating with them. You wonder if they're reading your mind or your palm. Venus in Scorpio promises primal, transformative intensity, sexually, emotionally, or psychologically. "See how tempestuous I am. I simmer with volcanic emotions. And I won't let you hide from yours." If you're an "honesty junkie" or an "intensity junkie" too, you're hooked. If you're not, look elsewhere. Venus in Scorpio lures you with an aura of the unknown, the hidden, which was the original meaning of the word "occult." Rolling Stone guitarist Keith

Richards, also known for his collection of skull rings, has Venus in Scorpio; so does rocker Tina Turner, of whom Mick Jagger said, "Standing next to her (on stage) is the hottest place in the world!" Sophia Loren, famous for her sultry looks, has Venus in Scorpio.

Venus in Pisces attracts through the Neptune-ruled archetypes: the Mystic, the Poet, the Dreamer, the Seer, and the Romantic. They want you to notice the pure, untrammeled Spirit looking out through their flesh-and-blood eyes. They offer escape from the dreary "real world" into a realm of awareness, fantasy, and illusion, where consciousness, rather than personality with its social security number and shopping lists, reigns supreme. Whether Venus in Pisces impresses you with this visionary quality in or out of church, temple, mosque, or ashram doesn't matter; these people tempt you with first-class tickets to Inner Space. Make sure those tickets aren't one-way. "Merge with me. Renew your spirit with me. Listen to my albums, play Dungeons and Dragons with me, or let's just watch the Moon on the water together. You can let your innermost Self breathe in my presence, and I won't chase it away with bright lights and harsh questions." New Age writers Ram Dass and Shirley MacLaine have Venus in Pisces, as does ballet dancer Mikhail Baryshnikov. Poets Edgar Allan Poe and Elizabeth Barrett Browning had Venus in Pisces.

MARS IN WATER

Mars in Water pursues you with either an emotional onslaught or quiet waves of feeling, washing persistently and irresistibly over you, wearing down your resistance. Whoever invented Chinese water torture probably had Mars in this element, so don't underestimate its ability to get what it wants.

Mars in Cancer sets out to prove to you how utterly nurtured you could be, how your every emotional need could be met, by this relationship. These people offer protection, security, and a "nest" where they will soothe and heal all your frazzled nerves–and they'll wrestle anacondas to keep it that way. You may feel totally safe, or crowded, depending on your nature. They provide emotional support and understanding, and much like Pisces, a participant in your inner life. For example, Mars in Cancer will ask you what you dreamed last night. When you tell your dream, Mars in Cancer doesn't yawn and look the other way. These people will actively listen and suggest insights of their own, provide you with a notebook for a dream journal, hold you when you wake up from a nightmare. They pay attention to your personal mythology. For example, suppose you tell your Mars-in-Cancer lover that violets have always symbolized spring to you, because you used to pick them as a child. On May first, Mars in Cancer arrives at your house with a huge bunch of violets, handpicked for you. Humphrey Bogart, who excelled at playing tough, crabby men with soft hearts under their hard shells, had Mars in Cancer. William Shakespeare and Lord Byron, a Romantic poet, had Mars in Cancer. A Mars in Cancer woman who literally acted out her fantasies was Marie Antoinette, who had a peasant's hamlet built at Versailles before the French Revolution.

Mars in Scorpio floods you with a tidal wave of passion, or fixes you with a penetrating gaze, biding its time. They hypnotize you or analyze you or overwhelm you with intensity. They offer fulfillment on a sexual, emotional, and transpersonal level. "This relationship will change both of us and make a bond that will never be broken. I'm ready for it; are you? Let me tell you why you're frightened." Mars in Scorpio makes a point of its honesty, its realness, its ability to deal with potentially touchy issues, its desire to share its depths with you. They tell you about their hospice work. They take you to a psychology lecture or a seance or a horror movie or an X-rated one, or simply to their house for dinner and soul-revealing, mesmerizing conversation until three in the morning. These people demonstrate that they will always be right there for you, closer than your skin, and if you long for that kind of closeness, you'll find them irresistible. Rock star Jimi Hendrix had Mars in Scorpio; so did author Henry Miller, passionate in every sense of the word.

Mars in Pisces pursues you under the banner of the Spiritual Warrior. It's a crusade, and your heart is the Holy Grail. They try to touch your soul, gently, with their bare hands. They may not ride up to your door on a white horse, but they secretly wish that they could, and they ask you to science fiction and fantasy conventions as a poor substitute. They write you poetry; they take you to *Star Wars*; they do everything possible to aid and abet you in your escapes from reality. In the play *A Thousand Clowns*, one of the characters, asked by his lover to return to reality for a moment, instantly replies, "I will only go as a tourist!"–a good example of Mars in Pisces. Poet-songwriter Bob Dylan has Mars in Pisces in the House of Career, and in many ways he has become a public symbol of this configuration. Read his lyrics or some of his song titles, reflecting Piscean fantasy: "Blowin' in the Wind," "Visions of Johanna," "Mr. Tambourine Man," "You Angel You."

VENUS AND MARS IN THE BIRTHCHART

Venus and Mars in the signs are not the only indicators of how a person will choose to relate. Always consider Venus and Mars in the context of the chart as a whole. Suppose that timid little Mildred, the grade-school librarian, has seven planets in Libra and Mars in Aries. Her Mars in Aries will not make Mildred the Zorro of the singles bars. In this extremely Libran chart, Mars in Aries might translate into demonstrating that Mildred will always apply energy to keeping the peace, always be willing to take the lead in kissing and making up. Her courtship style may be more active than is usual in a woman with so much Libran energy; she might, courteously, approach a man with tickets to an event she knows interests him, but in a way that makes it easy for him to refuse without embarrassment to either of them. But Mildred's courtship style will not be so insistent as is usual with Aries; she won't leave a string of urgent invitations on his answering machine or camp out on his doorstep.

After you consider Venus and Mars as indicators of relating style, look beyond these planets and consider them in the context of the chart as a whole. If you can remember that, you are doing fine. Charts are not made up of only planets. Our next step is to examine some **houses** that possess special significance in intimacy, in Chapter Six.

THE ARC OF INTIMACY

Where do you spend most of your time? Relationships? Career? Psychological work on yourself? Creative projects? What kinds of experience "hit you where you live"? Answer these questions, and you'll start to grasp the concept of houses.

Houses. What are they? In dream work, a house is a symbol of the self. In astrology, a house is an arena where that self operates. In a birthchart, houses are the twelve prominent "pie slices." Physically, they are sections of space above and below the horizon of the birthplace, six above and six below. A planet's position in the houses tells us whether that planet was rising, setting, or somewhere in between. But that's not all.

We learned in Chapter Two that houses symbolize territories–internal or external–that can be entered and explored. Planets, you will recall, answer the question **what:** what part of the mind you are considering. Signs answer the questions **how** and **why:** what motivates that part of the mind, how it behaves. Houses answer the question **where:** in what arena of someone's life you can see that sign-planet combination in action. If you need any of these concepts reviewed, please see Chapter Two.

Houses show where the action is! Houses reveal where someone's life happens. They are experiential; a separate, specific life drama unfolds in each one. The scripts vary and include "Developing a Social Persona"; "Establishing a Personal

Myth"; and "Planning the Future," to mention only three. There are twelve of these ongoing dramas active in everyone's life, but some are more emphasized than others. Think of it this way: your birthchart is like a TV set with twelve soap operas in perpetual broadcast, but a few are your favorites and get more attention.

FIGURE 2: THE TWELVE HOUSES

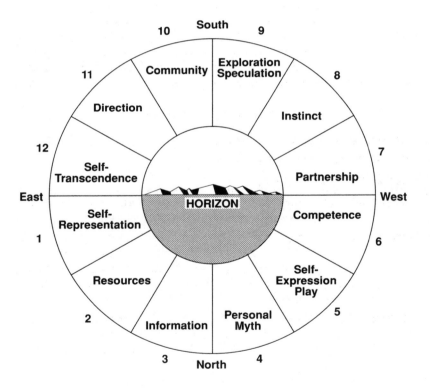

Four houses in particular form a "mini-series" pertinent to relationships. Houses five, six seven, and eight constitute an **arc** of intimacy in the birthchart. Each of these houses can be considered a special dimension of the relationship-forming process. Each is a stage in that process, containing its own potential hazards and stepping-stones, building on the preceding house or houses within the arc. Each house must be mastered if we are not to suffer a repeating cycle of frustrations. You learn to sit before you crawl, crawl before you stand, and stand before you walk. The arc of intimacy represents another sort of developmental sequence in the growth of relationships.

Briefly, house five emphasizes playful, self-renewing romantic activity. House six focuses on issues of responsibility, humility, and self-sacrifice–essential to the survival of any relationship. House seven highlights issues of commitment and trust. House eight is sexual and rooted in the unconscious. Issues of "chemistry" and "electricity"–and how to sustain them in the long haul–arise there. At the end of the chapter we'll give some examples of how planets and signs might behave in a particular house. First, let's examine the houses in this arc, one at a time.

The Fifth House

TRADITIONAL NAME: House of Children

CORRESPONDING SIGN: Leo

ASSOCIATED PLANET: Sun

TERRAIN: Pleasure; Creative self-expression; Falling in love; Playfulness

PROCESS: Sharing one's history with an interesting stranger. Enjoyment of spontaneity, pleasure and relaxation. Willingness to be enchanted by another; openness to falling in love. Ongoing discovery and creation of the relationship.

ABORT SEQUENCE: Inability to initiate contact with people or to respond. Rigidity, control, seriousness, iciness, inability to play. Addiction to constant newness and excitement in relationships; refusal to accept routine or boredom. Insistence on living only in the present.

Welcome to the House of Love Affairs–one of its traditional names. Step right this way into the House of Pleasures, another of those names. Enjoy yourself. Indulge. Play all you like in the House of Creative Self-expression, but if you get stuck here, you'll wind up an adult lost in the house of Children.

This is the house of falling in love, of romance, where the sparks first start flying. This is the house of the first date or the second or the third. The early stages of a love affair are ruled by the fifth house.

What happens in those early stages? Without fail we go through a ritual that could be called The Trading of Life Stories. We're fascinated by the other person, his or her novelty and mystery. "Tell me the epic, the drama, the saga of you. Tell me about yourself." We make our first connections to our partners here. We rediscover, through someone else's marveling eyes, how interesting we are, how colorful. We play. We feel giddy, smitten, and besotted. The other person seems endlessly perfect, and couples delight in every new discovery they make about each other. The fifth house stage of a union is full of excitement, fresh, wondrously new, and feels like manna from heaven to our egos.

Planets or signs, but especially planets, in your fifth house indicate what qualities you need to have present in the other person at the beginning of a love affair, as an omen that the relationship could last. When a planet lies in this sector of the chart, it is a trigger for the falling-in-love mechanism. Early in the relationship, the other person must figure into the **courtship**, which is what happens in the fifth house. Other factors must be present for the long haul, but the fifth house of both people must be activated if the relationship is even to begin.

How can the fifth house go wrong? We may not learn how to play, relax, and have fun. If the planet or planets we have there are unlike the tone of the rest of the chart, this house may seem like alien territory. But to learn the language of love, you must start with the language of the fifth house, even if seven of your planets lie in solitary Capricorn, and you feel awkward about expressing your romantic fifth-house Venus. Another possible malfunction of the fifth house can be the refusal to leave it. Typically we enjoy the fifth house. Some people crave the thrills of the early stages of intimacy and become hooked on telling their stories, addicted to the enraptured attention of a first-time listener. Others are uncomfortable about having their faults subjected to the scrutiny of a post-fifth-house relationship, once the glow of apparent perfection has worn off. Some people have a low tolerance for anything or anyone who has become at all routine, and they avoid the sameness or responsibility inherent in longer term intimacy. The art of loving does not consist solely of play and wonder, but many of us refuse to accept that truth. Such a person ventures into the sixth house of responsibility–humility and working on the relationship–and frightened, runs back to the fifth house, which has become his or her prison.

The Sixth House

TRADITIONAL NAME: House of Servants

CORRESPONDING SIGN: Virgo

ASSOCIATED PLANET: Mercury

TERRAIN: Responsibilities; Competence and skill; Devotion and self-sacrifice

PROCESS: Acceptance of equal responsibility for the relationship. Willingness to work out the practical details of intimacy. Realization that no one is perfect; tolerance of each other's faults. Development of relating skills.

ABORT SEQUENCE: Unequal roles; dominant-subordinate pattern; one partner contributing far more than the other. Refusal to accept responsibility or compromise. Constant criticism, belittling or sabotaging each other. Poor relating skills.

Monday morning. The alarm clock whoops sadistically in your ears. You stumble toward the bathroom and crash into your mate in the smallish doorway. Your mate beats you to the shower. You pour yourself the last of the orange juice and blearily toast a slice of bread. Your mate walks into the kitchen and is hurt, because you made toast for only one and polished off the juice. You go into the bathroom and discover the sink festooned with hair, towels crumpled on the floor, and the toothpaste cap nowhere to be seen. The two of you conclude your breakfast and start your week with a fight.

Sound familiar? In adult love we experience the sixth house as often as the fifth, but we celebrate it less in songs and stories. Yet a strong response to the sixth house is just as necessary as a strong response to the fifth, if we want a relationship to last and thrive.

The basic sixth-house question is: How do we work this? How do we work out the details of this partnership? How do we combine two unique individuals, each with his or her own quirks and differences, and make sure their daily lives flow smoothly together?

We need to do three things: hold an ideal for the relationship, work conscientiously and mutually on attaining it, and avoid blaming one another when we fall short of that ideal. In other words, we need to accept our own and each other's imperfections, while trying to overcome them. That's the core of the sixth house.

In a birthchart this is the house of competence, of proficiency, of carrying out personally meaningful responsibilities. A weak response to this house can make a person feel inadequate, trapped in inferior roles, weighted down with meaningless tasks. In a relationship, this house symbolizes the development of relating skills. Perhaps the most important are communication skills; Mercury rules this house. Other responsibilities involve the willingness to contribute equally to the relationship; to the housework, to the budget, to the give-and-take of affection and emotional responsiveness. Neither partner should "serve" the other exclusively; in the traditional House of Servants, the idea is to learn to "serve" one another equally. Neither partner should carry the major share of responsibilities in any area of the relationship without a compensatory trade-off in another area. Signs and planets, most particularly planets, in your sixth house indicate what relating skill you should strive to develop.

Steve Forrest is an enthusiastic and inspired cook. He doesn't memorize cookbooks, although he looks at them sometimes. Mostly, he says, "God speaks to me." Jodie Forrest, when left to her own devices, put down the book she was reading and cooked a meal on the rare occasions when the mood struck her, but for the most part she lived quite happily on canned tuna, raw vegetables, and rice cakes. It occurred to Steve and Jodie that, considering his talent and her disposition, it was ridiculous to divide the cooking-and-washing-up chores equally. Steve has taken over as chef, Jodie as dishwasher, and each is sure he or she has the better end of the bargain. That's one sixth-house drama that ended well!

A relationship that works perfectly is the goal of the sixth house, but **insisting** on perfection is its danger. Common mistakes in the sixth house are shirking responsibilities, or requiring that your partner be your clone, who fulfills all your expectations and anticipates your every whim–certainly not a relationship of equals! Another mistake is acquiescing to such a demand. The sixth house can malfunction if one or both partners incessantly try to "improve" the other by a stream of criticism, fault-finding, and nagging, dwelling on everything that is wrong with the relationship and the mate, and ignoring the other's good qualities and the relationship's potential.

The sixth-house process continues, in different forms, throughout the life of the relationship as couples adjust to each other's changing roles and responsibilities. Failure to respond to the sixth house spells a poor chance of succeeding in the seventh, the house of commitment.

The Seventh House

TRADITIONAL NAME: House of Marriage

CORRESPONDING SIGN: Libra

ASSOCIATED PLANET: Venus

TERRAIN: Commitment; Intimacy, trust; Identification with others; Partnership, cooperation; Healthy interdependency

PROCESS: Establishment of long-term, committed relationships. Equal, flexible sharing of duties and pleasures of the relationship. Day-by-day attentiveness to the relationship and each person's changing needs.W

ABORT SEQUENCE: No firm commitment from one or both partners. Mistrust, guardedness, lack of intimacy. Unequally shared responsibilities and benefits. Rigid role-division. Selfishness, self-absorption. Loss of one's identity in the partner. Stagnation.

For the first time in the arc of intimacy, we have moved above the horizon as we pass from the sixth house into the seventh. That passage from the subjective to the objective areas of the chart carries symbolic meaning: to make an adult commitment we must lose our egocentricity. We must become aware of other people, sensitive to their differences. In the house of "the other," the house of the "not-self," we must recognize that other people are not replicas of ourselves. Nor should they be. That realization–this person is different from me–leads to a question: What might he or she have that I lack? What does he or she know that I don't know? How could my life be enriched by this person? We recognize that the person who embodies our seventh-house qualities seems, in some mysterious way, to complete us.

In the fifth house we experience the magic of attraction, the headiness of romance. In the sixth house we are humbled, as each partner realizes that the other is not perfect. In the seventh house we have accepted our shortcomings and our need to grow beyond the confines of our egocentric selves, through the input of another person. We discover our blind spots in the sixth, and we seek partners to help us overcome those blind spots in the seventh.

We always feel pulled by someone who represents our seventh-house qualities, and it's quite normal that we do. In a healthy response to this house we identify with the other person who is exhibiting traits that we already have, to some extent, but that we need to develop further. Our seventh-house partner functions as a role model for those traits, bringing them out in us, encouraging us to express them more and more. Without this type of identification we can't sustain a seventh-house relationship. There is a difference, however, between liking certain characteristics in a partner and thinking we don't possess any of them ourselves, and therefore demanding that the partner make up for our perceived lack. But the partner is the role model, not the supplier. Signs and planets in your seventh house paint a picture of the person who beckons you with that promise of wholeness, but you must remember that it is your seventh house, and its signs and planets belong to you, not to someone else. You will be drawn to those qualities in another, but your seventh house is not a gaping hole in your chart that cannot be filled except by another person. If you feel that way, then you are no longer identifying, you are projecting.

Here's an example of projection: Rachel can't understand why she's always getting involved with men who aren't willing to make a commitment, who insist on "space" and autonomy. She likes freewheeling, zany, Monty Pythonesque men who keep her in stitches but never want to stick around. Street-theater players and distracted geniuses flit in and out of her life with alarming regularity. What's going on? Hint number one: Rachel is an Aquarian, working on developing independence and individuality. Hint number two: Rachel has Uranus in Leo in her seventh house.

Projection is what happens when, usually unconsciously, we take one of our own positive or negative characteristics that we find difficult to express and place it onto another person who "acts it out" for us.   Once Rachel starts to "take back her projections," in psychological jargon, and express her individuality, she will feel more whole and complete. Until she does, she will need a Mork to play next to her Mindy–in other words, she will require her own projected Uranian qualities in someone else to make her feel complete, and a Uranian person will be irresistibly attractive to her. Will she stop liking eccentricity once she has taken back her projection? No, nor should she. When Rachel realizes her individuality, she will identify with another strong personality and enjoy how that quality in her mate helps her express her own unique style, rather than projecting that trait and insisting on an exaggerated version of it in her lovers.

The ability to identify with someone else, without losing your own identity in the other person, is essential to a seventh-house relationship. To make a successful passage through this house, we must develop empathy, sympathy, understanding, the capacity to put ourselves in someone else's shoes–and to remember which shoes belong to us: in other words, to discern clearly between the "self" and the "not-self." We must lose our self-centeredness and become aware of and sensitive to another person, his fears, her needs, where they correspond to and vary from our own. We must agree to make rational, fair compromises about our differing hopes and dreams. We must take frequent inventory of the relationship, allowing it to change as each partner changes. We must acknowledge what each can offer the other in the journey toward wholeness. This house has also been called the House of Open Enemies, an interesting name, in view of the fact that we can project qualities we dislike in ourselves, just as much as those we like. The relationship as a mirror of the best and the worst that is in us is a theme in this house. The seventh-house partner is someone whom we view as our equal, in whom we meet our match, who pushes us to the limits of our growth, who makes us respond as deeply as we are capable.

How do we deal with these seventh-house "significant others"? We accept them as they are, not as we want them to be. We respect their differences. We don't polarize over personality issues. "You're the crazy one and I'm the sane one; you're the spiritual one and I'm the worldly one; you're the feeling one and I'm the thinking one"–that kind of split in how you view each other is a seventh-house danger signal.

How do we achieve such a partnership? We trust. We share, openly and honestly, our genuine nature, our needs and wants. We commit to each other. Trust and commitment are interdependent, as interdependent as a couple in a seventh-house relationship. Can you commit to someone whom you do not trust? Can you trust someone with whom there is no commitment? These relationships feel normal, equal, honest, familiar, fair and stable, sometimes even from the beginning. A seventh-house couple is one that lasts after the initial fifth house fireworks die down, sixth-house glitches are ironed out, and seventh-house projections lift. Seventh-house intimacy is a slow-blooming flower, unfolding over time, nurtured by equality, interdependency, trust, and commitment.

The Eighth House

TRADITIONAL NAME: House of Death

CORRESPONDING SIGN: Scorpio

ASSOCIATED PLANETS: Mars, Pluto

TERRAIN: Formation of the bond to one's mate

PROCESS: Imprinting on another person, sexually, mentally, emotionally. Acceptance of feelings arising from instinctive levels of consciousness. Honesty, psychological nakedness.

ABORT SEQUENCE: Sexual dysfunction. Lack of depth, relationship feels like friends but not lovers. Avoidance of psychologically charged issues.

Until now in the arc of intimacy we might have been discussing how you get along with your best friend. But to arrive at the eighth house, we cross the line into sexuality. This is the house of **instincts**, of motivations whose roots run deeper than our conscious minds: sexuality, death, and the "occult," or whatever notions we have about survival after death.

Volcanic stuff.

Now those seventh-house partnership bonds are tested, now we abandon logic and rationality, and simply feel: is this my mate? Have I bonded to this individual, deeper than mentally, not just emotionally, more than spiritually, more than sexually? On a gut level, with every cell in my body, with all my reflexes, from the reptile part of my brain, have I imprinted on this person?

Sex is part of this bond. More than physical sex is necessary to form it, but physical sex is essential for its creation and sustenance. Sexuality and bonding are multilevel processes, and physical sex is only one factor in them.

Planets and signs in the eighth house show the qualities you need in a mate to maintain this level of connection, through and beyond your sexual circuitry. If your Moon falls in your eighth house, for example, your mate must have certain lunar qualities: imagination, sensitivity, tenderness, intuition. Imagine that you've been dating someone for a relatively short period of time, and you discover that this person is sexy, intelligent, gutsy, and amusing, but he or she has the emotional sensibilities of a two-by-four. If you have an eighth-house Moon, the thrill is gone, and it won't return. You may continue to like the person, certainly, but he or she is a bad bet for a life mate.

Healthy sexuality involves more than memorizing all the positions in a paperback "marriage manual." It also includes releasing and accepting overwhelming feelings. Sometimes this is easy and joyful; other times it's painful and embarrassing, but in any case, acknowledging all the emotions aroused by the partner is essential to the formation and continuation of the bond.

You are at a party. Your mate spends the entire evening huddled in a corner with an attractive member of the opposite sex. Whether you casually inquire about their conversation or have a glorious fight in the car on the way home, you are bound to have had some twinges originating from your eighth house. What if your mate leaves you? The ancient primate in you knows that such abandonment means lessened chances of survival, and its hackles rise, growling, "Kill the interloper!" If you're a card-carrying New Age citizen, you may be mortified at this reaction, but mortified or not, it's better to deal with it, gently or directly according to your style, than to repress it.

Eighth-house feelings come from other levels than those that motivate the primate. Your personal psychological issues are also triggered by your partner. Your reaction to that conversation at the party, for example, might also be rooted in childhood desertion by one of your parents. If you don't face those emotions, you can pour salt on that early wound, never seeing its connection to your present insecurities. But if you broach the subject with your mate, who knows your life story (remember the fifth house!), he or she might point out that your reaction has some roots in your personal history.

One of the two planets that rule this house is Mars, planet of sexuality, assertion, aggression, initiative, will, drive, courage, and enthusiasm. The other is Pluto, ruler of psychic depths. In adult love we accept that blinding passion does not burn constantly, but Mars' association with this house is extremely significant. An eighth-house bond must have Mars present. The God of War, not just the Goddess of Love! How can this be?

Certainly it takes will, drive, and courage to maintain an eighth house relationship. It takes maintenance of a good sexual relationship, compromise over differing drives, and some realism in assessing what is and is not a "good" sexual relationship. A couple is in needless trouble if they assume that something is drastically wrong because after ten years together they no longer pant in each other's presence and somehow manage to keep their hands off one another. But severe sexual dysfunction–chronic dissatisfaction, frigidity, impotence–is definitely a problem. Why do relationships head in that direction? A complete answer to that question is obviously beyond the scope of this book. We can answer the question astrologically, however, and say: lack of Plutonian honesty in facing emotions, usually rooted in a lack of Martial courage. Popular culture contains endless examples of one partner, angry (Mars) at the other, withholding sex (also Mars). That's reacting with passive aggression, rather than actively confronting the conflict. When unresolved anger lingers in a relationship, it can block a lot more than physical affection. A festering Mars blunts enthusiasm, snuffs out intensity, cripples honesty (because it's too dangerous), stifles initiative to deal with issues, and can lead to a slow undermining of the core of the relationship, sexually and otherwise. Moral: deal with your anger, face your issues together, feed your Mars and Pluto functions, if you want to deepen and preserve the bond between you.

We've looked at the arc of intimacy, houses five, six, seven, and eight, where relationships begin, are worked upon, committed to, and tested. Now its time for some examples of planets and signs in these houses. We want to introduce a way to understand what it means to have, for instance, Mercury in Scorpio in the seventh house. Once you've learned this method, you can apply it to interpreting the impact of any planet in any sign or house.

Teachers, Methods, and Classrooms

A planet in a house is your teacher, advising you how to master the material of that house. Personify that planet. Think of it as human. Imagine a personification of Venus, the Goddess of Love. You react to her as a teacher rather differently than you react to Saturn, the Lord of Solitude. Planets in a house focus your experience in that area of life. It is the nature of the planet, the teacher, that most determines your experience of that house.

What if you have no planets in a house? In astrological jargon, these houses are referred to as "untenanted." An untenanted house does not mean that you have no events in your life related to that house. Everyone enters all twelve of these territories. All that an empty house means is that you're on "independent study" in that area. Do you have five planets in the seventh house? You needed five teachers for that subject, and they may or may not get along, as team teachers sometimes do and sometimes don't work well together.

You can tell what methods the house's teacher (its planet) uses by what **sign** the planet occupies. If the house contains a planet in one sign, and also contains another sign not occupied by a planet, the course for that house is taught partly by the planet with its sign's methods, and partly by independent study, using the methods of the untenanted sign. If you have no planets in a house, you are on independent study, using the methods of the sign or signs in that house.

Ready for an example? Imagine that you have Mercury in Scorpio in the seventh house. Mercury is teaching you how to form committed relationships (seventh house). Mercury says, "Communicate! Talk! Establish a dialogue!"

You are the pupil, questioning Mercury, and you ask, "What kind of dialogue? How can I do that?"

"Use Scorpio methods," Mercury answers. "Be honest, be intense, be emotional. Use that level of vocabulary. Ask penetrating questions. Broach gut-wrenching topics of conversation. The people who can hold their own in these exchanges are your soul mates."

What if there is more in your seventh house than just one sign? How do these methods change?

Suppose that your seventh house starts at twenty degrees Libra and ends at twenty-five degrees Scorpio, with Mercury at six degrees Scorpio. In this case Mercury is your teacher, using Scorpio methods, and you are also on independent study, using Libra methods. Your seventh-house classroom contains a manual titled *How to Form Relationships the Libra Way*. You read in this Libra workbook about politeness and graciousness and sensitivity to others, without a specific teacher, and you also learn direct questioning methods from your Scorpio Mercury.

Suppose that a house starts at twenty degrees Libra, contains all of Scorpio and ends at three degrees Sagittarius. When a sign is completely contained within a house, astrologers say that the sign is **intercepted** in that house. What do intercepted signs mean? Some medieval traditions maintain that you have no entry or access into an intercepted sign, but we disagree with that notion.

Think of the sign on the cusp (beginning) of a house as your introductory method (sign) for that subject (house), in this case, *How to Form Relationships the Libra Way*. You have a teacher, which is Mercury, and its methods are Scorpionic. That Scorpionic Mercury is the focus of your work in that house; it is your teacher. However, you are also on independent study in that house, using Libran and Sagittarian methods.

Are you starting to get a feel for this metaphor? It can be applied to any house in the birthchart. A planet is your teacher, teaching you about the affairs of its house. Signs are the methods. The house is the course or the subject.

Let's try another example. Bill has Jupiter in the fifth house. Jupiter is teaching him how to fall in love, and Jupiter has an eye out for likely prospects.

"Bill! Over there! See that woman juggling on the street corner?" Jupiter, ruler of Sagittarius, makes Bill notice the Gypsies among us. And that's not all. Jupiter pulls Bill toward the woman he met buying a copy of *Let's Go: Europe* (the Explorer, the Anthropologist), or toward the Philosopher holding forth at the university or the corner bar.

While Bill is talking to one of these women, Jupiter keeps up a running commentary from his fifth house. "You've had more fun in a half-hour conversation with this person than you've had for weeks. That's a good sign! Doesn't she lift your mood?" Falling in love, for Bill, always starts with a Jupiterian experience with another person. An exuberant, good-natured, curious, expansive personality will start his fifth-house circuits humming. What next?

His Jupiter lies in the sign Pisces, so Bill uses Piscean strategy to prolong the Jupiter contact. For example, he enlists the woman in some escapist fantasy or pastime (Pisces) that promises to maintain the silly connection (Jupiter) between them. He asks her to go to the circus, or to enter an "Anything That Floats But Is Not a Boat" race with him. He continues the Jupiter atmosphere in a Piscean way, to encourage what is growing between them. There will be plenty of time to trade life stories, too, while building the non-boat and floating down the river.

Now that we've explored the arc of intimacy and learned a technique for understanding how planets operate in signs and houses, let's turn our attention to the interaction between two complete birthcharts, in Chapter Seven.

Part Three

SHARING THE SKY

CHAPTER SEVEN

HOW BIRTHCHARTS INTERACT

No matter how different two people might be, if we put them both in the pressure cooker and close the lid, they'll work out a pattern of relation. It may be joyful. It may be mutually destructive. But a pattern will appear–and no matter who they are, that pattern can be analyzed through a study of the interplay between their birthcharts.

The first step is to observe how the planets in one birthchart impact upon the planets in the other chart. There are many techniques for accomplishing that, and we'll be exploring all of them. But the core of the process doesn't lie in mastery of technicalities. Far more centrally, it has to do with common sense, imagination, and a willingness to plug astrology into that wonderful library of human experience you carry in your head.

If a mouse and a cat are locked up together, what happens? In the world of animals the answer is obvious. But in the world of men and women the games are more subtle. Maybe the "mouse" still gets eaten, but maybe not. Perhaps the "cat" adopts a posture of benign authority, content to merely display its teeth rather than using them. Perhaps we get a distinctly **nice** mouse. Many stories are possible, and none of them are difficult to imagine.

Cats and mice are familiar characters. Once Mars and the Moon are just as familiar, you'll be an astrologer.

A man has a very prominent Mars at the beginning of the sign Aries. It lies in his first house in a conjunction with his Sun. For purposes of generating a story, we might liken that Mars to a "cat"–it's a hunter: competitive, willful, and passionate. Maybe his wife has her Moon in early Libra–a milder, more vulnerable motif: a "mouse," in other words, at least relative to his fierce Mars placement.

What happens? No way to know exactly. Like the rest of us, those people can do as they please. Astrology offers them many behavioral options, and trying to guess the one they will pick is not the astrologer's work. But translating "Mars" and "Moon" to "cat" and "mouse" starts the interpretive ball rolling.

In the previous section of this book we went into great detail about how to understand the individual from an astrological perspective. Once you've accomplished that, much of synastry takes care of itself, at least if you are willing to rely heavily on your old friends–common sense, imagination, and your own human experience.

That man's Arian Mars and his wife's Libran Moon form an **opposition** aspect to each other, suggestive of tension (see Chapter Two if you're fuzzy about aspects). But if you need to actually calculate that aspect before you sense tension between this particular cat and mouse, you probably also need a blow with a two-by-four to help you awaken in the morning! If you've really understood the individual birthcharts, that tension leaps out.

Hesitant? Don't feel dumb! This is one of those places where the great advantage of speaking about astrological symbols out loud becomes clear. If you had sat down with those two people to explore their relationship from an astrological perspective, you naturally would have dwelt on the brusque ferocity of the man's "mask" as you developed the meaning of his Arian Mars in the first house–it's such a salient feature of his individuality. For similar reasons you would have also expanded upon the delicate sensibilities and profound relationship needs of the woman's Libran Moon. With all those words hanging in the air, the potential clash between the two configurations would be inescapably obvious–even if you didn't know a thing about how to calculate aspects between charts.

Still, these **interaspects**–aspects formed between the planets of two charts–are the workhorses of synastry. Why? Simply because not all interactions between birthcharts are quite as evident as the particular "cat" and "mouse" scenario we've been considering. Some are far more subtle. Without any knowledge of interaspects you'd still pick up the broadest interactive themes without any difficulty. And if you were able to give warm, wise human advice about how to handle those broad themes more lovingly, you'd be a fine astrologer and help whoever came to you for insight. The advantage of understanding interaspects is that they telegraph to you all the interactive patterns, even the ones you might otherwise miss.

Too much technique, not enough human reality: that's one of the astrologer's riskiest pitfalls. Be careful you don't get lost in the labyrinths of theory. Interaspects are powerful, but they can also be a one-way ticket into that labyrinth. Later in this chapter and all through Chapter Eight we'll go into them, but first things first: our initial step is to absorb both birthcharts, summarize them inwardly as feelings, then compare them on that gut level. What do we get? Cats and mice. Dreamers and realists. Homebodies and gypsies. That's the level where the magic happens. That's the level where astrology becomes human.

Here's the practical principle: **Carry your synastry analysis as far as you possibly can on the basis of the "feel" of each birthchart, then further refine your understanding by resorting to the use of interaspects.**

In harmony with our guiding principle, we'll use a few specific examples to flesh out this idea of getting the "feel" of various kinds of astrological interactions before we dive into the more technical side of interaspect work.

Saturn In Love

Saturn can be a symbol of blockage–a "feel" that arises all too often in intimacy. It represents what we refuse to experience. More deeply, Saturn symbolizes an area where we are challenged to overcome our blockages through the application of positive Saturn virtues–self-discipline, patience, determination. But those virtues never arise automatically, personally or in loving relationships. We have to work toward them. And if we don't work, then the blockage remains, usually protected within a steely casing of stubbornness and self-righteousness.

Two lovers might have Saturn in Fire signs. No single astrological feature can be safely interpreted in isolation from the rest of the birthchart, but abstractly Saturn in Fire suggests a shared blockage (Saturn) in terms of assertiveness, tolerance of risk, and the expression of anger (Fire). Since the blockage is shared, there is harmony here: He: "The O'Rileys called and asked if we'd like to go shark-wrestling with them this weekend. Care to go?"

She: (emphatically) "Are you crazy???!!!"

He: "I was hoping you'd say that."

So far so good. But like most kinds of astrological "harmony," there are dangers here too. In this couple, their hesitation to take risks could lead to a deadening collusion in which all possibility of newness and change was systematically eliminated from their relationship and everything collapsed into ritual and predictability. Once again, that's not their "fate," it's just a danger that comes with this particular kind of "harmony."

In a little while we'll learn that the harmony between those two Fire-sign Saturns is connected to the fact that they make a trine aspect to each other. Perhaps we might miss that linkage in our preliminary and more intuitive analysis of the two birthcharts. No problem. When we came to the technical figuring of interaspects, we'd pick it up then. Interaspects, in other words, are a wonderful safety net–but like most tightrope walkers, your first priority should be staying on the tightrope.

Jodie Forrest may someday write a horror novel relating her early safaris into the darker reaches of Steven Forrest's apartment. *Tales of Mildew* is the working title. Steve has Saturn in Virgo, and one of his blockages is connected with the distinctly Virgoan process of housekeeping.

Steve, on the other hand, experienced great frustration with what he perceived to be Jodie's lack of proper enthusiasm for life's adventures: scrambling up cliff faces, hiking out into the snowy woods with the wind still howling, sleeping ingloriously in a mud puddle amid otherwise glorious natural circumstances. Jodie's Saturn lies in Sagittarius–the sign of exploration and robust engagement with experience. That's where **her** blockages lie.

Clearly, there is friction between these Saturns. Steve's Saturn blockage bothers Jodie and Jodie's Saturn blockage bothers

Steve. So what happens? Divorce is one option. But so is adult compromise. Since their marriage, Steve has become a (somewhat) more industrious housekeeper and Jodie has become a (somewhat) more adventuresome woman. To make their marriage work, each had to respond strongly to Saturn's call for self-discipline and determined effort. Otherwise, the blockages would have remained unchallenged and unmodified, and the static high-jinx prophecies of the fortune-tellers would have been right on the money.

If you start with a clear understanding of Saturn in Virgo and Saturn in Sagittarius, then the friction between them is rather obvious–provided you obey the cardinal rule of synastry and remember to feel the ideas as you think them or say them. And if you miss the connection, no problem–you'll make it when you calculate the interaspects and discover that Steve's Saturn squares Jodie's Saturn–the ninety degree aspect of friction.

How to Recognize Interaspects

Now that we've put interaspects in their place, let's look at them carefully. They are a powerful tool, and you would have to be a very intuitive astrologer indeed to do high quality synastry interpretations without their help.

Many neophyte astrologers are daunted by the prospect of picking out these geometrical angles around the birthchart. There's no need for that hesitancy. Once you get off on the right foot, aspects are not hard to grasp. The trick is to begin with a crystal-clear mental photograph of the wheel of signs. Once you have that, everything else falls into place.

Aspects are geometrical angles formed between planets in various signs. Each angle suggests a different **pattern of relationship**–friction, harmony, tension. (Look at Table Four in Chapter Two on page 19 for a summary of all the major aspects.)

Let's consider the birthcharts of two of Hollywood's most successful real-life lovers: Katharine Hepburn and the late Spencer Tracy. Astrologer Marc Penfield included them in his fascinating compendium of birthcharts, *An Astrological Who's Who*. As we would suspect, their destinies were linked by many powerful interaspects.

FIGURE 3

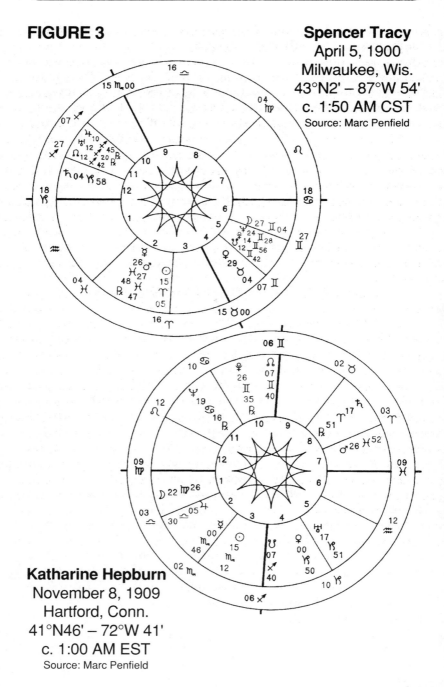

Spencer Tracy
April 5, 1900
Milwaukee, Wis.
43°N2' − 87°W 54'
c. 1:50 AM CST
Source: Marc Penfield

Katharine Hepburn
November 8, 1909
Hartford, Conn.
41°N46' − 72°W 41'
c. 1:00 AM EST
Source: Marc Penfield

Katharine Hepburn's Neptune lies in the middle of Cancer. Spencer Tracy's Sun lies in the middle of Aries. Is there as interaspect between them? To find out, refer to your mental photograph of the wheel of signs. Cancer and Aries make a right angle to each other–one glance at the zodiac tells you that. Immediately you know that her Neptune and his Sun are in a square aspect.

What if her Neptune is in mid-Cancer but his Sun had been in mid-Leo? Is there an interaspect? There two signs are adjacent, so the two planets are separated by about thirty degrees–the width of one complete sign, in other words. Once again, look at Table 4 in Chapter Two on page 19. No major aspect exists between planets separated by thirty degrees, so in this case, there would have been no interaspect.

Here's a methodical way of proceeding. Pick a planet in Katharine Hepburn's birthchart, say her Saturn, which lies in the middle of Aries–in a conjunction with Spencer Tracy's Sun. Count **one sign** on either side of Aries–you'll come to Pisces and Taurus. Tracy has planets in both signs. Is there an interaspect? No–because counting one sign in either direction only moves us thirty degrees, and thirty degrees is not a major aspect. (It's what's called a minor aspect, but we don't need to be concerned with minor aspects here–the major ones will give us plenty to think about.)

Now count **two signs** on either side of Hepburn's Saturn. You'll come to Aquarius and Gemini. Two signs' separation means a sextile aspect–and if Spencer Tracy has planets in the middle of either of those signs, they are linked to Katharine Hepburn's Saturn through that interaspect. Does he have planets there? Nothing lies in Aquarius–but he has three planets in the sign of the Twins: Pluto, Neptune, and the Moon. Do they form the sextile with Hepburn's Saturn? As we'll soon see, just being in the correct sign doesn't guarantee that the interaspect exists. We need to be in the right part of the sign as well–in this case, the middle, since Katharine Hepburn's Saturn is in the middle of Aries and that's the point from which we are counting. Only Pluto qualifies.

Similarly, counting **three signs** brings us to the square.

Four signs means a trine interaspect.

Five signs is another minor aspect called the quincunx or the inconjunct and we can safely ignore it for our purposes.

Finally, counting **six signs** brings us to the opposition.

Remember to count both clockwise and counterclockwise around the chart: Aspects work in both directions!

In our example we were careful to say that Hepburn's Saturn lay in the **middle** of Aries–and that Tracy's Moon in **late** Gemini did not make a sextile to it. Let's look at this point more carefully. The problem is that the two planets are "outside the orbs of the aspect" and no interaspect links them. In other words, a sextile is technically an angle of sixty degrees. It need not be exact–an error of a few degrees on either side of the perfect sextile won't alter the basic meaning of the interaspect, just water it down a bit. But an error of more than seven or eight degrees is too much: the aspect won't work anymore. It's "out of orbs."

There is nothing particularly rigid about aspectual orbs. In Table 4 of Chapter Two we give some working suggestions, but there's no need to follow them slavishly. Stricter orbs have the advantage of creating fewer interaspects and limiting your attention to the truly significant ones. Looser orbs give you many more aspects to consider. Greater subtlety is generated–and perhaps greater befuddlement. Take your pick. We suggest tighter, stricter orbs for starters.

In either case, remember to add a couple of extra degrees to the orbs of any aspect involving the Sun or the Moon, and to be two or three degrees stricter with aspects involving the North or South nodes of the Moon.

To work precisely with interaspects, our procedure is essentially the same as what we just outlined–two signs means a sextile, three signs means a square, and so on. We simply add one more step.

Spencer Tracy's Moon lies in 27 Gemini. Katharine Hepburn's Moon is in 22 Virgo. That's a separation of three signs (Gemini **zero**, Cancer **one**, Leo **two, Virgo three**), and we suspect that the two planets make a square interaspect. Do they? Reason like this: the point in Virgo that is precisely square to 27 Gemini is 27 Virgo. But Hepburn's Moon lies in 22 Virgo–five degrees away from the perfect square. Is this close enough to count? For squares, we suggest an orb of seven degrees. In this case the interaspect really does exist. With a five-degree separation the angle is sufficiently precise to operate effectively. Had Katharine Hepburn's Moon been in 15 Virgo, then the orbs would've been too wide and for practical purposes there would have been no interaspect.

A lot of numbers to juggle, but the essential reasoning is simple. First, count the signs separating the planets to determine whether an aspect **might** exist. Second, determine exactly what degree "Planet A" would have to occupy in order to be in a perfect aspect to "Planet B." Third, determine how far "Planet A" actually is from that **perfect** aspect. If it's within the orbs, you've got an aspect. If not, you don't.

Let's try another example.

Katharine Hepburn's Venus is in zero degrees of Capricorn–and that leads to a more complex situation. The point that precisely opposes her Venus is zero degrees of Cancer–and Spencer Tracy has no planets there. But his Moon opposes her Venus! How? The answer has to do with orbs. While zero degrees of Cancer is the point that **precisely** opposes her Venus, anything within about seven degrees of that point is also within the orbs of the opposition. That carries us forward to seven degrees of Cancer–still in a blank region of Tracy's birthchart. Counting seven degrees backward, however, backs us right out of Cancer and into the previous sign, Gemini. With Tracy's Moon in 27 Gemini, it's well within the orbs of an opposition to Hepburn's Venus, only three degrees away from precision even though it's in the "wrong" sign. Our simple rule about counting signs breaks down, in other words, when we're dealing with a planet very close to the beginning or end of a sign. The rule doesn't fail entirely: it still unerringly gives the degree of the **precise** aspect. Then it's up to you to remember that the orbs of the aspect might carry over into the next sign.

When such a situation exists, the aspect is said to be **out of quality**. This has the effect of diluting its effectiveness some-what, and you should be a degree or two stricter about your orbs in such a case.

The rule of thumb is to be extra careful when you're searching for interaspects linked to a planet in the early or late degrees of a sign. The rest of the time, if you can count to six, you can figure interaspects.

Aspects by Element Alone

Aspects are based on the four elements–Fire, Earth, Air, and Water. All Fire signs, for example, are trine each other. That is, they get along well, sharing the common goals and temperament of the fiery element. The same harmony exists for all three Earth signs, and so on. The elements form "families," and they enjoy each other's company.

Going further, Fire (will) mixes readily with Earth (Patience). Traditionally, Fire and Air were called the "positive" or "masculine" elements, while Water and Earth were seen as "negative" and "feminine." While the greatest harmony exists strictly within each of the four elemental families, the Fire-Air community is a peaceful one and so is the Earth-Water community. Each Fire sign, for example, makes aspects to all three Air signs–two exciting, harmonious sextiles and one tense (or complementary) opposition. Always, the opposition can be problematic, but of all the aspects it is certainly the most "romantic." Often when two people experience that "you are my other half" feeling, we'll see lots of oppositions between their birthcharts. So Fire mixes with Air, either in a spirit of mutual excitation (sextile) or through the tense fascination of the opposition.

Similar logic links each Air sign to all three Fire signs either through sextiles or oppositions. It also ties Earth to Water or Water to Earth in the same way.

But Fire doesn't know what to make of Water or Earth! They speak different languages. Fire, being "positive" or "masculine," can't readily connect with the temperament of the "negative" or "feminine" elements. The misunderstanding goes both ways: Water, for example, doesn't know quite what to make of Air. Earth can't easily find any common ground with Fire. Unsurprisingly, these are the elemental combinations we find in square aspects (friction) or in most of the various minor aspects where the interactive pattern so often boils down to missing each other's meaning or failing to connect.

Aspects then are intimately linked to an understanding of the four elements. Grasp one and you are well on your way to grasping the other. All this leads to a very practical insight into synastry:

Even when aspects are not technically present, comparing planets in two charts by element alone illuminates patterns of harmony, friction, or indifference.

In other words, keep an eye on the elements! Katharine Hepburn's Uranus in 17 Capricorn does not make a trine to Spencer Tracy's Venus in 29 Taurus–they're twelve degrees out of orb. But both planets lie in Earth signs, and they speak the same language. Her individuality (Uranus) seeks the goals of Earth–solidness, reality, steady growth, commitment. Exactly the same goals motivate his romantic instincts (Venus). The link would be stronger if the interaspect existed, but even without the numbers turning up quite right, there is harmony here.

For this reason, interaspects that are "out of quality" (in the "wrong" sign) should be viewed with special caution. Earlier we saw that there is an out-of-quality opposition between Tracy's Gemini Moon and Hepburn's Capricorn Venus. Normally Gemini (an Air sign) and Capricorn (an Earth sign) don't have any business together. They are from different "communities," and speak mutually incomprehensible languages. Gemini's frenetic search for experience seems pointless and random to orderly Capricorn. Capricorn's single-minded efficiency appears cold and hopelessly narrow to Gemini. In this case, the two planets are linked through an opposition aspect. They might still experience the feeling of simply missing each other's meaning and misunderstanding each other's intent, but because of the opposition, they are nonetheless bound together in the pattern of tension and mutual fascination characteristic of this interaspect.

If you've hung in there with us so far, congratulations! Most of the technical material is behind us now and we are almost ready to begin the more emotionally rewarding work of interpretation. But first, a subject that has perhaps been nagging at you...

Keeping Track of Interaspects

Typically a handful of supercharged interaspects dominate a couple's astrological interactions. Unsurprisingly, these interaspects generally involve the primal triad of Sun, Moon, and Ascendant. Hepburn's Saturn, for example, falls upon Tracy's Sun, while his Ascendant conjuncts her Uranus. These broad-stroke interaspects form the bedrock of intimacy, at least from an

FIGURE 4: SYNASTRY WORKSHEET

Tracy's Impact Upon Hepburn's Birthchart

His ☉ Falls in Her **8th** House ☌♄□♅□♆
His ☽ Falls in Her **10th** House □☽△☿☍♀□♂☌♇
His ☿ Falls in Her **7th** House ☍☽□♀☌♂△♆□♇
His ♀ Falls in Her **9th** House △☽⚹♂
His ♂ Falls in Her **7th** House ☍☽□♀☌♂△♆□♇
His ♃ Falls in Her **4th** House ⚹♃△♄☍☊☌☋□ASC☍MH
His ♄ Falls in Her **4th** House ⚹☿☌♀□♃△ASC
His ♅ Falls in Her **4th** House ⚹♃△♄☍☊☌☋□ASC☍MH
His ♆ Falls in Her **10th** House △☿☍♀□♂⚹♄☌♇
His ♇ Falls in Her **10th** House ⚹♄☌☊☍☋□ASC
His ☊ Falls in Her **4th** House △♄□ASC
His ☋ Falls in Her **10th** House ⚹♄□ASC
His ASC Falls in Her **5th** House ⚹☉△☽□♄☌♅☍♆
His MH Falls in Her **3rd** House ☌☉⚹♅△♆

Hepburn's Impact Upon Tracy's Birthchart

Her ☉ Falls in His **10th** House ☌MH⚹ASC
Her ☽ Falls in His **8th** House △ASC☍☿☍♂△♀□☽
Her ☿ Falls in His **9th** House ⚹♄△☽△♆
Her ♀ Falls in His **12th** House ☌♄□☿□♂☍♆☍☽
Her ♂ Falls in His **2nd** House ☌☿☌♂⚹♀□♆□☽
Her ♃ Falls in His **8th** House ⚹♃⚹♅□♄
Her ♄ Falls in His **3rd** House ☌☉⚹♇⚹♆△♃△♅△☊□ASC
Her ♅ Falls in His **1st** House ☌ASC□☉⚹□MH
Her ♆ Falls in His **7th** House ☍ASC△MH△☿△♂□☉
Her ♇ Falls in His **6th** House ☌♆☌☽□☿□♂
Her ☊ Falls in His **5th** House ☍♃☍♅☌♇
Her ☋ Falls in His **11th** House ☌♃☌♅☍♇
Her ASC Falls in His **8th** House □♃□♅□☊△♄□♇
Her MH Falls in His **5th** House ☍♃☍♅

astrological perspective. Achieving skill in synastry depends upon keeping these quintessential linkages clear. That's not as hard as it might sound; there are generally not very many of them.

The interpretive fish grows more slippery when we include all interaspects rather than limiting ourselves to the supercharged ones involving the primal triad. We leap from a handful of interconnections to dozens–and unless you can balance your checkbook blindfolded, you'll need a strategy just to manage all the astrological data.

Look at Figure 1. It's a Synastry Worksheet, filled out for Katharine Hepburn and Spencer Tracy. We know it looks about as comprehensible as something copied off the inner walls of Dhufu's pyramid–but don't be nervous. All of those hieroglyphics are already familiar to you. The worksheet simply shows all the interaspects linking Tracy and Hepburn, even some relatively inconsequential ones.

As we've seen, Hepburn's Saturn is conjunct Tracy's Sun. Look on Hepburn's side of the Synastry Worksheet. Find the glyph for Saturn (♄). Read the list of aspects that follows it. That list shows every major aspect that Hepburn's Saturn makes to Tracy's planets and sensitive points, as if her Saturn had been placed in his birthchart. A conjunction with his Sun. Sextiles to his Pluto and his Neptune. Trines to his Uranus, Jupiter, and North Node. A square to his Ascendant. At a glance you see how **her** Saturn is wired into **his** birthchart.

Why are there so many interaspects? The answer is easy. Look to the other side of the Worksheet. Find the symbol for Tracy's Sun (☉). There you see what aspects his Sun would make if it were placed in her birthchart. A square to her Neptune. A square to her Uranus. Plus the familiar conjunction with her Saturn– and that's our answer. Each interaspect is entered twice on the worksheet, once from the point of view of Katharine Hepburn's chart, and then again from the point of view of Spencer Tracy's birthchart. Her Sun conjuncts his Saturn. His Saturn conjuncts her Sun. As we'll see in the next chapter, both ways of phrasing the statement are instructive. Although this "double entry" procedure involves some extra clerical work, it's worth the trouble. One of the secrets of successful synastry is the ability to move fluidly from one person's frame of reference into that of the other person, without getting stuck in either viewpoint. Our double-entry technique on the Worksheet guarantees that.

In Chapter Eight, we'll offer specific procedures for interpreting these interaspects. Right now, our task is simply to provide ourselves with the raw information. How dó we proceed?

First, supply yourself with a Synastry Worksheet. You can easily make your own based on what you see in Figure 1. Or you can order some Worksheet blanks (see Appendices).

Next, choose one of the two birthcharts. Say you pick Katharine Hepburn's. You'll be working methodically down the list of her planets, nodes, Ascendant, and Midheaven. Start at the top with her Sun. It lies in 15 Scorpio. Remember that figure, then put her birthchart aside. Now look at Spencer Tracy's chart. What you're trying to do here is to put Katharine Hepburn's Sun into Spencer Tracy's birthchart. Where is 15 Scorpio in his chart? Right on his 15 Scorpio Midheaven–and you have your first interaspect: a conjunction between her Sun and his Midheaven. Enter it on the Worksheet–twice. Once for her Sun, once for his Midheaven.   Continue the process, using the procedures we outlined earlier in this chapter. Every time you find that her Sun is linked aspectually to one of his planets, make a note of it on both sides of the Worksheet. When you've finished with her Sun, do her Moon the same way, and so on until you've gotten down to the end of the list. If you've double-entered everything, then your work is over. No need to repeat the procedure for Spencer Tracy's planets–by double-entering, you've already accomplished that.

You now have a complete listing of all the interaspects that link these two actors. You can pick any point on either chart and in a glance see how it impacts upon the planets in the other chart.

If this seems like a lot of work, take heart: once you've gotten a bit of experience, you can fill out such a Worksheet in a few minutes. If it takes longer than that, you are probably having trouble thinking about aspects. The cure, as we saw earlier, is to develop a thorough, almost instinctive grasp of the wheel of signs.

One more note: while you are filling out the Worksheet, jot down where one person's planets would fall in the other person's houses. As you can see from Figure 1, there is a space for that information. Spencer Tracy's Sun, for example, lies in 15 Aries in his third house. Where would his Sun lie if it were placed in Katharine Hepburn's birthchart? Fifteen degrees of Aries lies in her eighth house, in other words. Therefore, we say that Spencer Tracy's Sun lies in that zone of **her** birthchart.

What does it mean to have X's Venus in Y's fourth house? That's a big subject. We'll deal with it in Chapter Nine. We introduce it now only for the practical reason that it's a part of the Synastry Worksheet and the information can be conveniently recorded while you are busy plotting the all-important interaspects.

One piece of fine tuning: although we define house cusps precisely, they are actually blurred areas a couple of degrees wide. Once a planet enters that territory it is in effect "thrown forward" into the next house. For example, Hepburn's Sun (15 Scorpio) technically lies in Tracy's ninth house, since his tenth house doesn't begin until 15 Scorpio. But for practical purposes, we would say that her Sun impacts upon his tenth house, not his ninth. Why? Because it is "on the cusp," and therefore its effects are "thrown forward."

Whenever a planet is within a degree and a half of a house cusp, its major impact is upon the following house.

With your Worksheet filled out–and with a grasp on the basic meaning of each of the two birthcharts individually–you are ready to dive into the crossfire of astrological intimacy. You've seen how to recognize an interaspect. Now let's figure out how to understand one.

CHAPTER EIGHT

INTERASPECTS

Rock 'n' Roll fans will never forget the band called The Who. From their humble London beginnings in the early 1960s right up until their breakup in the early 1980s, they stretched the boundaries of a new kind of music. Fronted by lead singer Roger Daltrey and driven by the damn-the-torpedoes guitar style of composer Pete Townshend, The Who lifted the spirits of a generation. Even today, when many of us aging "baby boomers" are feeling low, all we have to do is crank up the volume on "Baba O'Riley" or "Pinball Wizard" and we're sailing high again.

The general crashing and banging that is such an elemental part of the music of The Who was not limited to their musical performances. Pete Townshend and Roger Daltrey were notorious for crashing and banging against each other, especially in print. Their infamous feuding nearly broke up the band on many occasions. In many ways they simply seemed not to like each other very much. And yet some force held them together, kept drawing them back into collaboration. They were opposites. Townshend: mystical, intellectual, angry, Steppenwolfish. Daltrey: playful, worldly, a classic "teen idol." Yet they were bound together. Rage–and fascination. Rebelliousness–and yet dependency. Escapism–but no exit. Immediately upon discovering

FIGURE 5

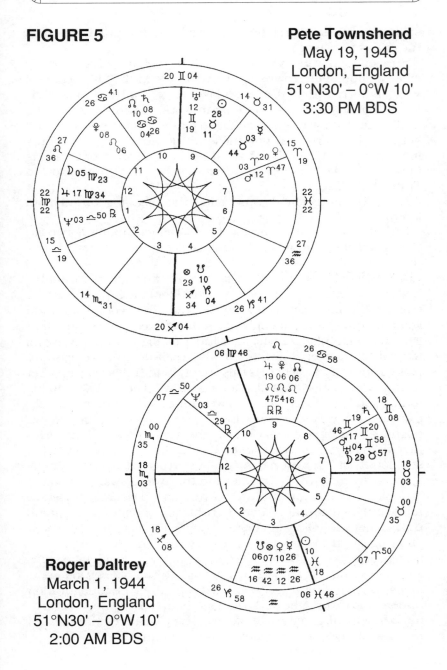

Pete Townshend
May 19, 1945
London, England
51°N30' – 0°W 10'
3:30 PM BDS

Roger Daltrey
March 1, 1944
London, England
51°N30' – 0°W 10'
2:00 AM BDS

such paradoxes in a relationship, we begin to think in terms of the opposition aspect...

Sure enough, when we look at their birthcharts, that's exactly what we find. Pete Townshend's Moon lies in the fifth degree of Virgo in his twelfth house. It opposes Roger Daltrey's Sun in his fourth house. A Sun-Moon link: in working with interaspects, that's like striking a vein of gold. No matter what else is going on between the charts, we know those people pluck sensitive chords in each other. (Townshend's and Daltrey's birth information is included in Debbi Kempton Smith's book, *Secrets From a Stargazer's Notebook.*)

How do we go about unraveling the meaning of such an interaspect?

Our first step is to understand each configuration on its own. Only then are we in a position to begin to unlock their interactions.

Townshend's soul (his Moon) is driven by an endless, insatiable hunger for perfection (Virgo). He feels (Moon) the gap between the real and the ideal, between what he's actually accomplished and what he could have accomplished–and he likely experiences that gap quite painfully. At best, this lunar configuration drives him toward excellence; at worst, it leads to self-destructiveness and picky annoyances. Where is this energy being released? In other words, what house does his Moon occupy? The twelfth–and his lunar "soul" is hungry for the twelfth house experience of self-transcendence. He can sense instinctively (Moon again) what we might call the presence of God, and he feels a transrational drive to remain in that elevated state. Trouble is, if he falls prey to the self-doubts of Virgo, he can settle for surrogates, such as simply staying drunk. To the medievals, the twelfth was "House of Troubles." That's an unduly narrow and pessimistic assessment, but it's true that planets there have a tendency to run amok unless they are solidly anchored in what we might broadly think of as spiritual disciplines. Pete Townshend, in other words, drives himself hard both materially and psychically. If he stays in balance, his accomplishments in both realms can be enormous. But if he fails to keep the shadowy side of the configuration under control, then he falls into moodiness, escapism, and self-punishment, along with a tendency to take his inner tensions out in picky attacks on the people closest to him.

Now put all that on the back burner. Let's move on and consider Roger Daltrey.

Daltrey's basic **identity (his** Sun) is shaped by Pisces and expresses itself into the fourth house. With the help of a little astrological knowledge, we realize that his public image as the archetypal hyper-hetero "rock star" is little more than a mask. Both Pisces (self-transcendence) and the fourth house (the unconscious mind) denote the blurring of Roger Daltrey's solar identity. The reason that he is so proficient at playing the role of a public symbol is **not** that his ego is so strong and well-defined, but rather the opposite: far more than most of us, Roger Daltrey is sensitive to the undercurrents that shape the mass mind. Ego, as we customarily understand it, never fully formed in him. He mirrors those social undercurrents. All in all, we find a sensitive, warmhearted man, eager for a well-defined role to play and devastatingly naked without one.

What happens when these two men interact? Townshend's Moon and Daltrey's Sun are linked by an opposition aspect–and right away we sense the dual qualities of tension and complementary characteristic of this astrological configuration.

On the tension side, Townshend's sharply critical perfectionism can be rough on Daltrey's sensitivity. Meanwhile, Daltrey's "vagueness" and "irrationality" can infuriate Townshend's taste for precision and intellectual rigor. On the complementary side, Daltrey's relative gentleness can perhaps soften Townshend's harshness–on others and on himself. Daltrey is sensitive to collective undercurrents; far more than Townshend, he has an instinct for what people want to see and hear. Townshend, on the other hand, is the consummate craftsman, driven by Virgoan dreams of excellence. Had they not met and collaborated, it is difficult to escape the notion that Townshend would have made creative decisions that alienated his audience–perhaps long before he even had an audience. Daltrey might have become simply a hack, parodying whatever styles were current. But together they were able to accomplish much more–and not in spite of their differences, but rather, because of those differences.

Shades of gray are the way of the world. Theoretically, this opposition interaspect between the two driving forces of The Who could have worked in blissful, conscious complementarity–or in homicidal tension. But in practice we typically find a mix of the

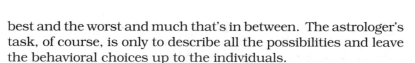

best and the worst and much that's in between. The astrologer's task, of course, is only to describe all the possibilities and leave the behavioral choices up to the individuals.

Let's dig a little deeper into the birthcharts of these two musicians, then try to deduce some elementary principles that apply across the board to all interaspects, even those belonging to people who spend less time in the fast lane.

Roger Daltrey's Moon lies in the last degree of Taurus in his seventh house (the "House of Marriage"). A fortune-teller would say that he was destined to "marry a Taurus," and probably an emotional one (the Moon's contribution). A more modern and certainly more accurate way of phrasing the prediction would be: Roger Daltrey has a lot of "soulmate business" to face, much of it with men and women who are lunar and Taurean in nature. That is, men and women of imaginative, moody, and subjective nature (Moon) who are concerned with Taurean issues (nature, music, security, concrete accomplishment, the body). These soulmates are guaranteed to appear in his life at critical junctures, often sending him careening off in directions he could not have anticipated before their arrival. He must learn to cooperate with these soulmates without being eclipsed by them. That's the heart of the seventh-house terrain: learning to establish equality and healthy interdependency in a long-haul partnership.

Into Roger Daltrey's life, at the tender age of nineteen, storms an emotional, creative Taurean–Pete Townshend–who catalyzed a set of events that would leave an indelible mark on Daltrey's experience. Where exactly is Townshend's Sun? Near the end of Taurus, less than two degrees from Daltrey's seventh-house Moon. A conjunction. The long creative partnership between the two men has proven to be the "marriage" the fortune-teller would have prophesied. Its existence is suggested by the nature of Daltrey's birthchart. But its results–those are as uncertain as next year's teenage fad.

Perspective: as we've already seen, an opposition links Townshend's Moon to Daltrey's Sun. Now we add the observation that Daltrey's Moon also conjuncts Townshend's Sun. Astrology predicts what history confirms: their destinies are interwoven. One Sun-Moon linkage is enough to imply that connection. Two make the observation irrefutable.

Although this Sun-Moon conjunction is a single configuration, it can be phrased in two ways. Each emphasizes a different interpretive point of view. We might say "Roger Daltrey's Moon conjuncts Pete Townshend's Sun," or we could invert it and say that "Townshend's Sun conjuncts Daltrey's Moon." This inversion is more than a word game. The statements are identical in meaning, but differ in nuance. The first phrasing of the sentence emphasizes the fact that Daltrey has an impact upon Townshend; the second, that Townshend affects Daltrey. Understanding the two-way flow of astrological interaction is the key to unlocking our general formula for all interaspects.

Daltrey's Moon falls on Townshend's Sun. What significance does this have? How does this interaspect feel? Something about Daltrey's instincts and emotions (his Moon) lines up with the core of Townshend's personality (his Sun). Daltrey floods Townshend's awareness with lunar energy–that is, with feeling. Townshend, in other words, always has an emotional response to Roger Daltrey, for better or worse. His solar ego is filled with uncharacteristically lunar qualities. Put simply, Daltrey makes Townshend moody–even more so than he would be otherwise. He also impacts upon him in such a way that Townshend's creative imagination is stimulated.

In a word, we would say that Roger Daltrey's effect upon Pete Townshend is to **lunarize** his Sun.

Turning the phrasing around, we recognize that Townshend's Sun also impacts upon Daltrey's heart, stimulating it to operate in a more solar way. That is, Townshend pushes Daltrey's Moon into active manifestation. Potentials locked away in the singer's psychic depths (Moon) are triggered into active, extraverted development. Specifically, we observe that, while Roger Daltrey is essentially a warm but withdrawn man (fourth-house Piscean Sun), he nonetheless was born with an instinct for relating to people (seventh house) in an earthy, emotional way (Taurus Moon). Left to his own devices, that quality would manifest cautiously in a tender but probably rather narrow personal life. Enter Pete Townshend; with his partner's Sun stimulating that Taurean Moon into a far more solar expression, history records that "shy" Roger Daltrey's hairy chest became a cultural icon for over a decade. His earthy seventh-house Taurean Moon was pushed into a far more aggressive stance than it ever would have taken naturally.

Townshend, thus, has the effect of **solarizing** Daltrey's Moon. Here's our general principle:

In any interaspect, the action is two-sided as each planet imprints the stamp of its own personality upon the other planet's nature and operation.

Thus, when the Sun in one chart touches a planet in another chart, its effect is to solarize the action of that planet–that is, to charge it with solar vitality and inspire it to action. The Sun, in turn, is suffused with the qualities of the planet upon which it is acting. That is, the Moon might lunarize the Sun, Mercury would mercurialize it, Jupiter jovialize it, and so on. Much of the rest of this chapter is devoted to a close analysis of each planet from this perspective.

Be careful never to assume that any such process is guaranteed to be dreadful or joyful. Ultimately everything depends upon the attitudes, determination, and level of commitment of the partners. In love, each planet can be a Gift-Giver–or a Thief. Which will it be? No way to answer that question astrologically. Everything depends upon the generosity, self-awareness, and motivation of the partners.

Townshend's Sun conjuncts Daltrey's Moon. The flow from Townshend to Daltrey is characterized as solarization. What if his Sun had **squared** Daltrey's Moon instead? The process would still accurately be described as "solarization," but the nature of the interaction would now have a different tone. Instead of the fusion associated with the conjunction, we would observe the friction that's connected with square aspects. In other words, solarization can happen in many ways, some of them harmonious, some of them explosive.

To put it all in subjective terms, we may like it when someone solarizes us–that's typically the case when the process occurs through trines and sextiles–or we may not like it a bit: often the case with squares and oppositions. Those statements are accurate...subjectively. But don't forget that being pushed and stretched in love is one of the qualities that keeps a partnership alive, and that too much easiness and comfort often lead to somnambulism.

The general principle: **The planets forming the interaspect determine the developmental issues at stake–solarization, lunarization, and so on–while the aspect linking them determines the specific tone of the process (tension, complementarity, friction, etc.).**

How intense will this process of "jovialization" or "neptunification" be? Three factors figure in our understanding here. First, consider the precision of the interaspect. Planets one degree apart from a perfect sextile interact far more vigorously than planets seven degrees away from the perfect sextile. Second, consider how centrally each planet figures in the individual birthchart. In other words, if Neptune in one person's birthchart is the ruler of the Ascendant and in a tight conjunction with the Sun, then it's a powerhouse, and any interaspect it forms might well prove to be the key to the whole synastry interpretation. On the other hand, maybe Neptune's role in the birthchart is relatively inconsequential. Then its interaspects are correspondingly less significant.

The third factor in determining the intensity of a interaspect is not a purely astrological consideration. It has to do with the intensity of the relationship itself. If you sit down next to a stranger on a bus and that stranger "mercurializes" your Sun, you'll likely have an interesting conversation in which you do a disproportionate amount of talking about yourself. (Mercury = Talk; Sun = Self.) Should you marry such a person, you might well write a semi-autobiographical novel. The relationship is more charged; so is the response to the interaspect.

These interaspects are the cornerstones of practical synastry. Let's delve into each one of them in detail.

Solarization

PLANET: The Sun

AS GIFT-GIVER: To charge and revitalize.
     To push into active manifestation.
     To encourage.
     To support.

AS THIEF: To eclipse.
     To overwhelm.
     To dominate.
     To burn out.

   You are the first astrologer who ever lived. There is no astrological tradition on which to fall back, no preconceived notions about
any of the planets, nothing but raw, direct experience.   King
Dog's-breath the Terrible appoints you to invent astrology–and
offers to cut off your head if you're not suited to the job. With that
kind of encouragement you quickly get very creative. The King's
first question is "What is the Sun's significance?" You've got three
days to answer. You reason: summer is green and full of life,
winter is dead and dreary. Cloudy days are sad days. Sunny ones
are happy. Plants turn toward the Sun and wither in the
shadows... **hmmm**... you have your answer: the Sun signifies
life.

   Now, ten thousand years later, no astrologer would disagree
with you. The Sun still means life. It is the purest, simplest
symbol of the life-force itself. Vitality. Energy. The gasoline in
your existential tanks.

   In synastry the Sun floods the contacted planet with a tidal
wave of energy. Spotlights it. Pushes it into dramatic development.

   Is this always an unalloyed good? Not necessarily. Sometimes
the Sun's force is overwhelming. Think of it like this: The
electricity fails in an unfamiliar room. You need a bit of light to
help you find the candles. You fumble in your pocket for a match.
All you find is a small nuclear warhead. Now, that'll make a flash,
but maybe a bit brighter than what you had in mind...and that's
exactly the danger with solar interaspects. The impact can be
powerful–too powerful.

At its best a solar interaspect can boost the contacted planet to a new energy level. One who solarizes your Uranus, for example, brings out your natural Uranian qualities–your independence, your capacity for creative, divergent thinking, your free-spirited ability to lead your own life. You'll likely share some distinctly Uranian experiences. Like winding up in Paris at two in the morning drinking Pernod with David Bowie, when you thought you were only stepping out to phone Mom.

All that Uranian excitement can be wonderful...if you can handle it. The dark side is that maybe the framework of your psychic structure is simply not sturdy enough to cope with this onslaught of boosted (solarized) Uranian juice. What happens then? The dark side of the planet begins to dominate your behavior. You become eccentric, cranky, unrealistic, stubborn–Uranian diseases.

The rule of thumb is that the healthier a response you are making to a planet in your birthchart, the happier will be your experiences with someone who solarizes that planet. Why? Because the Sun's action is to vivify, to emphasize, to bring out–and it makes no distinction between your virtues and your blind spots. The Sun simply forces your hand. Maybe that's a gift; maybe it's the work of the Thief, stealing your balance and good judgment like an unscrupulous fur trader selling "firewater" to unsuspecting, nineteenth-century Indians.

Sun is identity. Ego. When solarization occurs between two people, one person's ego is imprinted upon some aspect of the other person's individuality. Thus, there are two critical dimensions to the process of solarization. The first, which we have just explored, is that the solarized planet is simply pushed to the forefront of an individual's behavior, for better or worse. The second dimension is that the natural qualities of the solarized planet are not merely emphasized; they are also somewhat distorted. Something new, something alien, even unnatural, is added to the normal operation of that planet. A new voice, new values, new motivations appear.

Thus, to allow one's self to be solarized is to allow another person into one's life in the most central and intimate of ways. That individual's impact, especially in an intense, committed relationship, will prove to be incalculable. Life-shaping. Something of his or her individuality enters you and stays there. What if you don't like it? Then run! Get away! There is no other defense. Mere contact with the person guarantees impact.

In our society we are taught to value independence and personal freedom. And yet love inevitably implies a lowering of defenses, a merging, a willingness to touch and be touched. Solarization–this loving acceptance of another's identity into the fabric of our own being–is an act of ultimate trust. We are changed. The path of our life is turned.

Positively, as we internalize our partner's solar identity, our own life-process is fertilized, saved from the kind of psychic "inbreeding" that occurs if we never learn from anyone, never allow anyone to inspire or surprise us.

Negatively, our partner can so dominate us that we lose track of our own course. We can be eclipsed. Humiliatingly, we can be reduced to a mere clone of the other's personality. A puppet.

If you are solarized by someone you love, learn from him, trust her. Let that individual into your heart and mind. Don't worry if you find yourself picking up certain of that person's characteristic gestures or turns of phrase. It's normal in solarization. But guard your freedom too. Find a middle course. Listen to yourself as well as to your lover. Let yourself learn. Let yourself be changed. Then make those learnings and changings your own.

If you find yourself in a relationship in which you solarize the other person, be gentle. You probably don't fully comprehend the power you wield, and that makes you extremely dangerous! Recognize that however egalitarian your ideals might be, you still have awesome influence upon your partner's destiny. The planet you touch in that individual is like clay in your hands, ready to receive your imprint. Take that responsibility seriously. Imagine yourself to be quietly guiding the development of that dimension of your partner's life. Be a good guide. Not too dominant. Not too stultifying. Not too convinced of your own infallibility. And if your partner seems to be defensive, putting up mile-high walls, consider the possibility that he or she senses the overwhelming, solarizing danger in you and is undertaking a process of self-preservation in the only possible way: running away.

Lunarization

PLANET: The Moon

AS GIFT-GIVER: To sensitize.
  To deepen.
  To comfort.
  To inspire.

AS THIEF: To emotionalize.
  To upset.
  To smother.

What does Moonlight mean? Let the poet in you answer, not the rationalist. The Moon is a creature of the night. To decipher its significance you must respond from the night-side of your own being, from your unconscious, from your dreams and fantasies. Your day-self is useless here. It speaks another language, a more rational one. With Luna you must **feel** the answer.

The Moon's meaning? Magic. Romance. Passion. True enough. But even Hollywood's Moon-worshippers understand that much astrology.

Go further. There's more to the Moon than smooching in the Moonlight. Deep down, you know that already. The ghostly sickle shining through the bare trees on a black, windy night. Tattered clouds. The old graveyard. A cat startles at nothing. What do you feel? Something other-worldly. Something surrealistic. Something vaguely ominous. Something...unsettling. That's Luna too.

Once, in the minds of men and women, there was a Goddess. She was the Mother, and she was feminine. But she wasn't Betty Crocker. Long ago the "feminine" was a primal power, equal in every way to the masculine. But different. She ruled a distinct domain: the night. The realm of dreams–and nightmares. The realm of birth–and death. A realm of tender nurturing–and of inexplicable, lightning-swift violence. The Goddess, in other words, had teeth. As humanity lost its sense of the primordial feminine, a madness of unchecked, unbalanced power corrupted the decisions of active, aggressive "solar" people, and a corresponding madness of powerlessness overtook the "lunar" poets, dreamers, and visionaries.

In synastry, if we are to understand the process of lunarization, we must recover the old, half-forgotten Luna. We must recover our ancient respect for the powers of the night.

When the Moon in one birthchart contacts a sensitive point in another person's birthchart, that zone of life is flooded with emotion. That planet is made to feel itself like never before. Awareness itself is boosted. You might never think of your teeth...until you have a toothache. You might never consider your back...until someone is kind enough to scratch it. That's the kind of impact lunarization generates. All the inner, subjective processes associated with the lunarized planet are heightened. Much that was unconscious suddenly flashes into awareness. The volume is turned up on all the emotions, pleasant or unpleasant, sane or certifiably bonkers, connected with that planetary function.

Is lunarization a positive effect? Everything depends upon how we handle it. A parallel might be drawn with another lunar process: deep psychotherapy. Is psychotherapy "good" or "bad"? Doctrinaire people on both sides of the question have their position papers written, and they are ready to quote from them at the slightest provocation. Perhaps the wider truth is that psychotherapy can be helpful; it can also be a pointless, even perilous activity. Stirring up the unconscious is not terribly difficult, any more than opening Pandora's box was difficult. The problem lies in the next step. Now that all those demons and pestilences are stirred up, what are we going to do with them?

One of the best psychotherapists we know warns his clients in the first session: Are you sure you want to undertake this process? Are you confident you know what you are getting into? The same can be said for lunarization. It's potentially healing–and potentially very spooky.

The Moon is the Mother. In lunarization the Moons wants to nurture the planet it touches, bringing it from weakness to strength, from infancy to maturity. It wants to comfort that planet, to fill it with vision and imagination, to make it happy. How does Luna go about realizing her aim? Crudely, sometimes. She's like a person who believes passionately and dogmatically that psychotherapy is the answer to any question. "What do you feel?" "Why do you think you feel that way?" "How do you feel about feeling that way?" It's easy to lampoon this process, but it works nonetheless. It succeeds in opening up the unconscious: Pandora's box again. Trouble is, Luna might find the box is harder to close than it was to open.

A trusted friend fills your **bonding mechanism** (Venus) with emotion, helping you to understand more deeply your intimacy needs, nurturing your capacity to enter into ongoing, mutually supportive associations. So far so good. But imagine that your friend, "psychotherapizing" your Venus, helps you get in touch with some fundamental vacuums in your marriage. That too can be helpful–maybe. Everything depends upon what steps you take as a result of gaining that knowledge. Perhaps you bring that wisdom home to your husband or wife and begin to work actively on deepening your relationship. That's a practical example of the Moon's Gift. But maybe the Thief twists the healthy pattern, sowing only childish seeds of discontent.   You leave your marriage or wreck it with an affair–only to realize that, in this case at least, you were better off without the Moon's "wisdom."

Once again, the key principle is that the Goddess has teeth. The Moon–the unconscious–is a stormy, dangerous sea. We must sail those waters if we are to become wise. But we must sail them cautiously and know when to make for harbor rather than challenging hurricanes in our pea-green boat.

Positively, as we are sensitized to our own inner processes through lunarization, we can become wiser–that is, happier, less driven by neurotic, unconscious dimensions of our character. Our lunarizing partner might help lead us to new levels of self-understanding, new insights into our foibles and mad hungers. That's the good news.

The bad news is that, in lunarization, we can be driven regressively back into childishness and narcissistic emotional-ism. Why? Because lunarization empowers the unconscious to a dangerous degree. Irrational fears, self-damaging "needs," and developmental glitches rooted in our early years–all these can be energized, lifted from the crypt like some ancient zombie we thought we had successfully laid to rest. Then we deal with them. Or they deal with us.

If you are lunarized by someone you love, prepare for a very emotional relationship. You'll know tenderness and caring as never before. You'll also likely embarrass the pants off yourself from time to time with moodiness, irrationality, and childish tantrums. Let yourself be mothered, but don't allow yourself to be smothered. The child's task is to grow up, and that's a delicate, ironic process. The child needs the mother and also needs to not need her. Your lunarizing partner creates an incubator for your growth. Use it, but know when to climb out into the world, dry your eyes, and take a grown-up stand.

If you find yourself in a relationship in which you lunarize your partner, prepare to be very vulnerable. Whether or not you put it into words, the aura of your being seems to say to that person, "Feel, feel, feel." Perhaps he feels love and admiration for you. Wonderful. That's easy to get used to. But perhaps he also feels anger and frustration. Maybe decades ago mommy wouldn't let him have that third bowl of ice cream, and those enraged, violent "little boy" emotions are locked in his unconscious too. Arguably, they'd be better off remaining there, but you'll stimulate their reentry into awareness. Those darker feelings are part of the package. You are the "psychotherapist," at least in this part of your relationship. No escaping that role. So be a good one. Know when to love actively. And know when to back off. Know when to encourage emotion, and when to balance emotion with adult rationality and responsibility. Above all, don't fall into the trap of encouraging your partner to feel and grow and explore–and then leap down his or her throat the instant that unsettling process bothers you.

Ascendantalization
(accent the third syllable)

AS GIFT-GIVER: To socialize.
To stimulate.
To stylize.
To "egg on."

AS THIEF: To trivialize.
To caricaturize.
To "make a fool of."

There is a French expression for feeling good–"Je suis bien dans ma peau"–that can be translated as "I am at ease in my skin." Those words spring directly from the part of human awareness that astrologers call the Ascendant. "At ease in one's skin." What

does the phrase imply? Well-being, certainly. But more: Poise.
Centeredness. Self-acceptance. A state of easy normalcy.

To learn about the Ascendant there is no need for lofty
meditations or for long hours spent peering into obscure medieval astrology texts. Instead, just go to a party–and the brasher
and phonier that party is, the better. Watch how people act. The
word "act" is of course appropriate under such circumstances.
Who can be "real"–that is, engage in intense psychological
honesty–with the music at eighty decibels and the drinks mixed
strong, while circulating through a horde of strangers hurling
fusillades of witticism at each other? "Acting" is the only option.

Some of us like parties. Some of us don't. There's room in the
world for all of us. But in the everyday course of living, all of us
are compelled to streamline our psyches in a way that allows us
to relate superficially to the immediate social environment. If we
do that well, we feel "at ease in our skins"–and we make a strong
response to our Ascendant.

Someone might have Leo or Libra rising. Such a person will
likely appear to be right at home in social situations. Those are
friendly, expansive signs, good at parties unless the rest of the
birthchart pushes strongly in the opposite direction. But what if
a person has a more introspective sign on the Ascendant, such
as Scorpio or Cancer? He or she can still be "at ease in his/her
skin"–just more quietly. Not everyone in the room need be "the
life of the party." The trick with the Ascendant is not to be the
smooth-talking slick dresser who knows all the best jokes and
spends the party surrounded by a gaggle of admiring candidate
sex partners. Rather, it has to do with a self-accepting knowledge
of one's own natural style, a capacity to use that style effectively
in social circumstances, and a sure fix on the difference between
an honest adaptation to social reality and mere posturing and
phoniness.

In synastry the Ascendant plays a significant role. In keeping
with our general formula, the significance of the Ascendant is to
ascendantalize whatever planet it touches in a partner's
birthchart. In other words, qualities associated with the Ascendant–poise, style, social confidence–are grafted onto the
ascendantalized planet.

A woman is an eighth-house Pisces with Cancer rising and
Saturn in the first house: not exactly a social butterfly. She has
Mercury in Virgo in the third house, which is a highly verbal,

communicative feature. Clearly there is tension here. How does an introvert with strong language skills resolve that paradox? Perhaps she doesn't! Perhaps she simply feels "bottled up." Perhaps she's silent for long periods then bursts out with spells of pointless nervous chatter. But maybe her response is stronger. She makes peace with the inwardness, capitalizes on her vivid imagination–and becomes a fantasy novelist. And she's still quiet at parties.

Along comes a woman who ascendantalizes her Mercury. Initially, as their friendship is forming, the impact of this interaspect is simply to encourage the novelist to speak. She talks about book plans, feelings, the weather, politics...and quite unintentionally, through practice with this Ascendantalizing friend, she improves her verbal skills. Before long, she notices that when the two women are together in a group situation, she feels better about herself. More at ease. Words come to her more quickly. She knows what to say. She's urbane, entertaining, informative, interesting...and she's received a Gift.

In common with all astrological processes, ascendantalization has few guarantees. The Thief can strike just as easily as the Gift-Giver. The ascendantalized planet is pushed into more active, social operation. That's all we know for sure. At best this encourages poise and maturation. At worst the Thief can take over, simply trivializing the contacted planet, pushing it into premature, unconsidered activity. Our novelist can find that whenever she's with her friend in a social situation she tends to open her mouth before her brain is engaged, with disastrous, embarrassing results.

What determines whether we'll see the Thief or the Gift-Giver? It boils down to how solid a response the ascendantalized individual has made to the planet in question. If our introverted novelist has been taking her writing seriously, polishing her craft, feeding her intelligence with curiosity and openness, then she'll likely have reason to welcome ascendantalization. Her Mercury is healthy; one push from her friend and it shines. On the other hand, perhaps the novelist has been lazy. Perhaps she's settled for cliches. Perhaps she's not a novelist at all–there were darker possibilities in her birthchart. Then, when that starved Mercury is ascendantalized, its illness is made apparent to anyone who's listening.

In the previous chapter we looked at the charts of Spencer Tracy and Katharine Hepburn. Anyone who has seen their films has been delighted by their capacity for banter, good-natured combat, and quick-witted playfulness. Together they both radiated "style"–and once again, when we use that word, we don't mean fashionable clothes. Tracy's Ascendant is in the eighteenth degree of Capricorn. Hepburn's is in the eleventh degree of Virgo. Thus their Ascendants form a stimulating sextile interaspect. Each actor, in other words, ascendantalized the other one's Ascendant–and offered a feast of style for anyone who watched.

Mercurialization

PLANET: Mercury

AS GIFT-GIVER: To inform.
　　　　　To excite intellectually.
　　　　　To enliven.
　　　　　To encourage speech.

AS THIEF: To confound.
　　　　　To "tie in knots".
　　　　　To fluster.

In her book, *The Faces of Science Fiction*, photographer Patti Perret quotes one of the genre's grand old masters, Fritz Lieber: "I occupy one of the half billion or so stations in the speech web of story-telling, gossip-trading, observations-sharing, English-speaking minds...It's my job to keep my station in good working order, busily receiving and sending...and with my antennae burnished and honed to catch, embellish, reweave, and retransmit hints of the strange, the mysterious, the wondrous."

We don't know Fritz Lieber's birthchart, but it's clear that he is a master of Mercury. This is the planet of data-transfer. Pure information, coming and going. "Intelligence" is a key word here. So are "speaking" and "listening." But most central is that miracle-seeking, wonder-loving inner state we call curiosity.

In mercurialization, the contacted planet is asked to think. That's the heart of the process. How is such cogitation encouraged? By giving the planet something to think about! Information is everything. When we're bored, we're dull. Kids growing up in environments lacking stimulation have been proven to grow up less bright and alert than kids who are given access to varied experiences, interesting objects, changing viewpoints. Mercury floods the planet it touches with ideas and experiences. Sometimes it argues. Sometimes it offers books. Often it simply plays mind games. Not infrequently it shows up with tickets to a movie–or tickets to Lisbon.

Mercury encourages the planet it touches, once stimulated, to speak its mind. First it enriches the information environment. Then it forces speech, usually through dialogue. A man has Saturn in the tenth house (career; community). A tennis buddy mercurializes it. "You mentioned the other day that you were interested in incorporating your business. I happened to have some literature at home about that. Here it is. I had a friend who incorporated. They had to pump his lungs–nearly drowned in a sea of paper. But I know this other guy who really should've been incorporated. He's a painter. Or was. He spilled a can of paint on this old lady's marble-top antique chessboard. Belonged to Napoleon. Or so she said. Anyway she sued him for everything but his toenails...what do you think you're gonna do?"

Mercury the Thief operates by never shutting up–or by attempting to put prefabricated thoughts into the other person's head. With its verbal agility it can fluster the planet it contacts, tie it up in knots. It can win arguments, even when it's wrong. The Gift-Giver shares what it knows, then listens. The Thief insists upon agreement.

If you mercurialize someone you care about, first consider what planet your Mercury contacts in that person. What issues does it represent in that individual's life? The answer, of course, depends not only upon the name of the planet, but also upon its sign and house and its role in the larger patterns of the birthchart. Once you've understood the big picture, then realize that you have access to certain information or certain ways of thinking that can be extraordinarily useful in that department of your partner's life. Share them. Engage the partner in dialogue. You're not a teacher exactly...more like a library. Stimulate, inform, ask hard questions, facilitate clear thinking as best you can. But don't try to enforce any decisions.

If you find yourself in a relationship in which you are mercurialized, start by accepting that unless you're an Enlightened Being, the contacted planet in your birthchart is not all-knowing. It has a blind spot or two. There is something it's not seeing, something essential...and your partner can help. He or she has the information, or at least the method for finding it. The difficulty and the delight is that you must discover the missing pieces of the puzzle together. Think of that partner as a library–but a library in chaos. The books are scattered. There is no card catalog. Half the volumes are in Latin. To find what you need you'll have to search together, comparing notes, talking, exploring, questioning.

The poet Percy Bysshe Shelley mercurialized the chart of his wife, Mary Shelley. His Mercury stimulated her imaginative Neptune through a sextile interaspect and simultaneously complemented her shadowy Pluto through an out-of-quality opposition. Would she have written *Frankenstein* without him? Or did he help give voice to that creature from her Neptunian-Plutonian depths–just as her Neptune and her Pluto fed transcendental vision into his glib Mercury?

Venusification
(Ve-NOOSE-ification)

PLANET: Venus

AS GIFT-GIVER: To attract.
　　　　To refine.
　　　　To warm.
　　　　To soothe.

AS THIEF: To seduce.
　　　　To manipulate.
　　　　To lull.

Men have played a disproportionate role in establishing the myths and symbols upon which our culture is founded. One effect of that historical twist is that the planet Venus is universally viewed as a pretty woman. Ask a dozen men–five thousand years ago or today–to come up with images of attractiveness, irresistibility, and seductive warmth. What do you get? The Goddess Venus–feminine, curvaceous, misty-eyed, draped in a sexy marble Greco-Roman negligee.

You can hardly blame the boys. But if the balance ever shifts and women become the dominant symbol-weavers, you can safely predict that Venus will be packed off to Sweden for that famous operation...

Attraction: that's the key to Venus. When someone venusifies you, there's an excellent chance that you're going to like the sensation. How does it feel? That depends upon which planet in your own chart the other person's Venus contacts. If Venus contacts your Mercury, your mind is attracted. You find that person fascinating. If he or she venusifies your Neptune, then your sense of magic and wonder is alerted. Should Venus contact your Saturn, you will likely be drawn in by Saturnine feelings–that man or woman fills you with a combination of longing and respect, as if he or she represented some unattainable ideal.

The world is cold and treacherous in many ways, full of two-legged predators. Most of us, as a result of an accumulation of disappointments, hurts, and fears, gradually accrete a protective shell. Naively, some of us imagine that shell to be "bad." Cynically, others imagine it to be "good." A better, more neutral word might be "inevitable." However necessary that shell might be and however inevitable its acquisition, one observation is certain: finding someone with whom we can drop the shell is one of life's most blissful experiences.

Venus melts the shell. When we are venusified, we immediately sense warmth in our hearts, trust, understanding, interest, attraction...as if some great magnetic void has opened up between us, pulling us in, drawing us together.

At best our being is engaged in that most healing of activities: love. In fact, strong Venus contacts are perhaps the single most common astrological features in happy marriages and lasting friendships. Simply liking each other is essential if any two people are going to survive the bumps and wrinkles of intimate human interaction. Strong Venus links come nearer to guaranteeing that kind of affection than any other kind of planetary configuration.

So where's the catch? Don't worry, it's there. Have you ever really liked someone, really trusted, really opened yourself–and gotten nailed to the wall? And looking back, would you say that the catastrophe stemmed from misunderstanding and wishful thinking on your part, exaggerated by misrepresentation on the part of your partner? If you can identify with this scenario, you need no introduction to Venus the Thief.

The old saw "Love is blind" offers helpful insights into Venusian interaspects. If someone venusifies you, it is as if that mere man or woman were suddenly surrounded by a sparkling aura of wonderfulness. Violins sound in the distance. Sweet-smelling, intoxicating mists rise up from somewhere down around your Nikes. Before you know it, you get attached. Your thinking is not as clear as it might normally be. You want to see that person as the embodiment of all that is decent in the universe. This is a mixed blessing, or mixed curse, if you prefer. The up side is that you get a flash of something approaching unconditional love: a spirit of generosity, a quickness to forgive. And that's a fertile growth medium for genuine commitment. The down side is blindness. If you are venusified and if that person's motives are predatory or simply whimsical, you've really let the cat in with the parakeet.

If you venusify someone, strive to represent yourself honestly to that person. He or she expects a lot of you, probably more than you can deliver in the long run. Soften the blow in advance with the disciplines of truth.

The rock band the Rolling Stones have never been nominated as paragons of virtue, nor have they sought to appear that way. The undercurrents of violence and recurrent elements of sexism on their music have alienated a lot of people. Yet there is irony here. One of the saddest themes in this generation's history has been the erosion of the institution of male friendship. And yet the Stones' Mick Jagger and Keith Richards have quietly carried the torch as "pals" for over three decades, never publicly mythologiz-ing their relationship or capitalizing on it, and yet successfully weathering together the storms and temptations of fame, di-vorces, corporate politics, mid-life crises, wealth, changing mu-sical styles, and sundry legal difficulties, not to mention Keith's long, destructive bout with narcotics. Unsurprisingly, when we compare the two men's birthcharts, we find rampant venusification. For starters, the Venuses themselves share a sextile interaspect. Beyond that, Jagger's Venus conjuncts Richards's Moon and trines his Mercury, while Richards's Venus opposes Jagger's Mars and squares his Jupiter, his Mercury, and his Pluto.

Martialization

PLANET: Mars

AS GIFT-GIVER: To excite.
　　　　　To embolden.
　　　　　To arouse.

AS THIEF: To terrorize.
　　　　　To irritate.
　　　　　To enrage.

Passion. Adrenaline. Heat. Fire. Those are Mars words. Feel them in your body and you'll feel the ambiguous relationship the human spirit has with the red planet. We love it and hate it, fear it and seek it.

A passionless life. A passionless marriage. The phrases feel like indictments. Or maybe death sentences. Yet passion frightens us. We turn from it–and then look back longingly. We pay dearly for it–and then smother it as quickly as we can, just to control it.

The Martial thermostat has only two settings: freezing and boiling. That's the difficulty with Mars. Feast or famine. Too much intensity. Or too little.

Imagine that you and I are caricatures of suburban values in the 1950s. We share a back fence. We're both out there weeding our tomatoes, gossiping about another couple in the neighborhood. "I've known them for fifteen years. I tell you, those two have the best marriage I've ever seen. Fifteen years, and they've never once had a fight." You nod your head with a faraway look in your eyes.

In this scenario, of course, we both privately compare our own marriages unfavorably to that of our "blissful" friends.

Nowadays, hopefully, we're a little smarter. We might say, "Fifteen years without a fight! What are they saving up?" And if we're a little smarter still, we might add, "And how well do they even know each other?"

Intimate conflict is a thoroughly miserable experience. That much is certain. But if undertaken fairly and honestly it can also be a form of communication. It can break up the icy veneer of lies and half-truths that begins automatically to build up in any bond that's more than a few months old.

Like most experiences that threaten us, Mars–and martialization–is a process fraught with taboos. There are certain observations we're "not supposed to make," certain common human behaviors we've all agreed to ignore.

Scratch an old tomcat behind the ears. Stroke his back. He stretches, luxuriates–and then bites you. Why? He's aroused sexually. And he responds violently. Fighter pilots have spoken of getting erections as they flew into battle. Go to the typical movie. What do you see? Sex and violence. Why are they always linked? A sexy man or a sexy woman often exudes a certain undefinable aura of danger. Why?

Mars is the common denominator. All those energies are Martial. If astrology is the wiring diagram of the human mind, we learn that passion and rage–sex and violence–run on the same circuit.

As I write these words, I feel tremendous resistance in myself, as if I am not supposed to be saying these things. And yet the trick we must learn if we are going to deal effectively with shadowy issues is never to go halfway and then get paralyzed with fear or "morality." We must always go further, deeper.

No sex without violence. That is our taboo principle. A fool might take this idea as a vindication of rape, brutality, and sadomasochism. Most "good" people are likely experiencing a degree of shock at reading such smut in a nice astrology book.

Only go further: "violence," in the Martial sense, takes many forms. It goes without saying that physical violence has absolutely no place in any healthy sexual relationship. It kills trust, and without trust love dies. The same can be said of emotional violence. But there is another kind of violence: honesty. Difficult honesty. Honesty when it hurts to say it and it hurts worse to hear it. Honesty that confronts a person's precious defense mechanisms and cherished lies.

A couple has contracted that uniquely modern disease: drifting apart. He's deeply involved in his career. She's getting into astrology in a big way. Nominally they are supportive of each other, but deep down there are angers and fears. Naturally their sex life has begun to reflect the distancing that's taken place in their marriage. One night it all boils over. All that "supportiveness" flies out the window. All the tension that's built up between them gets released in one incendiary fireball. But they hang in there. The fight is ugly, but honest. It takes time and they both bleed, but conflict finally gets them down to the truth. She's afraid that, in the light of his worldly success, he's losing respect for her. He's afraid that, in the light of her interest in astrology, she's thinking of him as a psychological or spiritual cripple. It takes four hours of hell for them to rip away that numbing veneer of "politeness" that was eating away at the passionate heart of their marriage. But it's worth it. That night they make love, and it's the best sex they've had in months. Why? Because in the world of healthy adults, good sex and unchallenged defensive blockages are mutually exclusive.

When someone you love martializes one of your planets, you can count on conflict developing there. This statement is not nearly so pessimistic as it sounds. You need that conflict. That planet is not as alert as it needs to be. There is something it fears to see, fears to learn, some truth "so terrible" that an awful lot of the planet's energy is locked up in defensiveness. When the healing begins, you'll probably feel for a moment as if your martializing partner has turned into your enemy, or at best as if he or she is misguided. Maybe there is misguidance. Maybe there is cruelty. That's possible. But maybe there's truth too, a truth you'd rather not hear. Control your fear. Control your rage. Listen and judge. At worst you hear an untruth. That's not so bad: correct it. At best you restore to your partnership that dangerous, delicious, passionate edge of shared growth.

Should you find yourself in the martializing role, remember that whatever planet you touch in your partner is touching you too–right in your Mars. No matter what the identity of the other planet in the interaspect, your Mars is being stimulated. As a result, take a moment to mistrust yourself. Passion distorts, usually by magnifying: the person who's merely in a bad mood, through the eyes of passion, becomes The Most Negative Person in the World. The one who's left his underwear on the floor becomes The Filthiest Slob Who Ever Walked the Earth. Think before you speak. You probably see a truth, and you probably should share it, even if it won't be popular. But watch how you phrase it. Watch your tone of voice. Resist that hilarious, devastating one-liner that's sure to rankle. It would work beautifully in a comedy of manners; but it won't fly in the bedroom. No need to be overly gentle. But don't be foolishly extreme either.

Singer Linda Ronstadt and former California governor Jerry Brown raised a lot of eyebrows a few years ago when they had a relationship. There were those who felt that such conduct was "improper" in a man of his station. Looking at their birthcharts, we discover that Ronstadt martialized Brown's independence-loving Uranus through a supportive trine aspect. He had a certain native pluck and irreverence regarding social "proprieties" (natal Uranus in the tenth house); she merely emboldened it through the Martial interaspect.

Jovialization

PLANET: Jupiter

AS GIFT-GIVER: To brighten.
    To uplift.
    To expand.
    To cheer.

AS THIEF: To flatter.
    To intoxicate.
    To overextend.

"Faith" is one of those pretty words, like "love," that tends to get blurry when you hold it up close. What does it mean? One might have faith in a sound investment or in a particular spiritual teacher or even in a rickety set of stairs. What are the common denominators? Certainly faith implies confidence. That's part of the picture. But faith is more specific. It connotes a quality of confidence that extends beyond strict reason, as in religion–or rickety staircases.

With faith comes lightness. A burden is lifted from our shoulders, shared with whatever entity inspires our faithful feelings. With that easing of responsibility joy arises–and joy's sister: humor. We laugh. We smile like a bride. And like the bride, we look forward to our future with a heady mixture of triumph and delight.

The planet that has astrological dominion over these emotions is Jupiter, the proverbial "king of the gods." Naturally, throughout much of astrology's history, these Jupiter energies–faith, joy, humor, success–have been viewed as positive contributions to any birthchart. Jupiter was a "good" planet, and anything it touched was improved.

Or so went the theory. The truth is more complex. Not negative, just more complex.

Faith. Joy. Humor. A feeling of invincibility. They're all thoroughly wonderful as **feelings**. But reality sometimes has other plans. A kid got his driver's license a year ago. Now he wants to find out how fast his Camaro can take that curve. His Jupiter circuitry is cooking. Just before he rolls the car and kills himself. That's the dark side of the "lucky planet": unrealistic overextension, too much optimism, all the reality-denying, shadow-fleeing excesses of what's sometimes called "positive thinking."

Jupiter helps us to see opportunity. It puts us in a state of consciousness in which we are hypersensitized to positive possibilities and deem ourselves worthy of claiming them. That's its gift. The hook is that sometimes Jupiter has to get us half-drunk on expansive, world-conquering emotions before we get the message. And those emotions are dangerous.

When you jovialize someone you love, think of yourself as that person's cheerleader. Should you jovialize a friend's Scorpio Moon, for example, then your task is not merely to "cheer her up," but rather to help guide her toward real Scorpionic victories, to assist her in seeing new possibilities in her efforts to penetrate the heart of the psyche (Scorpio Moon process). Maybe you take her to a lecture by a famous novelist and thereby encourage her to discover a creative outlet for her pent-up psychological intensity. Maybe you introduce her to astrology.

Maybe you tell her jokes. Seriously...humor can be a potent agent in opening the deeper reaches of the mind. Woody Allen, arguably the greatest clown of the modern era, is a Sagittarian with Jupiter and Mercury both conjunct his Sun. Those three planets all form a sextile interaspect to Diane Keaton's Aquarian Moon. Thus, as she opened her heart to him in their glory days, he not only jovialized her experimental instincts (Aquarian Moon), but also mercurialized them and solarized them. Together, Woody Allen and Diane Keaton were masters of slapstick, but as a team they also used humor to pick the lock on a number of often painful, taboo subjects: insecurity, sexual vulnerability, fear of aging, psychotherapy, betrayal, ethnicity, and so on. That represents jovialization at its best: the ability simultaneously to brighten and to deepen your partner's perspective, especially regarding topics previously full of threatening impossibility.

One of the hazards of being human is that we tend to take ourselves awfully seriously. Should you be jovialized by someone close to you, let your partner teach you humor, even if it seems to be at your own expense. Humor opens the door to greater Gifts. Try to get the joke–if you do, you'll get a lot more. That friend or lover has an instinctive grasp of your highest potentials. He or she knows how you've been underestimating yourself. Your resistance to the humor is a measure of your attachment to narrower perspectives moored in darker, more hurtful periods of your life.

The Thief twists the process of jovialization, pushing his or her partner into foolish excesses or premature, ill-founded efforts. Flattery figures prominently in the Thief's strategy. So does humor's shadow: mockery. Often the most damaging aspect of jovialization arises when the partner feels bound to "say only positive things"–and encourages you, in the name of "supportiveness," to leap over the cliff.

Keep an eye out for the Thief, but enjoy the rest. Jovialization–bringing out the hidden best in someone who's sharing your life–is high on the list of reasons why love is worth the effort it takes.

Saturnization

PLANET: Saturn

AS GIFT-GIVER: To crystallize.
> To focus.
> To confront.
> To discipline.

AS THIEF: To repress.
> To control.
> To tantalize.
> To frustrate.

Saturn is the bogeyman. The planet of death. The lord of solitude. Or so say the traditionalists. Sepharial, an early twentieth century British astrologer, writes: "Saturn gives delays, impediments, defects, secrets, fatalities, falls from position, misfortunes, melancholy moods, chronic hurts, sorrows, disease, and hurts to women and children. It makes the native independent, unhappy, secretive, cautious, jealous, miserly, and governed by habit."

Not exactly "date bait," right?

You'd get no disagreement from Professor A. F. Seward, "the world's foremost astrologer," (if not the world's most modest) circa 1915: "Saturn's influence...causes its subjects many reverses, usually in middle life. Much of their trouble coming through marriage and love affairs."

Unsurprisingly, the "old school" astrologers' dark view of Saturn carried over into synastry. The ringed planet's interaspects were perceived as baleful influences upon marriage, prophetic of estrangements, emotional coldness, and the early demise of one of the partners.

Out of this tradition of horror and gloom a singularly odd perception is currently arising. In modern times strong Saturn contacts are more often than not found in long-lasting marriages. Again and again we see it: the birthcharts of a couple that holds together through thick and thin, slogging through the swamps and toasting the good times, are stitched together with a network of Saturnian links.

Any marriage, and most friendships for that matter, sooner or later comes upon stressful times. Once again, such tension is inevitable whenever two monkeys are stuck in the same small cage. Years ago the practical and social pressures that kept marriages intact were far more pervasive than they are now. Those pressures were a double-edged sword. Negatively, they kept many couples bound together in a semi-homicidal emotional wasteland throughout their adult lives, all as a result of a mistake they made as teenagers.

Positively, that pro-marriage social pressure helped many a couple survive the bumpy places in the connubial road. Now, with divorce practically a national sport, couples who stay together must **choose** to stay together, actively and consciously. With the door to "freedom" wide open, each lover must willingly accept the limitations inherent in the marriage vow. In bad times such a decision takes a big dose of the healthiest kind of Saturnine energy: self-discipline.

In a word, Saturn the Gift-Giver offers **commitment**. Saturn's message is that, while love is certainly an emotion, it is also more than an emotion. It is a promise to act in a responsible, open, honest way, no matter what kinds of tension are in the air.

Should someone you love saturnize a planet in your birthchart, you might not enjoy the feeling at first. Like a fine brandy, that contact typically must be given time to mature before its full flavor emerges. Your partner confronts that part of your own character, challenging it to "grow up," impelling that planet to make a mammoth push toward its mature potential. Often Saturn suggests a specific, concrete plan for that push, helping to crystallize and focus the energies of the contacted planet.

Subjectively you may experience saturnization as an apparent effort on your lover's part to control you or even to repress you. Is that true objectively? Possibly–that's the Thief's way. But even if the process is the work of the Gift-Giver, you might still sometimes experience those bad feelings. No one really likes to grow, especially the kind of growth that carries us from the delightfully vague world of dreams into the painfully limited world of reality. That particular transition is Saturn's speciality. Retrospectively you may appreciate the results of saturnization, but they can take their time to appear, and meanwhile the process itself is tiring, frightening, and often thorny. Typically it even feels unnatural, as if our saturnizing partner is asking us to become someone other than who we already are–which of course is precisely what's happening.

Saturn, subjectively again, fills us with feelings of hunger. Like the proverbial carrot at the end of the stick, it holds before us a sense of what we could be. Should someone saturnize your Mercury, for example, that person pushes you to speak and think (Mercury) more clearly and rigorously, pointing out inconsistencies in your ideas, holes in your logic. Should someone saturnize your Venus, he or she might similarly confront you regarding your romantic ideals, sexual assumptions, and intimate behavior (Venus). Should someone saturnize your Sun, then the authenticity of your entire way of being in the world is called into question. In all cases, if you accept reality and make a disciplined effort to change yourself, you've received a Gift.

On the dark side, the Thief can turn all that inspiration into frustration and self-criticism. How? By holding out impossible ideals. Never satisfied, always demanding, the Thief tantalizes, frustrates, and ultimately depresses whatever planet it contacts.

If you saturnize someone, scrutinize yourself. Be careful you're not the Thief. All of us are frightened sometimes. All of us live in a world we cannot control, dependent for our survival upon seemingly random forces we can barely influence—like the whimsies of warmongering politicians or the statistical reassurances of the people behind your local nuclear power plant. Those "out of control" feelings scare us. Therein lies the glitch: as a result of our fears of what we can't control, we might unconsciously seek to over-manage some zone of experience more under our direct influence. Like the decisions of somebody we love. That's where the Thief gets in. We displace our legitimate, but frustrated, urge to be in control of our own experience, twisting it into a compulsion to keep another human being under our thumb.

Should you saturnize someone who trusts you, study your motives. Are you trying to keep an unnecessarily tight rein on that person's behavior? Are you emotionally invested in keeping your partner safely predictable, in his or her "proper place"? Have you recognized his or her inalienable right to navigate independently in this mysterious world? If not, then the Thief is under your skin, using you.

Carl Jung and Sigmund Freud, the co-developers of psychoanalysis, worked well together for many years, pushing each other to new levels of precision and depth.   Such shared accomplishment alerts us to Saturn contacts between the men. Clinching our guess, we observe how their relationship soured once Jung, the younger man, began to diverge from Freud's "party line" regarding the nature of the human unconscious. Jung's sense of being "squashed" and Freud's feelings about Jung's "disobedience" or "betrayal" all point toward the activity of Saturn the Thief.   When we look at their birthcharts, we discover that Freud saturnized Jung's Jupiter and Saturn through trines, and his Mars through an opposition.   Turning the viewpoints around, we also learn that Jung saturnized Freud even more powerfully. Jung's Saturn trined Freud's own Saturn. It also contacted Freud's nadir through a conjunction, his Venus through a sextile, and his Sun, his Uranus, and his Mercury through square interaspects.   Thus, these two men, virtual studies in saturnization, illustrate for us the best and worst of what this contact can mean. And perhaps ironically, despite their personal falling out, Saturn won in the end: their names, in history, are now forever married. At one level, at least, their relationship endures.

Uranization
(accent first syllable)

PLANET: Uranus

AS GIFT-GIVER: To individualize.
To liberate.
To surprise.
To revolutionize.

AS THIEF: To disrupt.
To shell-shock.
To frazzle.
To deprave.

When we were kids, most of us were taught to pronounce "Uranus" like this: "yer-AY-nus" with an accented long **a** on the second syllable. In late January, 1986, when the Voyager probe flew by the planet, the newscasters all agreed to a different pronunciation: "YER-in-us." Astrologers have been known to use both pronunciations, but many use a third: "yer-AHHHH-nus."

This linguistic mess is hardly a major moral issue, but it's certainly a delight to anyone who understands the astrological significance of the planet. If Uranus could talk, its message would be, "Why don't all you people think for yourselves?" The synchronicity, of course, is that currently if you so much as open your mouth to utter the name of this planet, you must "think for yourself." How will you pronounce it? No matter what your choice, you've got enemies. Somebody is going to accuse you of mispronunciation.

Thinking for one's self. What does it mean? Certainly it goes far beyond figuring out how to say "Uranus." All of us are subjected to overwhelming social pressures, squeezed into pre-fabricated roles, with prefabricated opinions, tastes, lifestyles, even thoughts. Men are taught not to cry. Women are trained to cry perhaps too easily. We are all encouraged to equate happiness with success and success with money. Each society is different but ultimately the same. Only the customs vary. The essential process–socialization–is universal.

And that's why God made Uranus.

This is the planet of rebellion. It refers to the ability to break rules. To question authority. To crack the mold into which culture tries to pour our lives.

Uranian energy is, above all else, exciting. It fires us up, puts a sharp edge on our senses, accelerates the mental processes. Also, for reasons that are difficult to comprehend logically, this planet brings in "long shots." Someone buys the right lottery ticket and wakes up a millionaire. Another person is transferred to northern Iceland. A third unexpectedly inherits an estate in Australia. Despite the fireworks, the key to understanding Uranian energy is to recognize that the planet promotes **individuation**, the effort to become truly one's self. The long shots appear to function as "cosmic matching funds" that support and amplify the core Uranian process.

In intimacy, uranization is a giddy feeling, not for the fainthearted. The rug is pulled out from under the uranized planet. Everything is questioned. Idols fall. Comforting certainties evaporate. A voice exhorts us, "Don't follow leaders!"

A woman comes from a strict, puritanical background. A man appears in her life who uranizes her Venus. He pushes her to rethink her sexual mores, asking her to separate what she feels from what she's merely been trained to think. Another man is a nonviolent Quaker. A woman appears who uranizes his Mars. She makes him angry–and forces him to rethink his position on aggressive behavior. Does he abandon his Quaker ideals, become abusive and violent, simply because someone's Uranus happens to contact his Mars? No–not unless he's been hiding those kinds of feelings behind a thin facade of pacifism. She merely encourages him to go beyond the Quaker "position" that he has learned and to replace it with direct personal experience, independent analysis, and absolute honesty. She might have no idea that that's what she's doing, but those are the effects.

If you uranize someone, remember that conventionality is not simply a destructive, limiting force. It is also a stabilizing, even deepening influence. Very few individuals are so inherently strong and wise that they'd be better off had they been left solo in the jungles at an early age. Life is full of quagmires and puzzles. For a million years men and women have been mapping them, passing their wisdom down the line of generations. That wisdom is far from perfect, but most of us can benefit from using it until we gradually develop better, more individualized answers. In uranization you might push your partner too fast, exciting him, pressing him to claim a level of freedom he is currently unprepared to handle responsibly. The woman from the puritanical background might find herself unintentionally pregnant. The Quaker might humiliate himself by hitting the woman who uranized his Mars. In either case the uranized individual might react regressively, fleeing into safer territory in shocked response to the frightening–the perilous–Uranian freedom.

Should you find yourself strongly uranized in an intimate relationship, get ready to move into uncharted territory. You've found a partner who is going to push you, cause you to ask dangerous questions, encourage you to stretch toward the limits of your true individuality. To hold up your end of that exiting process, concentrate on keeping your balance. Be willing to doubt everything you've ever taken to be true, but at the same time, be wary of giddiness and blind, bulletproof enthusiasm.

Freud's Uranus conjuncted Carl Jung's Moon, while Jung's own Uranus sextiled Freud's Moon and squared his Sun. This solar and lunar uranization is a central element in the synastric bond between the two men. Each stimulated the other's Uranian capacity to crash through the post-medieval picture of how the human mind operated and pushed themselves–and the world–into the era of modern psychology. Pierre Curie uranized his wife's Mercury through an opposition; the corresponding intellectual breakthroughs led to a Nobel Prize. Illustrating the "long shot" dimension of Uranian activity, a woman was born on the Caribbean island of Martinique in 1763. A fortune-teller looking at her birthchart would've noticed a conjunction of Venus and Mars on her midheaven and predicted "fame through marriage, but troubles there too." Along came a man named Napoleon, uranizing that configuration through a sextile. He married her, and for a while she was empress of France.

Neptunification

PLANET: Neptune

AS GIFT-GIVER: To inspire.
　　　　To uplift.
　　　　To sensitize.
　　　　To enchant.

AS THIEF: To confuse.
　　　　To dissipate.
　　　　To weaken.
　　　　To glamorize.
　　　　To deceive.

You're lying in your bed at night, drifting off. Suddenly a jolt runs through your body. You've "caught yourself falling asleep." One question: Where were you three seconds before the jolt? Space. Spirit. The Unconscious. Or, as a saxophone player we used to know once put it: "backstrokin' in the Sublime."

Whatever your personal answer, the astrological answer is Neptune. This is the planet of consciousness itself. Pure being. Whatever you choose to call that spaciousness that stares out through your eyes–and through your personality: that's Neptune.

Neptune figures prominently in the charts of saints (and drunks), visionaries (and dreamers), mystics (and people who stare into the television set for six hours every night of their lives). **Self-transcendence** is the common denominator. Usually that's taken to be a positive attribute. That's half the truth. The other half lies in recognizing the hallucinatory, fog-bound pit that lies directly beneath the fragile human ego.

Psychoanalytic theory places great emphasis upon the child's struggle to emerge from that Neptunian pit. Or, to use proper theoretical language, it emphasizes the infant's struggle to differentiate ego from unconscious. As a result, mainstream psychologists look askance upon any "regressions" into the blurry Neptunian state.

Mystics take a different view. To them, the elemental purpose of living is to explore that mysterious inner landscape and to make peace with it.

As astrologers we must recognize that the Neptunian coin has two sides: mystical rapture and oblivion. Our primary difficulty, strange as it may seem, lies in learning to tell one from the other. The crux of the problem centers on an old, misunderstood word: glamor.

Nowadays "glamor" has become a cheap label. To call a woman glamorous is to praise her, faintly, as if to say, "you're beautiful...in a tacky sort of way." We might even be tempted to think that "glamor" is a modern word, since it seems so inextricably woven into pop culture. Actually the roots of the word "glamor" are ancient, linked to the Celtic traditions of fairies, wizards, and magic. If a leprechaun needed a horse, he might "cast glamor" over a bucket of stones. To the hapless farmer, those stones would then appear to be priceless gems–and an eminently fair trade for his swayback mare. Glamor, thus, is the capacity to make something appear to be other than what it actually is.

Each one of us actually **is** other than what we appear to be. But what exactly are we? That's Neptune's message: "You're not an ego. You're a **consciousness**, and that's far vaster and more exciting." Glamor gets in and wreaks havoc when, instead of melting ego for a while, pulling back its curtain and glimpsing those shimmering inner terrains, we misread the message and seek merely to glorify ego through inflated, unrealistic fantasies about ourselves.

The perfectly competent postal clerk fancies himself to be a "rock star." He leaves his job and his family and winds up down and out in L. A., screwed up on cocaine.

The housewife from Nebraska imagines herself to be a movie star and winds up in the gutter next to the postal clerk.

That's the dark glamor of Neptune, the one we must avoid unless we want all those mainstream psychologists telling us "I told you so."

In synastry, neptunification can be ecstasy. It can also sensitize every nerve in your body, and then kick you hard in the stomach. If someone neptunifies a planet in your birthchart, that part of you feels enchanted, lifted to a new level of vision. It also likely feels disoriented, as if the waiter has been more zealous than you had imagined in keeping your champagne glass topped off.

All of us, in the process of living, get a bit crusty. Habits develop. Walls go up. We need to be reminded of that softer, gentler, more magical place buried beneath the rituals. Why? If only because that Neptunian region is the true source of life's happiness. Think about it like this: no matter how fortunate you might be in every outward sense, it's still possible that you might be sad. And conversely, no matter how ill-starred your life might seem, it is still possible that you might be far happier than the more outwardly fortunate person. Happiness, in other words, is in Neptune's domain: consciousness, not circumstance. If someone neptunifies you, he or she touches that part of you that lies behind all the dramas of life's surface. He or she goes right to the heart, bypassing your crust–and bypassing all your defenses too.

If you find yourself neptunified, especially in the early stages of intimacy, be careful. Try to keep a clear fix on reality. You might not be seeing your partner very clearly, despite the warm feelings you're experiencing. You might instead have a super-clear fix on some romantic ideal you've been carrying around in your unconscious–and you might have pasted that ideal over some convenient target...that's not the point. Only that it requires balanced judgment. Perhaps the most practical rule of thumb is that when neptunified, go slowly. If the partnership has a sound basis, it won't disappear overnight.

Should you, on the other hand, neptunify someone who's important to you, try to create an environment of gentleness and support for that person. More specifically, consider what planet in his or her birthchart your Neptune touches, and recognize that you have the capacity to nurture the development of that function in an almost magical way. Your lover, for example, might have a Sun-Saturn conjunction in his fifth house. His identity (Sun) is dependent upon establishing some kind of self-expressive, creative outlet (fifth house), but he was born with a frustrating sense of inadequacy and blockage there (unconscious Saturn) that can only be overcome through application, effort, and persistence (conscious Saturn). You neptunify that configuration. What should you do? Follow your heart, but what comes out might well resemble this scenario. Look right into his eyes, open your heart, lock souls, and tell him that you see a poet in there.

Elizabeth Taylor has a Scorpio Moon in the second house. She feels (Moon) a Scorpionic hunger for a profound, dramatic sense of connectedness with a mate, perhaps complicated at times by feelings of personal insecurity (second house). The late Richard Burton, her longtime lover and husband, solarized her Moon. That interaspect alone is enough to account for the intense reactions they apparently created in each other, as he drove her Moon into active manifestation, and she, in lunarizing him, flooded his awareness with emotion. But Richard Burton also had a prominent Neptune, lying conjunct his Ascendant in his first house. That Neptune formed a close square to her Scorpio Moon. Thus he neptunified as well as solarized her, filling her heart (Moon) with other-worldly emotions and a sense of soul-contact. But did she perhaps see a "perfect man" in him, only to feel cheated again and again as his humanity asserted itself?

Plutonification

PLANET: Pluto

AS GIFT-GIVER: To penetrate.
    To reveal.
    To transpersonalize.

AS THIEF: To tyrannize.
    To corrupt.
    To horrify.
    To darken.

Pluto stares right through you.

Pluto asks you, "How much time do you spend thinking about what you're going to eat next? With whom you might get to sleep? How much money you have? What the other monkeys think of you?"

Most of us, if we have the courage to answer honestly, answer embarrassingly. For most of us the "big four"–food, sex, money, and power–are mightily fascinating subjects.

Then Pluto laughs in your face. He shows you galaxies, burning quasars, aeons of time. He calls you a microbe on a dust mote. He tells you that your whole life is a joke. And then he walks away.

What answer can we make? How can we defend ourselves against Pluto's chillingly empty analysis of our lives?

One answer is to make no answer. To simply accept the elemental pointlessness of existence. Down that road lies despair, though one of the stops along the way is "existentialism" with its emphasis upon life as the "theater of the absurd."

Maybe we have a better answer for Pluto. Maybe we say, "Wait a minute. Yesterday I sent twenty-five bucks to the Sierra Club. Show me a monkey anywhere who would do that."

In sending money to the Sierra Club–or in undertaking any similarly selfless action–we **transpersonalize** ourselves, that is, we become identified with a set of motives and needs that have absolutely nothing to do with the "monkey" in us. And in so doing we shrink the monkey and thereby offer Pluto a smaller target for his icy barbs

Altruism. A sense of mission. A feeling of transcendent purpose. These are the Gifts of the high Pluto. But to attain them we must first face the low Pluto and wrestle with the self-aggrandizing, hungry monkey whose appetites motivate so many of our actions.

When someone plutonifies a planet in your birthchart, that part of you is going to be pushed hard. Challenged. Asked to face its own shadow. How are you kidding yourself in that area of your life? What are your most comforting lies? If you can tolerate that kind of scrutiny, then your plutonifying partner offers more: a way to lift that planet to a new and higher level of meaning, a way to transpersonalize it, help it serve a purpose in the larger world– which in turn helps you by offering that uniquely Plutonian feeling of **cosmic legitimacy**. That plutonified part of your life may have once been "a joke," but no longer. Now it reflects something beyond monkey motives.

A woman has a Cancer Moon in the eighth house. She has introspective, nurturing instincts (Cancer Moon) that are locked into an exploration of a realm of the unconscious characterized by many social taboos (eighth house). Her response to the configuration is less than optimal. She becomes moody and preoccupied with her own emotions, hungry for sexual fulfill-ment (eighth house), and yet intimidated by the vulnerability that intimacy creates (Cancer Moon). She's fascinated with the idea of death (eighth house again) but shrinks from the unpleasant-ness of its actuality, perhaps slipping into morbid fantasies (Cancer Moon).

A man comes into her life who plutonifies her Moon. Like a theater-goer in a horror film, she reacts to his message with both hands covering her face–but one eye peering between spread fingers, glued to the screen. He points out her self-absorption. He picks apart her rationalizations. He's intuitively keyed into all her defenses. With his help she faces a part of herself that in the harsh light of the Plutonian perspective is intolerably wasteful and absurd.

This Plutonian "facing of the shadow" is only the first part of the process. The second part is to lift the contacted planet toward some transpersonal expression. Perhaps her new love encourages the woman in our example to volunteer in the local rape crisis center. Perhaps she becomes involved with a hospice, helping people who are dying. In either case her Cancer Moon is plutonified, lifted from mere introspection into the higher Cancerian world of active nurturing and healing

Is plutonification always so glorious? Not at all. Perhaps the same man comes into the Cancer Moon woman's life and simply horrifies her with his intensity, driving her deeper into her shell. How? Perhaps by dumping the illness of his own Pluto on her, corrupting her spirit with cynicism and bitterness.

Perhaps he does worse: perhaps he tortures her with truth, penetrating her defenses, but doing so without compassion, seeking only to assassinate her character. Perhaps he tyrannizes her, power-tripping and guru-tripping until their relationship looks like a case study in spiritual fascism.

If you find yourself plutonifying someone, start by trying to remember the last time anyone complimented you on your halo. If it's been a while, then be scrupulously careful of preaching to your partner. You've probably got some valuable insights into the shadowy side of the planet you're plutonifying. Don't overestimate them! That planet in turn is stimulating your own Pluto, and therefore whatever tendencies you have toward taking on too much authority in another's life are being emphasized. So go lightly. Honestly and confrontively, but lightly too.

Be sensitive also to the notion that a half-truth that someone really hears and uses is vastly more helpful than a whole truth so threatening that it is rejected. In plutonification one can cut too close to the bone and only stimulate the development of even more elaborate defense mechanisms in the partner. There is a fine line between a truly transpersonal urge to help another human being and a merely self-aggrandizing urge to appear uncannily wise and penetrating.   Cross that line and you've walked right into the lair of Pluto the Thief.

The nineteenth century pro-slavery politician Stephen Douglas was a charismatic speaker and wielded powerful influence. His support of slavery was so repugnant to Abraham Lincoln that Lincoln felt compelled to make a public stand against him. The famous Lincoln-Douglas debates that followed pushed Lincoln into national prominence and ultimately into the presidency. Douglas's Pluto opposed Lincoln's midheaven (public position), plutonifying him into characteristically altruistic action.

Abraham Lincoln and his wife, Mary Todd Lincoln, also illustrate the dark side of Pluto in a particularly poignant way. He plutonified her Saturn through a conjunction and her Mars through a square. These are challenging configurations, involving the two "malefic" planets of medieval astrology. Their marriage was a stormy one, and this plutonification is sufficiently thorny to account for that fact. Was there something of Mary Todd Lincoln's urge to control everything (Saturn) and her own unconscious violence (Mars) that Abraham Lincoln was helping her face? And when he was assassinated while sitting next to her in the theater, did she glimpse a brutal example of the seeming pointlessness of our existence, the legacy of the Thief?

CHAPTER NINE

YOUR PLANETS, MY SKY

Lois is a graduate student in philosophy, a reserved, calm young woman with a taste for books and rumination. Six months ago she discovered Mike, and she's laughed more in those six months than she has since she was a little girl. She's not taking the petty wars of academia so seriously. Her increased enjoyment of life shows in a more relaxed teaching style, and she's full of new ideas for her doctoral dissertation.

Mike's Sun falls in Lois's fifth house, the house of love affairs, playfulness, pleasure, and creativity. That is, if **his** Sun were placed in **her** chart, that's where it would fall. At the end of Chapter Seven, we discussed how to recognize these configurations. Now let's learn to interpret them.

Mike had been bored with the monotony of his life, habituated to a routine existence. Now Mike has realized that there's a world of ideas and experiences that he's never explored before. Since he met Lois, he's rediscovered his curiosity and is happily indulging it, at the library, lectures, movies, concerts, and in conversations that last until two in the morning. He feels as though Lois let him out of a cage.

Lois's Sun lies in Mike's third house, stimulating his appetite for communication, perception, and the exchange of information. She solarizes (brings out, emphasizes) that part of his life.

The placement of one person's planets into the other person's houses is a fundamental device in synastry. It helps us see the impact that each person has on the other's circumstances and behavior (houses). This procedure is called **transposing** one person's planets into the other's houses.

Mike and Lois are imaginary people. Let's see how this technique works in reality by considering the charts of Eleanor Roosevelt and Franklin D. Roosevelt.

Eleanor Roosevelt's Moon lies at eighteen degrees and fifty-five minutes of Cancer. FDR's eleventh house begins at nineteen degrees Cancer. Although Eleanor Roosevelt's Moon is mathematically in FDR's tenth house, its themes are felt primarily in his eleventh. Why? Because the cusp of a house is a very sensitive zone. Like the event horizon around a black hole, a cusp pulls a planet technically in the preceding house, but within approximately two degrees of the cusp, into the following house.

Suppose that your friend Spenser's Sun is one degree and fifty-nine minutes away from his girl friend Susan's fifth-house cusp. Do you place his Sun in her fourth house or her fifth? We could argue this point from a theoretical perspective until doomsday, but there's a better way. Tune out astrology. Tune in reality and simply ask Susan, where in her life does she actually experience the impact of Spenser's Sun? Does he "light up" her self-understanding? Is she more able to put down roots since she's been with him? Those are fourth-house themes. If Susan has gone into psychotherapy and joined a dream analysis group, and if they're buying a house together, that clinches it: his Sun falls in Susan's fourth house. If, on the other hand, Susan goes on vacations with him, has resumed work on her novel and dines out more often since she met Spenser, his Sun probably falls in Susan's fifth house. In this case, forget about how Susan feels and watch what she does. Look for how one person's behavior (houses) has changed since they became involved.

Pay particular attention to the houses affected not only by each partner's Sun, but also by the Moon and Ascendant. Where your Sun falls in your partner's houses, you solarize that house. Where your Moon falls in his chart, you lunarize that territory.

In transposition we consider not only the primal triad, but also all ten planets and the Midheaven. With so many factors involved, more than one house is usually accented in transposition. The houses that receive the most impact from your partner's planets are the areas of your life that are most affected by him or her. Like it or not, you'll spend more time wrapped up in the affairs of those houses if you commit to this person. Your mate will be like an actor in the theater of that house, beckoning you onstage.

Suppose that your lover puts six planets in your third house. We know that, like Mike in our example at the beginning of this chapter, your third house activity is increased. Third house **behavior** is what changes, quantitatively. How does it change in quality? The natures of the planets falling in your third house tell you how your behavior changes. Refer to Chapter Eight, "Interaspects," to see what the venusification of your third house, for example, might be like.

We can sum up what we've learned in two simple principles.

In transposition, the more planets that are transposed into a house, the more the behavior and activity of that house increases.

The mood or tone of the changed behavior is indicated by the nature of the transposed planets.

Let's try an example. Someone who venusifies your third house may enhance your verbal creativity, increase your eloquence, and improve your writing style, even if all you've ever written is grocery lists. On the other hand, this person may make it difficult for you to assert yourself verbally and speak unpleasant truths–that's Venus too. Someone who uranizes your third house may spark your originality, helping you to tear up those grocery lists, forget your writing group's criticism, and finish your novel in your way. Or you may develop a case of foot-in-mouth disease around such a person, blurting out inappropriate comments. Third house behavior is increased in both example, but the tone of the behavior varies with the planet involved, Venus in one case and Uranus in the other.

Writing a "cookbook" of examples of every possible planet in every house is beyond the scope of this book, but if you can remember the basic rules above, you can apply them to any planet in any house, and you'll be doing fine.

Let's discuss the "transposed houses" one by one. Remember the metaphor introduced in Chapter Six: the house is the lesson, planets are teachers, and signs are methods. Imagine that you are reading about a classroom (house) visited by new teachers (planets), not your own. Will these newcomers inspire you to learn more? Will they coach and enlighten you, sharpen and amplify your experience of that house? Or will they behave in incomprehensible ways, prevent you from learning at your own pace, or exhaust you with propaganda? The choice, at least in part, is yours.

The Transposed First House

TRADITIONAL NAME: House of Personality

WHEN STRETCHED: Enhanced personal style. Strengthened will. Improved poise. Increased sense of control over one's self and one's direction in life.

WHEN CONFUSED: Blurred, false, or missing sense of identity. Awkwardness, lack of self-assurance. Overly controlling or aimless behavior.

Your first house is the mask you wear in the world. Think of it as astrological clothing. Clothing is superficial, but it's absolutely necessary in our culture, used not only to protect and cover the body, but to signal something about the role we play, our job, our mood, our essence. We learn that certain styles and colors "look like us" or don't. Think of your Ascendant as your astrological energy wardrobe, a personal style that you project to the world. This or that behavior pattern does or does not suit you, does or does not facilitate your interactions with those around you, does or does not give you confidence and make you feel comfortable.

When your first house is strongly affected by your partner, a new "wardrobe consultant" has entered your life, and the impact hits more than your clothes. The Ascendant is how we **act**, the filter through which we express ourselves. We could call it our window on the world, and the person who affects it is a window washer–or smearer.

Prepare to be made more aware of your behavior patterns, both healthy ones that need encouragement and embarrassing ones you're ready to outgrow. Why do you sit in the back of the room during lectures? Why do you banter with the popcorn vendors at the movies? Why won't you stop and ask for directions if you're lost? Why do you carry a list to the grocery store and stick to it?

Why don't you walk down every aisle in that grocery store to see if looking at the shelves will remind you of forgotten items? Why do you hang out in the kitchen at parties? Why don't you camp out at the stereo instead?

How did you feel about reading those questions? Intrigued? Amused? Irritated? Thrown off balance? When you're with someone who bombs your first house, you'll feel all of the above and then some. You will find yourself examining your personal style more than before.

How will you react? Perhaps you'll overcome your extreme shyness or break your bad habit of dominating the conversation when nervous. Perhaps you'll develop more flair and self-assurance. Perhaps you'll decide you're a hopeless nerd and refuse to budge from your fetal position, unless it's to break a Ming vase. Perhaps you'll get into ridiculous fights over where you part your hair or the way you laugh. But perhaps you may need to.

Why? When someone puts planets in your first house, your style can be enhanced, but you should watch out for attempts, conscious and unconscious, to force your feet into shoes that don't fit you. Listen to the wardrobe consultant's suggestions, but resist, politely but firmly, if you know quite well you can't wear yellow. The Ascendant is the way in which we have to behave if we are to feel sane and effective in the world. It can be improved, but don't let it be blocked.

If you have a strong influence on your partner's first house, realize that you must tolerate his or her mask. It's not phony, it's how that person needs to present himself or herself. You can point out ways in which that behavior might be changed, but not eradicated. You must tolerate the essence of the person's style, rather than mock it or malform it–unless you want to live with someone who feels psychologically naked around you all of the time and will eventually improvise defenses or fight back or leave. Don't question every move your partner makes, see the humor in all masks, and help polish that window.

Woody Allen's Sun, Mercury, and Jupiter are conjunct and fall in Diane Keaton's first house. He solarizes her style, literally, since the "Annie Hall look" became a fashion after the movie's release. We could also say that he mercurializes and jovializes her style, giving her roles as high-strung, talkative (Mercury), giddy clowns (Jupiter). Keith Richards's Pluto in Leo lies in Mick Jagger's first house, and Richards has certainly played a part in the development of Mick's Leonine rock-and-roll mask and the cultural icon (Pluto) it's become. Similarly, Linda Ronstadt's Mercury-Pluto conjunction falls in Jerry Brown's first house, and one side effect of their romance was to make Brown's personal style and personal life a matter of public (Pluto) commentary (Mercury). Wallis Simpson's Ascendant fell in Edward VIII's first house; he asserted himself (first house) by abdicating to marry her.

The Transposed Second House

TRADITIONAL NAME: House of Money

WHEN STRETCHED: Increased self-esteem, based on who one is rather than what one has. More efficient management of material resources.

WHEN CONFUSED: Decreased self-esteem. Preoccupation with status symbols and financial security to prove self-worth. Fear of personal or material risk.

Your friend Jennifer is telling you the history of her love life. Andrew made her feel like a worm. He cut her down in subtle ways. When she noticed the pattern and dumped him, he even told her she'd never amount to anything without him. Bob was different. She felt really secure around him at first, because he was so sensible and down-to-earth, but after a while she got tired of his obsession with brand names, retirement funds, and being seen in all the right places. Chris was a thoroughly nice guy, good-natured and gentle, but always broke and always hitting her up for a loan. Finally she found Daniel, her husband, and she's happy she did. "He makes me feel like the most gorgeous, fascinating, capable woman in the world, like there's nothing I couldn't do. He's great for my ego. And my life has really stabilized since we've been together. I never thought I'd be able to buy a house and put down roots. I've stopped putting things on hold."

Did Jennifer just have a string of bad luck until she met Daniel? Maybe, and maybe not. These four men had something in common besides Jennifer: they all transposed a substantial number of planets in Jennifer's second house. One undercut her self-image; another improved it.   One was a drain on her resources; another supported them.

When your second house is heavily influenced by your partner, it can be one of the most painful of contacts, carrying great psychic costs.   This person can undermine your self-esteem, constantly bringing you face-to-face with how worthless you think you are.   It may not be said out loud, but an examination of the events in your life since you've been together can reveal a persistent pattern of your crippling devaluation by yourself and your partner.

Don't run away before you consider the corollary: A person who affects your second house can also be your partner in one of the most life-enhancing relationships you'll ever have, wonderful for your morale, and for your outer resources as well as your inner ones.   If you want a cheerleader, your best backer and your biggest fan, someone to encourage you to develop your untapped potential, someone who'll see potential you never dreamed of, look for someone who activates your second house.

How that house is activated depends on many things: the maturity of the two people involved, their honesty, their willingness to work together, to be honest when necessary and gentle when appropriate.

If you energize your partner's second house, be truthful and careful.   You are a kind of astrological bellows that can inflate or deflate your partner's sense of personal worth. Don't commit the cruelty of encouraging nonexistent talents. Don't sharpen your claws on your mate just for the pleasure of the exercise, either. You can give your lover a wonderful gift: in a culture where low self-esteem is the psychological equivalent of the common cold, you can help improve your lover's self-esteem.   But remember that you are holding a double-edged sword, and you can also inflict more than the usual share of misery on your mate by the ability to devalue him or her, to strike right at the heart of his or her sense of dignity.   If you have a strong influence on your partner's second house, you should memorize one of the Buddha's observations: Before you say anything, ask yourself, "Is it true, is it kind, and is it necessary?"

The late Richard Burton's Mars and his Sun-Saturn conjunction fell in Liz Taylor's second house, with his Sun-Saturn conjunct her second-house Moon. Their turbulent relationship probably attests to something of the nature of the transposed second house: it can be wonderful or terrible or both. Perhaps he solarized her emotional need (Moon) to develop a strong sense of personal worth and dignity, validating and enhancing (solarization) those feelings with concrete reasons (saturnization), and perhaps he empowered an exaggerated (another type of solarization) her irrational fears and moods (Moon) in this area, depressing and devitalizing her (also saturnization).

Paul Newman's Jupiter and his Ascendant-Mercury-Venus conjunction fall in Joanne Woodward's second house, the latter configuration on her Saturn-Venus conjunction. Newman has reviewed (Mercury) some of Woodward's dance routines (Venus) and added steps (Mercury) for her film *The Stripper*, (Ascendant-Venus!) certainly a second-house fan-and-cheerleader activity. Woodward's Sun, incidentally, lies in Newman's second house conjunct his Moon, so in their case, second-house transposition works in each direction, with each partner supporting the other's confidence in concrete ways.

The Transposed Third House

TRADITIONAL NAME: House of Communication

WHEN STRETCHED: Open-mindedness and non-judgmental perceptiveness enhanced. Curiosity stimulated. More information and experiences gathered. Communicative abilities strengthened.

WHEN CONFUSED: Bigotry and intolerance increased. Confusion, "disinformation," lessened ability to distinguish and maintain one's own point of view. Scattering of energy, over-scheduling, time wasting, disorganization.

In the 1960s TV show *My Favorite Martian*, Bill Bixby's life is invaded by "extraterrestrial" Ray Walston, complete with retractable antennae. The Martian makes Bixby ask a lot of questions that might never have occurred to him in the ordinary way. When we check books out of the library, why use a card when it would make better sense to trade in one of ours instead for the duration of the loan? Why does your political system work the way it does?

Why not elect two leaders and let them slug it out on an asteroid? Bixby gets a new viewpoint on earth culture and also becomes curious about how they operate on Mars–or beyond.

A partner who activates your third house arrives in your life and presents you with an encyclopedia full of questions about the world around you, and with an extra set of antennae to soak up possible answers and new experiences. The affairs of this house include its traditional name, "communication," but its definition is wider than speech and writing and intellectual activity. This is the house of perception, observation, and of gathering information–not the house of deduction and sorting information. Someone who transposes many planets into your third house can throw open new windows on the world for you. A mate who influences your third house can broaden your horizons, diversify your perceptions, expand your experiences, arouse your curiosity, challenge your assumptions, and sharpen your wits.

He or she can also bewilder you, bias your opinions, wear you out with endless talking, censor you or your sources of information, thereby weakening your reality testing, and exhaust you with the increased pace of your life. His or her world view may be imposed on yours, and you may feel brainwashed, rather than visited by an intelligent alien.

If your third house is energized by someone you love, be prepared to reevaluate some of your most deeply cherished notions. Enjoy the new experiences. Be willing to accept some confusion and some shift in your world view. Unless you're so wise that you can no longer learn anything, it will probably be good for you. But make sure that you reserve your right to think for yourself, and give back any propaganda leaflets.

If you stimulate your partner's third house, you can give your partner the pleasure of never being bored. Be careful of appointing yourself teacher, however, and respect his or her opinions when they vary from yours. It's possible to share the same facts but have different interpretations of them.

Author Simone de Beauvoir's Uranus-Mercury-Sun conjunction falls in existentialist writer Jean-Paul Sartre's third house. They met while both were studying for advanced degrees in philosophy (Mercury) and maintained a lifelong, unconventional (Uranus) professional and personal relationship. De Beauvoir is probably best known for a landmark feminist work, *The Second*

Sex, published in 1949, but also wrote novels, memoirs, and essays, some on Sartre. She solarized this writer's third house and also mercurialized it, encouraging his work and analyzing it for others, and their relationship had a Uranian flavor.

While researching this section, we were amazed at how many writers, thinkers, artists, or other professional collaborators transpose one another's third house. Keith Richards's Neptune (glamor, illusion), Moon (imagination), and Venus (creativity, appeal) lie in Mick Jagger's third house. Elizabeth Barrett Browning's Mercury-Mars-Pluto-Sun conjunction fall in Robert Browning's third house, conjoined his Pluto, and her Venus also falls in Browning's third house. She was better known as a poet than he was before their marriage, and certainly that combination of planetary energies contributed to his destiny (Pluto) as a poet (third house). Browning's Uranus and Neptune-Ascendant conjunction in Sagittarius fall in Elizabeth Barrett Browning's third house, inspiring some of the most idealized (Sagittarius and Neptune), romantic (Neptune) poetry (third house) written in English.

The Transposed Fourth House

TRADITIONAL NAME: House of the Home

WHEN STRETCHED: Increased self-understanding. Heightened sense of "rootedness" and security.

WHEN CONFUSED: Entrapment in unresolved psychological dynamics from one's personal history. Extreme withdrawal, psychological isolation from others.

The furniture in this house is the furniture in your head. The fourth house is subjective, internal, and complex. Think of its central activity as the search for roots: the psychological roots of home and the biological family. Someone who has access to this part of your nature has a hand on the door to your personal unconscious—and the skeletons in your closet.

Line up a hundred astrologers and ask them if this house symbolizes a person's experience of the mother or the father, and they'll probably be split fifty-fifty in their reply. We don't know who's right. The atmosphere of the parental home in general can be described by the contents of the fourth house, and sometimes it seems to refer to one parent more than the other. A partner who energizes your fourth house can evoke that atmosphere, bringing up mother issues or father issues in your life.

We do **not** mean that you should make tracks in the other direction when you meet someone who stirs up your fourth house, in order to avoid committing astrological incest. But it doesn't hurt to be aware of the fact that this person's presence in your life may hook you back into old family behavior patterns. Your partner's gift to you may, in fact, be precisely the illumination of those issues, which can lead to your emancipation from them, because you can't change something that you don't know is happening. Someone who energizes your fourth house can hold a key to your self-understanding, helping to heal old wounds, contributing to the feeling of security that comes from being reconnected to your true self. A mate who transposes several planets into your fourth house makes a good companion on journeys of inner exploration, and probably a pretty good roommate as well.

Such a person can also help drive you crazy, uprooting you in every sense of the word, rattling the skeletons in that closet, locking you into the painful repetition of scenes from your past. You can withdraw from the partner, from the world, from your own sanity.

Like it or not, when your lover activates your fourth house, he or she is deeply under your skin, and material from that subjective layer of the unconscious stirs and moves, demanding attention. You can react by reconnecting your inner and outer selves, or by watching passively as they drift farther and farther apart.

If your fourth house is strongly impacted by your mate, you don't have to earn a Ph.D. in psychology, but you had best spend some time understanding what sort of family dynamics influenced your childhood, and how you may or may not be repeating these patterns with your partner. On the other hand, the self-knowledge you can attain with such a person is priceless. Your lover is automatically fluent in the language of your innermost heart, your dreams and visions. If you want to know yourself and to be deeply known, you have found a good traveling companion.

If you stimulate your partner's fourth house, it's wise for you to have some psychological "basic training" too, and for the same reasons: so that you don't unwittingly become cast in a drama that your partner may need to recognize and release. Be very careful about the unconsciously manipulative effect you can have on your mate. You should also be wary of the way your partner might look you straight in the eye but see his or her mother or father. What you stir in that person goes back to childhood and is therefore not always a model of rationality. You're entrusted with something close to the core of this person's being, and that fact should produce something like reverence in you. Be a good steward. You can contribute to a profound sense of belonging and identity in your mate, and that goes beyond the traditional "nesting" interpretations of this house.

Examples for the transposed fourth house are rather difficult to obtain, since we're not on a fourth-house level of closeness to the people in our research. Freud's Moon fell in Jung's fourth house, and Jung's Saturn fell in Freud's fourth house. Books have been written about their relationship; an extremely brief version is that they split over the question of the unconscious, which Jung thought was a source of wholeness and wisdom (the intuitive Moon), and Freud thought was the container of material that needed repressing (Saturn). Nineteenth-century French poets Paul Verlaine and Arthur Rimbaud had a brief, turbulent affair, terminating with a drunken Verlaine wounding Rimbaud with two shots from a revolver. Each put Neptune (fantasy, illusion, poetry, intoxication with the Spirit or spirits) in the other's fourth house. Verlaine's Saturn also fell in Rimbaud's fourth house. Did that placement contribute to the adolescent, in revolt against the world, seeing Verlaine as an authority figure (Saturn)?

The Transposed Fifth House

TRADITIONAL NAME: House of Children

WHEN STRETCHED: Creativity stimulated. Enjoyment of life enhanced. Childlike spontaneity encouraged. Increased ability to "fall in love"–with life, a person, a creative act.

WHEN CONFUSED: Insistence on living in the present, at the cost of future plans or other relationships. Inability to delay gratification, childishness. Prima donna behavior, self-dramatization, acting out. Infatuation.

How would you like to be a child again?

Chances are that you have mixed feelings about that question. The child issues of the fourth house revolve around childlike feelings, needs, and fears. The fifth house has more to do with childlike self-expression and spontaneous, playful behavior. It would be wonderful to go back to the days when you had a sense of wonder for new experiences and new people, when it was easier to play, to laugh, to love, when your imagination was more active. On the other hand, childhood had its drawbacks, among them the eerie feeling that time dragged on forever, that you had little control over your life or future, and that you were a frustrated captive in a country bordered with incomprehensible "thou shalts" and "thou shalt nots". Childhood is an egocentric, self-indulgent time, partly because the boundaries of the world aren't, understandably, much bigger than the self.

A partner who affects your fifth house by transposition can put you back in that childhood place, with all the beauty and delight– and regressive self-indulgence–possible when your House of Creative Self-Expression, Love Affairs, and Joy is stimulated. Are you ready to fall in love, playfully, headily, breathlessly? Your romantic ideal can well be met by someone who activates this house. Do you want to have more fun, to forget about Monday morning and just enjoy a relaxing, silly, nonconstructive week-end? Would you like your creativity reawakened? Would you love it if someone encouraged you to drag that unfinished novel out of your filing cabinet, enroll in a pottery class, and get your camera out of the closet? Would you like to be able to reach out and connect with people more easily and unself-consciously? Then you need a mate who energizes your fifth house

On the other hand, someone who stimulates your fifth house can also pump up all your childish, irresponsible behaviors, feeding the part of you that wants what you want when you want it, regardless of what it costs you: your best interests, your future plans, your integrity, your primary relationship. More is needed for a long-term commitment than your fifth-house romantic ideal. Someone who affects this area of your chart can give the hungry child in you a voice, a microphone, and center stage, encouraging a "play now, pay later" mentality.

If your partner affects your fifth house by transposition, enjoy the relationship! Here's someone who is always able to make you laugh and to spark your originality. But take care that he or she doesn't contribute to your **childish**, rather than **childlike**, behavior.

If you energize your mate's fifth house, you can act like a tonic or a Muse, enhancing play and creativity. There need to be positive reasons for staying in a couple, and you can supply plenty: life is more fun with you. Take advantage of your direct line to that person's smile muscles. You can also invoke the sappy romantic in your partner, now and twenty years from now.

But if that sappy romantic demands that life always be as magical as your first month together, you may need to disillusion him or her, gently. A similar dynamic exists with your ability to release the child in your mate. Encourage that child's spontaneity, but don't encourage it to tyrannize the adult by demands for constant attention or instant gratification.

Art Garfunkel's Venus falls in Paul Simon's fifth house, adding an aesthetic grace (Venus) to Simon's house of play. Roger Daltrey's Venus-Mercury conjunction lies in Pete Townshend's fifth house, and Townshend's Mars and Venus lie in Daltrey's fifth house. They shared the transposition of the creative function (Venus) in the house of creativity. Daltrey mercurialized Townshend's fifth house, probably turning Townshend's attention (Mercury) more to that area, stepping up Townshend's production of lyrics (also Mercury). Townshend martialized Daltrey's fifth house, adding drive (Mars) to Daltrey's house of performance. Bess Truman's Mars-Sun conjunction falls in Harry Truman's fifth house, and the dynamic of that marriage was a playful one (fifth house). Edward VII and Wallis Simpson each placed the Sun into the other's fifth house; theirs is a famous (solarized) romantic (fifth house) story. Simone de Beauvoir's Saturn-Mars conjunction and her Moon lie in Sartre's fifth house, adding endurance and realism (Saturn), spark (Mars), and imagination (Moon) to their long-term association and, probably, to Sartre's creative energies. Finally, Keith Richards's Sun falls in Leo Mick Jagger's fifth house of performance, which should need no explanation!

The Transposed Sixth House

TRADITIONAL NAME: House of Servants

WHEN STRETCHED: More confidence in one's competence and skills, increased recognition of them by others. Greater sense of responsibility. Improved understanding of one's strengths and weaknesses.

WHEN CONFUSED: Decreased confidence in one's abilities, lack of understanding of one's faults or virtues. Lack of clarity about one's "job description," due to preemption by partner or to insufficient recognition for one's own skills. "Earning" love by performing tasks, or refusal to assume enough responsibility.

You might think that someone who transposes several planets into your sixth house would make a good teacher, coach, or supervisor for you. These traditional interpretations make sense, but the fundamental issues of the sixth house lie deeper than work or health. They are competence, usefulness, and responsibility. The sixth house contains echoes of the second; its questions are similar. What use am I? What can I do well? Am I recognized for that or not? How does that make me feel about myself?

If your mate makes a strong impact on your sixth house, prepare to ask yourself those questions more often, and prepare to have some good answers.

Helen's Sun falls in Barry's sixth house. They meet at the small college where Helen teaches American Literature, when Barry does a human interest story on the revamped English department for the paper where he's a part-time reporter. The rest of the time he writes fiction. So does Helen. They fall in love.

What effect could Helen's Sun have on Barry's sixth house?

One scenario looks like this: Helen reads Barry's material and praises its originality, characterization, dialogue, and immediacy. She lists famous writers whose work resembles his, delighting and encouraging him. She also points out that he gets so lost in his characters' heads that he has trouble stringing a plot together, suggests authors to read for role models, recommends an editing service, and wonders why he doesn't try his hand at a play like *Spoon River Anthology*, where characterization rather than plot is essential. Barry takes these comments to heart and his work takes off. He wins first prize at a drama festival, and there's talk of a Broadway production.

This is the wonderful side of sixth-house transposition. Helen has given Barry affirmation of his writing ability, confidence in what he does well (characterization and dialogue), understanding of where his skills need improvement, and practical help in improving them. She has encouraged him to take his talent seriously and to take responsibility for developing it, leading to recognition from others.

Darker sixth-house scenarios are available too. Everything depends on Helen and Barry and the choices they make. Helen could just as easily have read Barry's material, compared him scathingly and unfavorably to the geniuses whose work she teaches, and advised him to stick to the newspaper. He might have found that his faith in his ability to write a news story was also shaken. He might have decided that he'd better study **all** of the authors that Helen had to read for her Ph.D., before he wrote another word of fiction. Demoralized, he might have quit the paper, given up writing altogether, and found another line of work, while at night he humbly helped Helen grade papers and wished he were more talented. How lucky he is that Helen saved him from spectacular failure. How kind of her to let him ghostwrite her articles. But part of him resents the demoralization to which he consented and takes passive-aggressive revenge by failing to live up to his other responsibilities in the relationship.

If you stimulate your partner's sixth house, you are not necessarily his or her teacher, but your influence can lead to that person's mastery of whatever skills are most personally meaningful to him or her–or to their substitution with empty busywork.

Criticize constructively and don't make indiscriminate assignments.

If your mate transposes several planets into your sixth house, make sure you have a good grasp on what does and does not comprise your personally meaningful abilities, and be prepared to resist efforts to draft you into other areas. Be prepared as well for some review of those skills that can lead to their improvement. Be careful not to accept or reject new responsibilities without thought. Neither of you should have to expend efforts to receive love, and neither of you should carry all the load.

Paul Verlaine's Mercury-Uranus-Sun conjunction fell in Arthur Rimbaud's sixth house; Verlaine brought Rimbaud's astounding poetic genius (sixth house, and Uranus) to the attention (mercurialization) of the French public. Mary Shelley, author of *Frankenstein*, transposed her Mars-Sun-Uranus conjunction into poet Percy Bysshe Shelley's sixth house, conjunct his Mercury. Her Venus-Mercury conjunction also fell in Shelley's sixth house on his north node. Their common passion for (Mars) and genius in (Uranus) literature (Mercury) was a major part of their marriage and extended to a circle of friends (Venus). Jimmy Carter's Mars falls in Rosalynn Carter's sixth house. She attended his Cabinet meetings (sixth house), causing some controversy (Uranus) for him and undoubtedly some stress and challenge (Mars) for herself.

The Transposed Seventh House

TRADITIONAL NAME: House of Marriage

WHEN STRETCHED: Improved ability to relate on an equal basis. Relationships become open-ended and mutually supportive. Emotional depth of partnerships enhanced, increased intimacy.

WHEN CONFUSED: Blurred sense of identity, overidentification with partner or attempts to dominate partner. Unequal relationships. Too many relationships, leaving no time for self. Dependency or fear of dependency; fear of intimacy.

House of Marriage. House of Open Enemies. Will you love or hate someone who affects your seventh house by transposition?

Your reaction may not approach either extreme, but we can guarantee that it won't be indifference. A person who lights up this house commands your attention, calling it away from yourself (first house) to the not-self (seventh).

If your mate or friend energizes your seventh house, realize that in one sense he or she represents something you need and are drawn toward. That feeling of identification, that sense of oneness, is essential for committed love, and your mate can bring you that feeling. Appreciate the depth of that connection to your heart, but don't lose yourself in it.

Traditional astrologers say that you'll marry someone whose planets fall in your seventh house. Is that true? Maybe, maybe not. This is the house of intimacy, and formal marriage is only one kind. In the best of all possible worlds you will feel a sense of kinship with someone who illuminates this house. You are natural allies, partners, buddies. You have business together, perhaps metaphorically, perhaps literally. Such a person makes it easy to forget about yourself and identify with him or her.

If that sounds like the basis of a great romance, you're right, it is. If that sounds like trouble, you're also right: it might be. The problem with forgetting yourself is that sooner or later you have to remember yourself again. A person who energizes your seventh house can give you amnesia, robbing you of the sense of your own identity and leading you to sacrifice your legitimate concerns.

What happens then? You don't have a romance, you become a parasite. You may realize it but be too frightened to do anything, terrified that if your partner goes, what little sense of identity you retain will go too. Perhaps you fight back by trying to dominate the relationship, locking your transposed seventh house into a battle of "open enemies." Or you may make genuine, sustained efforts to sort out your own wants and needs from those of your mate, and to compromise rationally so that both sets of requirements are met, allowing each of you to enjoy the feeling of completion and fulfillment that a transposed seventh house can bring. Your lover can then seem like your long-lost other half, finally found. And that's a wonderful feeling, especially when you don't have to pay your identity for it.

Keep working. Think of your partnership as a sailboat whose steering requires constant attention as the boat yaws from starboard to port. The sailor's phrase "One hand for yourself, one hand for the ship" is applicable to the transposed seventh house: keep an eye on your partner's needs and an eye on your own, too.

Another side effect of the transposed seventh house can be an increase in the sheer number of new people that you meet. Make an effort to welcome your mate's friends into your life and be ready to cultivate new acquaintances together. If you're starved for companionship, you'll love this. But if your social schedule already makes you fantasize about a year on an isolated island with no telephones, mail, or plane service, you may need to take steps to keep that schedule under control.

If you stimulate the seventh house of someone you love, transposing many planets there, your partner can feel a selfless concern and tenderness for you that is hard to match elsewhere. Don't take advantage of it and try to turn him or her into your clone, or you can activate the house of open enemies instead. You deserve resistance if you try to preempt someone's identity.

We've already mentioned Pete Townshend's Sun conjoined Roger Daltrey's seventh-house Moon; Townshend's Uranus (independence, autonomy) also lies in Daltrey's seventh house conjoined Daltrey's Mars (assertion, drive), accounting perhaps for some of the creative drive and tension in their partnership. A similar dynamic existed between Arthur Rimbaud's Uranus and Paul Verlaine's seventh house Mars-Venus conjunction, while Verlaine's Pluto fell on Rimbaud's Descendant. Wallis Simpson's Jupiter fell in Edward the VIII's seventh house, jovializing it enough for him to abdicate the British throne for "the woman I love." Zelda Fitzgerald's Sun-Ascendant conjunction fell in F. Scott Fitzgerald's seventh house, and his Jupiter in her seventh, accenting their feelings of closeness and connectedness.

The Transposed Eighth House

TRADITIONAL NAME: House of Death

WHEN STRETCHED: Feelings intensified. Psychological sophistication increased. Improved ability to imprint on or bond to partner. Healthy sexuality. Acceptance of death, openness to "occult" or religious feelings.

WHEN CONFUSED: Neuroses intensified. Morbid self-absorption. Sexual blockage. Denial or fear of death or of transpersonal dimensions of reality.

The House of Death–at least in medieval astrology. But a person whose planets fall in your eighth house is not necessarily someone who helps you write your last will and testament. There are all kinds of "death" symbolized by the eighth house. Physical death, and questions about what part of the human spirit might survive it. Death of the sense of separateness that comes from sexual merging; the Elizabethans called orgasm "the little death." There is the death of sexual innocence, and there are also psychological deaths, as previously cherished self-concepts are shattered and fall away.

This is the house of the instincts, survival instincts, sexual instincts, and other feelings that arise from profound layers of consciousness. We confront the bedrock of our psyches in this house–or are confronted with it by our lovers. We understand ourselves better; our former self-image dies. Is that good or bad? Perhaps what we have discovered sets us free, or perhaps it overwhelms us, scaring us so badly that we run from further insights and from anyone who might evoke them. Refusal to look at the truth about ourselves is another kind of death.

The other side of this house is rebirth: birth of enhanced self-understanding, of a deeper capacity for intimacy, of a stronger, wiser spirit. Someone who affects your eighth house offers you those possibilities, but you will not make them real without the willingness to face yourself honestly and to acknowledge your feelings, drives, moods, and instincts. If you're hiding from yourself, a mate who transposes planets into your eighth house has the key to the closet where you keep your skeletons, whether you like it or not.

John's Sun and three other planets fall in Mary's eighth house. Within days of meeting him Mary finds herself telling John all about her teenage bout with anorexia, something she has never discussed with anyone but her therapist. Perhaps she realizes she needs to do more work on resolving the issues underlying her former eating disorder, goes back into therapy, and feels better. Perhaps her talk with John was exactly the catharsis she needed, no more and no less. Perhaps she's terrified by the feelings their conversation has stirred up, and she runs away from John and has a relapse. No way to tell how she'll react. All we know is that John's impact on her eighth house puts Mary in touch with that part of herself. How she handles it is up to her.

Is that the only way John affects Mary's eighth house? Probably not. His presence in her life also results in Mary's spending more time considering her sexuality, what it is and what it isn't. Perhaps she'll find John attractive and perhaps not, but his influence directs more of her attention to sexual issues. If Mary commits to John, she will also find herself more preoccupied by thoughts and feelings about death, the survival of consciousness, and other transrational subjects. Again, whether those topics disturb or fascinate Mary depends on her, not on John.

If you energize your mate's eighth house, you can make an unforgettable impact on him or her, physically, emotionally, and psychically. Make sure it's not through psychological dynamite; you're not necessarily your partner's therapist, nor should you be, although you can help bring those skeletons up to the light of day.

Elizabeth Taylor's Sun-Mars-Mercury conjunction lies in the late Richard Burton's eighth house, increasing the passionate intensity in their marriage. Freud's Mars fell in Jung's eighth house, challenging Jung in his explorations of eighth-house terrain. Van Gogh's Midheaven-Mars-Venus conjunction, and his Sun, fell in Gauguin's eighth house; their association certainly exposed Gauguin to some of the more turbulent aspects of the eighth house. Spencer Tracy's Pluto and Neptune-Moon conjunction fell in Katharine Hepburn's eighth house; she has remarked about Tracy, "I have had twenty years of perfect companionship with a man among men."

The Transposed Ninth House

TRADITIONAL NAME: House of Long Journeys Over Water

WHEN STRETCHED: Increased openness to new experiences. Well-considered but flexible world view.

WHEN CONFUSED: Loss of one's belief system. Rigid defensiveness of personal philosophy. Intolerance, dogmatism. Boredom. Nihilism.

What is the meaning of life? What are we doing here?

Did you have your reply ready? Could you have jumped onto a soapbox and delivered a speech? If you've got life all figured out, you may not appreciate someone who energizes your ninth house. But if you don't have all the answers and you don't mind new questions, you'll love that person.

You might expect someone who lights up your "House of Long Journeys Over Water" to call you from the airport with two tickets to Easter Island. That's entirely possible. But there are mental journeys as well as physical ones. You could also spend an evening together in your living room poring over an Easter Island picture book, looking at the giant statues gazing eyelessly out to sea, speculating about why they were built and what happened to the builders. Your conversation could take several interesting twists. Were the statues idols? Why do religions create icons? Is the urge to create linked with the capacity to feel awe, or simply with the need to express oneself? Do you do anything creative? Have you ever played with modeling clay? Well, it just so happens that your friend has some out in the car....

And you spend the rest of the evening up to your elbows in clay and new ideas.

Be prepared to stretch with someone who transposes your ninth house. Let go of your viewpoint on the world, because you're about to be handed a telescope, a microscope, and a kaleidoscope. Allow your perspective to change. Welcome experiences that are foreign to you, whether you have them in another country or with people whose nationalities–and natures–are different from yours. This house is also known as the house of higher education, religion, and philosophy. A partner who stimulates your ninth house can "educate" you in the broadest sense of the word. You are led to question your pivotal values–another term for "religion"–and the principles by which you live.

You might feel like Galileo did the first time he saw the Moons of Jupiter. You never again see the universe the same way.

On the other hand, you might understand how cult members feel when someone is brainwashing them. The horror of it is that you might allow that to happen. A mate who energizes your ninth house may consciously or unconsciously, substitute his or her world view for yours. We could all be wiser than we are, and it won't hurt you to try somebody else's beliefs on for size. But if they don't fit, don't keep them. The delicate line you are walking is to avoid defensiveness and understand your mate's ideas first, before you reject them out of hand.

If you affect your partner's ninth house, don't proselytize. Your influence can give your mate a smorgasbord of experiences and a renewed sense of wonder at the fascinating complexity of life. Life with you will not be boring. Your presence may help your mate open up to entirely new ways of thinking. But that doesn't mean that you're right, he or she is wrong, and you're on a mission to convert the savage. Also, if your partner's birthchart indicates an above average requirement for reflection or solitude, realize that you are increasing the pace of his or her life and understand that need for time to process new thoughts and activities.

Freud's Ascendant lies in Jung's ninth house, stimulating Jung's adherence to his own theories. Jung's Mercury-Venus conjunction, Sun, and Uranus occupy Freud's ninth house, contributing to their exchange of ideas and eventual rift. De Beauvoir's Jupiter and Neptune fall in Sartre's ninth house, with her Neptune conjunct his. It's interesting that a tenet of existentialist philosophy (ninth house) involves becoming conscious (Neptune) of one absolute given, the simple fact of one's existence, rather than one's essence or the possible meaning of that existence.

The Transposed Tenth House

TRADITIONAL NAME: House of Career

WHEN STRETCHED: Public identity better reflects total self.

WHEN CONFUSED: Inauthentic social role. Narrow attachment to status.

Follow someone around for a week. Find out all you can about that person without a face-to-face meeting. Talk to friends, colleagues, neighbors. Monitor mail. Search through garbage. Look up credit records and tax returns and voter registrations. At the end of that week you have constructed a working description of that person's tenth house: the public identity, the role in the culture; status; reputation; what he or she stands for; what others know about him or her, without personal acquaintance.

When your mate's planets stimulate your tenth house, they stimulate your public identity and how much time you spend dealing with it. Run for public office. Work in the drive to close or convert the nuclear power plant proposed for your area. Marry someone of another race. Move into an upscale subdivision. Play in a band on the weekends. These are all tenth-house activities. There are many ways to establish your public myth in the minds of others. The trick is making sure that the myth isn't too far from reality. Be wary of a relationship promising status, power, and notoriety if the nature of that status, power, and notoriety is irrelevant to you personally.

You are a painter, and a good one, and your oils have achieved some local recognition. People are prodding you to send slides to New York City. Dealers are sniffing around your studio. Along comes a friendship with an art critic who has connections in the city. Sounds wonderful, right?

Yes...if your heart and soul are expressed through those paintings, and it's important to you to have them recognized. No...if you've decided that you've learned all you can from painting, and now you're obsessed with photography. Don't avoid the art critic if other factors in the relationship seem right, but don't be bamboozled into hauling those canvasses up to Soho. Invite the critic into your darkroom instead.

If you energize the tenth house of someone you love, you can help this person gain recognition and affirmation for being herself. In the medieval sense, you can act as a "king-maker" who helped a monarch gain his birthright. But first you should understand exactly who your mate is, what he or she values, where the core of the identity lies, so that you don't put an impostor on the throne. A relationship with someone who is maintaining that uneasy balance with the outside world is like loving someone who's living under a false identity–strained for both of you, with little room for authentic intimacy.

The tenth house, opposite the fourth house, also symbolizes a person's internal, subjective experience of the parents. Astrologers disagree about which house refers to which parent. Each version of the theory appears to work some of the time. In any case, someone who energizes your tenth house by transposition can also act as a reminder of any psychological "unfinished business" you have with a parent. Be careful not to respond to your mate out of those old scripts, and if you light up your partner's tenth house, don't allow him or her to reenact childhood dramas with you standing in for a parent. Much as with someone affecting your fourth house, you can feel "at home" and comfortable with a person who affects your tenth. Enjoy the feeling, but be conscious that your mate might trigger some parental dynamics you may still need to understand.

Woody Allen's Moon falls in Mia Farrow's tenth house, conjoined her Sun. Farrow's roles in Allen's films have had a distinctly lunar cast: the softhearted floozy in *Broadway Danny Rose*, and the timid star-struck woman in *Purple Rose of Cairo* whose dream world comes briefly to life. Aristotle Onassis's Mercury-Ascendant-Sun conjunction falls in Jacqueline Kennedy Onassis's tenth house; one result of their marriage was to make her even more a subject of public scrutiny than before. F. Scott Fitzgerald's Moon falls in Zelda Fitzgerald's tenth house; the former debutante's social position was affected by their romance.

The Transposed Eleventh House

TRADITIONAL NAME: House of Friends

WHEN STRETCHED: Enhanced sense of purpose. Clarified goals. Relationships and contacts that support our aims.

WHEN CONFUSED: Loss of purpose. Confusion about direction in life. Hesitance about commitment. Associates who waste our time.

House of Goals. House of Friends. House of the Future. What do you want to be doing five years from now? What sort of person do you want to be? What kind of lifestyle will you have? What will you have accomplished?

Are you taking steps to get there?

Do you have any help?

All of these issues are raised in a relationship with someone who transposes planets into your eleventh house. The person may or may not bring them up, but the nature of the interaction will be such that you will ask yourself these questions, whether your partner does or not.

Jane has been ice skating since she was four years old. She's training for the next Olympics. Her coach transposes a cluster of planets into Jane's eleventh house. So does her best friend, who wants Jane to quit skating, devote herself to ballet, which she's also been studying since she was small, and move to New York with her friend to audition for ballet companies. Jane's boyfriend Philip also affects Jane's eleventh house by transposition. They sincerely love each other, and he's supportive of whatever choice she wants to make. They've been involved for over a year when Jane gets pregnant. Now what?

The choice is Jane's. Her career, her residence, her marital status, her pregnancy, her decisions, all belong to Jane. People who stimulate her eleventh house force her to define her goals and make choices, sometimes helping and sometimes hindering her, but in the long run those choices–and the responsibility for their consequences–are Jane's and Jane's alone.

Someone who energizes your eleventh house brings you face-to-face with what you want to do with the rest of your life. You are like the horse in the proverb; your mate leads you to the water, but you have to decide whether you want to drink. You choose the goals and move toward them yourself. Perhaps your mate supports you or perhaps not, but his or her presence in your life catalyzes your making those decisions–or backing away from them.

Not to choose is also a choice. Refusal to commit to a specific future still creates a future: drifting, time-wasting, aimlessness, daydreaming about what you're going to do "one day."

Goals are seldom reached alone. The traditional association of this house with friends has some validity, if we substitute for "friends" the notion of associates, like-minded others, colleagues, mentors, and protegees, or simply those who have similar goals. A mate who energizes your eleventh house can bring those people into your life, helping you create a network, a support system of people all moving in the same direction. On the other hand, if you've allowed your mate to make your choices for you, or if you've made none at all, someone who affects your eleventh house can pull a lot of people into your life to help you waste your time and distract you from your essential lack of purpose.

If your lover activates your eleventh house, plan to spend some time considering what you want to do with the rest of your life. Discuss your thoughts with your lover. Listen to the feedback, but make up your own mind what you'll do. If you stimulate your mate's eleventh house, have that same conversation, but do more listening than talking. Do you know what your mate really wants? Are those goals ones that you can support without sacrificing your own? Look at your mutual friends and acquaintances. Are those associations positive for everyone involved, or are they merely taking up your time?

Keith Richards's Saturn falls in Mick Jagger's eleventh house, adding the potential of practical strategies (saturnization) to Jagger's attainment of his goals. Gauguin's Venus fell in Van Gogh's eleventh house; Van Gogh admired Gauguin's work and the two had artistic goals (Venus) in common. The late Richard Burton's Ascendant-Neptune conjunction fell in Elizabeth Taylor's eleventh house, adding style (Ascendant) and glamor (Neptune) to her future and direction in life. Humphrey Bogart and Lauren Bacall's Moons fell in each other's eleventh houses, adding to shared feelings and a similar vision of their future.

The Transposed Twelfth House

TRADITIONAL NAME: House of Troubles

WHEN STRETCHED: Enhanced ability to transcend the smaller self and sense the eternal. Increased openness to spiritual, psychic or meditative experiences. More willingness to let go of ego attachments and identifications.

WHEN CONFUSED: Blurred sense of identity, mental and emotional confusion. Increase in escapist, self-destructive, numbing behavior. "Bad luck," as attachments are stripped away.

Wendy believes in prosperity consciousness. Her model of the world is that if you're hurting for money, it proves that you don't love yourself, because we all have the right to abundance as God's children. Wendy isn't Scrooge, nor is money her highest value, but prosperity consciousness still permeates her myth of herself and the world.

Wendy meets Thomas while contributing to a charity drive that he directs. Five or six of his planets fall in her twelfth house. She quickly recognizes that Thomas is more conscious, more open, more loving and clearly happier than she is. Yet Thomas is chronically broke. He devotes his time and energy to administering organizations that give to the poor, and he keeps almost nothing for himself. To her credit, Wendy is intrigued by Thomas and makes an effort to know him better. Thomas doesn't talk much about his beliefs, but she learns from one conversation, and a lot of observation, that he regards the love of money as an attachment that holds him back.

We don't necessarily mean that poverty is holy; the example could just as easily have been Thomas's encounter with a prosperity advocate. The point of the story is that someone who energizes your twelfth house comes at you from your blind side, undercutting your myth of yourself and the world, presenting you with new perceptions that invalidate your premises.

How do you react? At a lower level, we react badly, disliking the person who pulls the rug out from under us and kicks away the props that support our ego. It can be an enormously stressful and unsettling encounter. But there is rich potential in such an encounter. Someone who activates our twelfth house walks into our life saying, "Where you have put your treasure, there your heart is also." We are forced to look at our attachments and our rigid identification with our egos. If we are willing to grow and to acknowledge our need for alignment with our higher selves, this person strikes a spiritual, mystical chord in us. If we're not, we feel more as though he or she slammed a grand piano lid shut on our fingers. We feel confused, robbed of our personality. We react defensively, clutching at straws to affirm our identity, insisting loudly on our right to our narrow definitions of ourselves. Or we choose numbness through repetitive, addictive, stupefying behavior, to ignore that call from the deeper self. Less energy is available to live an outer life efficiently.

If your mate affects your twelfth house by transposition, and you want to avoid the preceding scenario, be willing to question yourself. All of us are playing a role in the world: our personalities, our outer selves. Be willing to look at what you portray. The life, the heart, the soul comes from the actor. Learn to identify yourself with that inner being, and the character's costumes and props and speeches become less important–and you feel more free. Do actors worry about what will happen to their wardrobes, or to the stage setting when it's struck at the end of a play? They know that they are the creators; they are what is real, and the play is a creation that comes and goes, interesting while it lasts and worth acting well, but not what is truly important. That sense of engaged detachment from life, and the buoyancy that accompanies it, are the gifts you can receive from a partner who stimulates your twelfth house.

If you activate your lover's twelfth house, remember: you are not his or her guru. Your presence in your mate's life can facilitate confrontation with that level of reality, but you are not there to force growth to happen your way–that's another form of egotism. Your effect on your mate's life is to increase the likelihood that he or she will cease to identify totally with the outer personality. That influence can frighten your partner, and with good reason. We all need to have an outer self that functions effectively in the world; complete lack of one spells insanity. Don't try to strip your partner of his or her personality.

Gauguin's Sun-Mercury conjunction fell in Van Gogh's twelfth house; their association had tremendous potential, but an unnerving effect on Van Gogh.   Rimbaud's Sun-Ascendant conjunction fell in Verlaine's twelfth house; Verlaine once referred to Rimbaud as "that devil of an adolescent."   Jimmy Carter's Venus-Neptune conjunction lies in Rosalynn Carter's twelfth house conjunct her Sun-Neptune; this transposition undoubtedly has something to do with the shared faith that is part of their marriage.   We were struck by the number of creative collaborations of one type or another with twelfth house transpositions; creativity can flow from the twelfth house source.   Besides the previous examples: Mary Shelley's Jupiter fell in Percy Shelley's twelfth house; Elizabeth Taylor's Pluto and Jupiter fell into the late Richard Burton's twelfth house, and his Moon in her twelfth.   Also on the list would be Jung's Jupiter in Freud's twelfth, Garfunkel's Pluto in Simon's twelfth, Hepburn's Uranus-Mars in Tracy's twelfth, and Bogart's Mars in Bacall's twelfth.

You've had a look at how birthcharts interact, but synastry doesn't stop there.   When we put two charts together, a third factor, the **composite** chart, is also active in the couple.   Let's examine that factor in Part Four.

Part Four

THE ETERNAL TRIANGLE

CHAPTER TEN

THE WHOLE IS GREATER
THAN THE SUM OF THE PARTS

Or so goes the old proverb. And it's true, especially in affairs of the heart. When two people commit themselves to loving each other, the **whole** of that couple is something new, something distinct from either of the individuals.

Two shy little mice get married and quickly begin throwing elaborate dinner parties. Two aggressive extroverts get together and move to the backwoods of Alaska. The changes are not always so dramatic, but the point is that the "meta-personality" of a couple does not always derive logically from the personalities of the individual lovers. Sometimes that meta-personality appears to have a mind of its own.

Every couple, then, is a threesome: you, me, and what we are together. Unraveling the sometimes Byzantine politics of this "eternal triangle" is the third and final step in our synastry pyramid.

In Part Two of this book we explored the first step in that pyramid: dissecting each of the individuals separately, as if each existed in a vacuum. In Part Three we added the second step: analyzing the interactions of the two birthcharts. Now, in Part Four, we complete the picture by recognizing that, in love, there is always an invisible third party, casting its votes, throwing its tantrums, offering its insights, just like the two visible lovers.

(Part Five, by the way, puts the three steps into perspective, merging them into an orderly interpretive strategy. If you're nervous about remembering all these details well enough to unlock the astrological dimensions of intimacy, don't worry: you don't yet have the master key. That comes in Part Five.)

The Composite Chart

The invisible "third party" in every partnership may be impossible to see, but it reveals its nature and its hidden agenda very clearly in the "composite chart." This chart, a synthesis of the two individual birthcharts, is the third leg of love's eternal triangle. Arbiter, deadlock-breaker, wild card, it moves behind the scenes to establish the framework of opportunity within which the two lovers navigate for as long as they remain together.

What does a composite chart look like? Exactly the same as an ordinary birthchart.

How do you interpret one? By the same rules you use with individual charts–except that you need to remember that now you're talking about the personality of the couple, an entity separate and distinct from either of the flesh-and-blood human beings who compose it.

How is the composite chart constructed? In essence, it is an **averaging** of the two birthcharts. The point precisely midway between your Sun and mine is our "composite Sun." The midpoint of our Moons is our composite Moon. If your Mercury lies toward the end of Scorpio and mine lies toward the end of Capricorn, the point exactly halfway between them–late Sagittarius–is the location of our composite Mercury.

Full instructions for setting up composite charts are given in the appendices at the end of this book. And if you're fainthearted when it comes to arithmetic, you'll also find an address there where you can order computerized composite charts.

As always in astrology, setting up the charts is merely a mechanical process, interesting for some, daunting for others, boring for most.

The challenge–and the reward–lies in learning to cajole insight and understanding out of those primordial symbols of earth and sky.

Let's look at a composite chart in action.

Zelda and F. Scott Fitzgerald

Few couples in history have managed to embody so perfectly the spirit of an age. The "roaring twenties" are forever mirrored in the colorful but tragic lives of Zelda and F. Scott Fitzgerald. When they met in 1918, he was the classic "dashing young lieutenant," while she was the eighteen-year-old southern debutante. From the beginning, Scott expected literary fame and its attendant fortunes. Although his plans were thwarted for a while, by 1920 he had published his first novel, *This Side of Paradise*. Shortly thereafter he married Zelda, and together they came to epitomize the manic high living and cosmopolitan chic so characteristic of that glamorous decade.

Flitting between New York, Paris, and the French Riviera, they drank and spent and partied, often to excess, but always with a quality of style and charm that kept them one step ahead of the shadows that lie down those roads. Of that period in their lives F. Scott Fitzgerald later wrote, "I remember riding in a taxi one afternoon between very tall buildings under a mauve and rosy sky; I began to bawl because I had everything I wanted and knew I would never be so happy again."

Those words proved prophetic. If the twenties showed the Fitzgeralds on top of the world, the thirties showed them devoured by the very shadows they had managed to elude for so long. Scott's heavy drinking developed into full-blown alcoholism; Zelda became schizophrenic. They separated, although their love for each other never died. Reading their letters, one gets the impression of Greek tragedy: two lovers, given a taste of paradise, then pulled apart, battered, and broken by elemental flaws in their own characters. Four days before Christmas 1940, F. Scott Fitzgerald died of an alcohol-related heart attack; seven years later, Zelda died in a fire in the sanitarium where she was interned. She was buried by his side.

As always, our initial astrological step is to get acquainted with the bedrock: we must absorb the birthcharts. Only in that context does the composite chart take on practical significance.

Figures 3 and 4 show the Fitzgeralds' birthcharts. Immediately the astrological energies that operate between them are apparent. Quickly scanning, we discover that Scott's Sun in early Libra formed a near-precise sextile aspect to Zelda's Sun, in early Leo. A stimulating sextile also linked their Moons: his in early Taurus, hers in early Cancer. Zelda's Sun, Ascendant, and Mercury all fall in Scott's "House of Marriage"–hence his instant attraction to her. Intensifying the bond, we discover that their Mars placements were virtually identical, both around the twentieth degree of Gemini. Throughout the good years of their marriage they had an almost legendary enthusiasm (Mars) for staying up until dawn simply talking to each other (Gemini). Their minds were on the same wavelength (conjunction).

Digging more deeply, we discover that Zelda's birthchart displays pronounced duality. On one hand, we find the Sun and Ascendant in demonstrative Leo, trined by an ebullient Sagittarian Jupiter and an iconoclastic fifth-house Uranus. Colorful stuff. On the other hand, we see a sensitive Cancer Moon in conjunction with gentle Venus, bolstered by the withdrawn qualities typical of a twelfth-house Sun. In her early years Zelda dealt with these astrological ambiguities in much the same way that adolescents everywhere do: she simply repressed the more problematic side of her psychological equation. In her words, "When I was a little girl I had great confidence in myself...I did not have a single feeling of inferiority, or shyness, or doubt, and no moral principles."

The tension between the "Performer" (Leo) in Zelda and the "Invisible Woman" (Cancer) would ultimately contribute to the madness (twelfth-house shadow) that destroyed her. In Zelda's own words, "It's very difficult to be two simple people at once, one who wants to have a law to itself and the other who wants to keep all the nice old things and be loved and safe and protected."

To Zelda's words "loved and safe and protected" we might add the word "noticed." In Montgomery, Alabama, Zelda was an enviable figure: a judge's daughter, a lovely, popular debutante. Her Leo "Performer's" need for applause was satisfied. When she met and married Scott, their glamorous New York life met those

FIGURE 6

Zelda Fitzgerald
July 24, 1900
5:33 AM CST

Montgomery, Alabama
32°N23' - 86°W19'

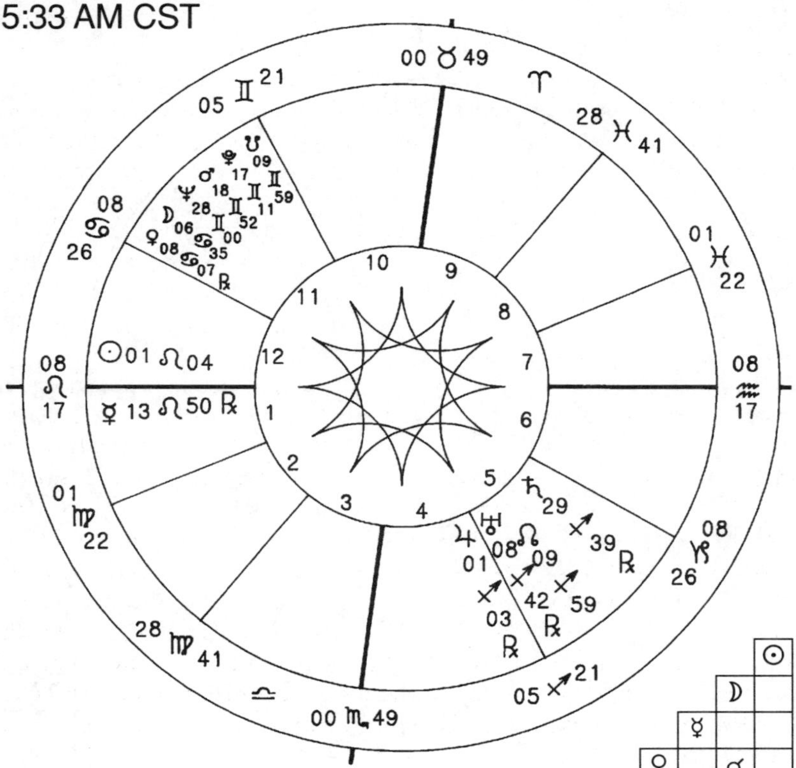

Angular: ☿ ♃
Succedent: ☽ ♆ ♅ ♄ ♇ ♂
Cadent: ♀ ☉
Cardinal: ♀ ☽
Fixed: ☿ ☉
Mutable: ♇ ♃ ♅ ♂ ♆ ♄
Fire: ♃ ☿ ☉ ♅ ♄
Earth: –
Air: ♇ ♂ ♆
Water: ☽ ♀

	MH	☊	♇	♆	♅	♄	♃	♂	♀	☿	☽	☉
☉												
☽												
☿												
♀											☌	
♂										✶		
♃												△
♄												
♅							☌			△		△
♆						☍						
♇								☌		✶		
☊					☌					△		
MH				✶		△					✶	□
ASC		△			△					☌		☌

FIGURE 7

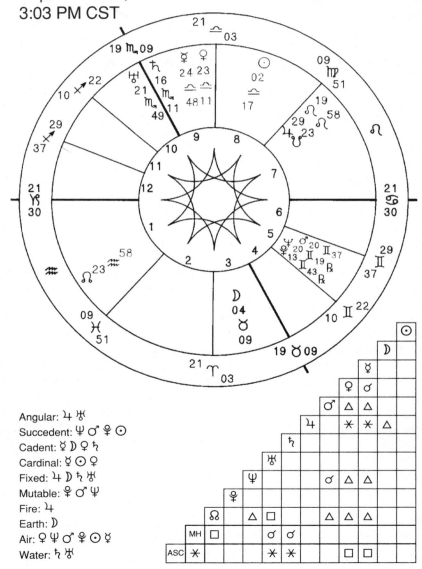

F. Scott Fitzgerald   St. Paul, Minnesota
September 24, 1896   44°N57' - 93°W06'
3:03 PM CST

Angular: ♃ ♅
Succedent: ♆ ♂ ♀ ☉
Cadent: ☿ ☽ ♀ ♄
Cardinal: ☿ ☉ ♀
Fixed: ♃ ☽ ♄ ♅
Mutable: ♀ ♂ ♆
Fire: ♃
Earth: ☽
Air: ♀ ♆ ♂ ♀ ☉ ☿
Water: ♄ ♅

same needs admirably–at first. But as Scott came to be increasingly lionized as a major literary voice, Zelda's Leonine instincts were thwarted. The resultant competitiveness between them is often cited as a central factor in the painful years that followed their spectacular rise.

Scott transposed three planets–his Sun, Mercury, and Venus–into Zelda's third house (communication). This configuration enormously stimulated her capacities as a writer. A good thing? Potentially, yes. But genius is a hard act to follow, and try as she might, Zelda was never able to achieve anything near her husband's literary success, financially or artistically. Would she have even tried, had not Scott so stimulated her third house? And would she have attained more of a sense of her own worth had she not diverted so much energy into the medium of literature? Difficult questions. Certainly Zelda was creative in her own right, and she did have a flair for language (Mercury in Leo conjunct her Ascendant). F. Scott Fitzgerald, however, was one of the great voices of his generation, and head-to-head competition with such a talent is no formula for self-esteem.

Turning to F. Scott Fitzgeralds' birthchart, we find a study in the prominence of the planet Venus. It rules both his Sun sign (Libra) and his Moon sign (Taurus). Venus itself was placed in its own natural sign, Libra, in a conjunction with Mercury. What can this mean? That Fitzgerald was one of history's consummate artists (Libra) goes without saying, as does the fact that his art (Venus) took the form of language (Mercury).

But there's more to Venus than beauty. She's also the "goddess of love." With the planet so central to his character, Scott radiated an intensely Venusian presence: warm, charming, magnetic. And critically, his romantic Venusian love for Zelda was a central feature of his life. His powerful mating instinct is exaggerated even further through the placement of his Libran Sun in the sexual eighth house. With his identity (Sun) motivated so elementally by the search for love (Libra) and destined to gather so much pivotal experience through the process of bonding (eighth house), it is clear that Zelda's catalytic impact was a central theme of his destiny. Thus, although there is little evidence to support the oft-repeated allegation that she "wrote his books for him," we can fairly say that from the astrological perspective, he likely could not have written nearly so poignantly and truly without her.

In typical eighth-house fashion the Fitzgeralds' marriage was psychologically profound–and often profoundly upsetting. Still, in 1925, Scott was able to write: "Zelda and I sometimes indulge in terrible four-day rows that always start with a drinking party, but we're still enormously in love and about the only truly happy married couple I know." And later, one sentence that captures so much of the dark side of his Libran, eighth-house spirit: "I left my capacity for hoping on the little roads that led to Zelda's sanitarium."

Serenity, the highest realm of Venus, is the unconscious, spiritual goal that motivates the behavior of anyone with the planet strongly placed. At the most elemental level of astrological interpretation, we observe that F. Scott Fitzgerald, despite his sensitivity, was learning how to establish and maintain inner peace. Beauty and love are Teachers there, and he studied under them. But there are Tricksters too, promising peace but delivering agony. The abuse of alcohol is one of them, and Scott fell prey to its temptations.

Can we see alcoholism astrologically? Emphatically we cannot. We might see a predisposition toward the problem, but ultimately the cornerstone of all modern astrological work lies on the human capacity to choose among a wide range of possible behaviors. No astrological feature leaves us without options–or leads us inescapably toward the gin bottle.

The Venusian peace-seeking qualities of F. Scott Fitzgerald's birthchart suggest at least the possibility that he'd be tempted by the desensitizing effects of drink. Furthermore, he has Neptune (altered states of consciousness) in his fun-loving fifth house, tightly conjunct Mars. The red planet's explosive enthusiasms, coupled with Neptune's lower proclivities, offered him many possibilities. The one he chose was a cycle of alcoholic "benders," sometimes lasting for days. His pattern of self-destructive drinking waxed and waned throughout his life and certainly contributed to his untimely death at the age of forty-four.

In a chilling line from his own notebooks, F. Scott Fitzgerald wrote his own sad epitaph: "Then I was drunk for many years, then I died."

Summarizing, in Zelda and F. Scott Fitzgerald we see two highly sensitive, creative people, both with somewhat indrawn characters driven by primordial hungers into unnaturally extroverted manifestations. In Zelda's case that hunger was the Leonine need for recognition and applause. In Scott's case it was the Libran hunger for love. The essential introspectiveness of Zelda's character is suggested by the Cancer Moon and her twelfth-house Sun; in Scott it is indicated by his Taurus Moon and his inward-probing eighth-house Sun. Thus, despite the many differences between their birthcharts, we find distinct parallels between Zelda and Scott. Coupled with the striking interaspects and transpositions we discussed earlier, it is no wonder that they immediately fell in love. These two, if nothing else, were kindred spirits.

That they contributed to each other's destruction is also true.

To deepen our understanding of this complex marriage, we now take the third synastric step. Let's consider...

The Fitzgeralds' Composite Chart

A composite chart is ultimately no different than a birthchart. Like a birthchart, it details the kinds of experiences that best nourish the spirit of a particular entity. It describes the available resources, the entity's strengths, its potential weaknesses and blind spots. The composite chart, like a birthchart, illuminates the happiest, most rewarding patterns of experience for the entity and cautions us about darker possibilities. If there is any "trick" to working effectively with composite charts, it lies in remembering that the "entity" in question is only indirectly related to the personalities of the two individuals; rather, it symbolizes the processes and personality of that far less tangible creature: the couple itself.

Consider Figure 5. This is the Fitzgeralds' composite chart. Whatever they were–or could have been–as a couple is reflected in its symbolism.

Begin interpretation, as always, with the Sun. That represents the entity's core and its ultimate source of vitality. Zelda and Scott, together, had the Sun in Virgo in a near-precise conjunction with Venus. Their identity (Sun) as a couple was dependent upon exposure to healthy Virgo experiences: craftsmanship,

FIGURE 8

Composite Chart
The Fitzgeralds

Montgomery, Alabama
32°N23' - 86°W19'

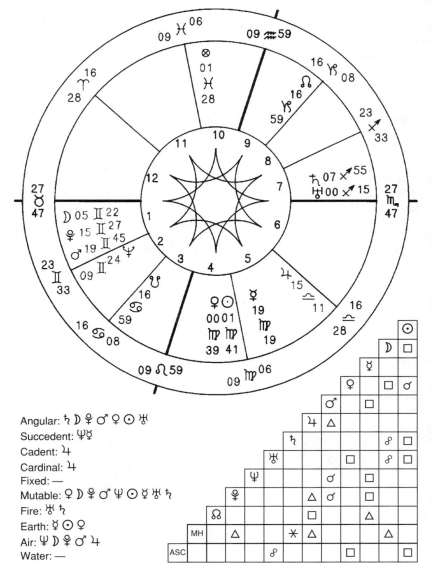

Angular: ♄ ☽ ♀ ♂ ♀ ☉ ♅
Succedent: ♆ ☿
Cadent: ♃
Cardinal: ♃
Fixed: —
Mutable: ♀ ☽ ♀ ♂ ♆ ☉ ☿ ♅ ♄
Fire: ♅ ♄
Earth: ☿ ☉ ♀
Air: ♆ ☽ ♀ ♂ ♃
Water: —

competence, meaningful responsibilities, accurate self-appraisal. **Perfection** is the endpoint of Virgo; its shadow is a **collapse** of confidence in the face of that goal.

The Venus-Sun conjunction is a common feature in composite charts drawn for romantic connections. The "goddess of love" (Venus) fuses (conjunction) with the identity and self-image of the couple (Sun).

Would their Venusian love survive time? Only if they nourished it with Virgoan virtues and experiences: personal growth, hard work, attention to reality. And if they failed? Then they fall prey to Virgo's shadow, losing faith in their marriage, descending into self-punishment and mutual psychological assassination.

Significantly, the Fitzgeralds' Sun-Venus conjunction lies in the fourth house (the deep unconscious; the "House of the Home"). Scott-and-Zelda were meant to draw much of their solar vitality from experiences of withdrawal from the noisiness of the world. As a couple, they were in desperate need of "roots": a home, perhaps a family.

What actually happened? Those fourth-house needs were at best only partially met. The Fitzgeralds never really had a home, living instead in hotels and transitorily in rented houses. In 1924, to gain hiatus from their hectic New York life, they sailed to France–but immediately duplicated there the same screaming social pace they had maintained in New York. They did have a daughter, Scottie, in 1921, but the child was raised primarily by nannies. Subsequently Zelda had several abortions. While it would be dogmatic to suggest that children and a traditional home life are essential to the happiness of every married couple, in the Fitzgeralds' case, based on their composite chart, we can state with certainty that commitments such as those could have had a healing, vitalizing effect on their partnership. Instead, they apparently succumbed to the darker side of Virgo by never developing the fourth-house Virgoan skills of home life, thereby allowing their confidence (Virgo!) in their union to slip away.

A relatively minor feature of their composite chart–Jupiter on the sixth-house cusp–adds corroborative evidence. For Scott and Zelda to maintain faith, hope, and a positive outlook (Jupiter), they would need to acquire sixth-house skills: practical competence, humility, responsibility.

In birthchart astrology, an individual with a fourth-house Sun is typically "hard to get a fix on." Often such a person is shy. Other times we observe a quality of inscrutability, as if we were viewing only a facade behind which lurked a very different character maintaining an impeccable "poker face." (Think of David Bowie and Boy George: two Rock 'n' Rollers with fourth-house Suns and highly slippery outward identities.) That is the way it was with Scott and Zelda Fitzgerald. The entity that they were together was essentially indrawn and quiet, even humble. But it wore a mask about as subtle as a ticker tape parade.

The Fitzgeralds' first house–which is the face they presented to the world–is highly charged. Their Ascendant is Taurus, normally suggesting a quiet outer "persona." But that Ascendant is heavily modified by the presence of three planets: the Moon and a conjunction of fiery Mars and intense Pluto, all in buzzing, talkative Gemini. Such a combination guarantees that Martial verve, Plutonian drama, and above all, Geminian animation and glibness would characterize their social behavior.

Mercury rules the Fitzgeralds' Geminian first house planets as well as their Virgo Sun–and Mercury itself is placed prominently, in Virgo, in the expressive, playful fifth house. Thus, along with their all-important Venus, this frenetic, restless, eloquent planet played a central role in portraying the tone of Scott and Zelda's life together. Unsurprisingly, their Mercurial quickness and verbal fluidity was legendary. A friend, Edmund Wilson, describes their impact upon people in these terms: "The remarkable thing about the Fitzgeralds was their capacity for carrying things off and carrying people away by their spontaneity, charm, and good looks. They had a genius for imaginative improvisations..."

Scott and Zelda's fabled unpredictability, as well as the fertility of their imaginations, we can trace to Mercury's significance, along with their prominent composite first-house Moon. Mars added passion and an edge of violence (recall their "four-day rows"). And Pluto? This is the planet through which individuals embody the forces of history. It is here that we observe the uncanny way the Fitzgeralds came to symbolize the *zeitgeist* of the 1920s.

A colorful Geminian mask. A quiet, insecure fourth-house Virgo core. The introvert wearing the mask of the extrovert. The tensions are obvious. Even if we were to miss them at first glance, a look at the aspect grid would quickly correct our oversight. The Fitzgeralds' composite Gemini Moon was less than four degrees away from a perfect square to their Virgo Sun: the aspect of friction. What they appeared to be outwardly (their first-house lunar configuration) and what they really needed in order to sustain their spirits (their fourth-house solar configuration) were working at cross-purposes. Understand this elemental clash and you've found the key to unlocking their composite chart–and the painful story of their marriage.

Scott: "We were the most envied couple in about 1921 in America."

Zelda: "I guess so. We were awfully good showmen.

Those lines, taken from a transcript of a talk with their counselor, Dr. Rennie, in 1933, capture the power of their outer persona...and also the falseness they perceived in it when viewed from the deeper perspective of their fourth-house Virgo center.

Balance was possible. Squares are not "bad" aspects; only challenging ones. The Fitzgeralds could, for example, have evolved a pattern of quiet home life in an isolated locale and punctuated it with stimulating "blitzes" into the cosmopolitan worlds of New York and Paris. That is what an evolutionary astrologer would have suggested had they consulted one. The secret with squares is to feed both sides of the question, creating reasonable compromises between contrasting legitimate needs.

Even though the dominance of the "mask" over the "core" is what led to the erosion of their marriage, it would be misleading to imagine that the Fitzgeralds' colorful, impassioned behavior is what killed them. Just as easily, they could have starved their outer Geminian self, living a quiet, responsible, middle-class life– and wound up just as alienated from each other. The whole is greater than the sum of the parts, and it is the whole that must be fed.

With composite charts there's an excellent rule of thumb to apply when you find yourself stumped: just pretend that you're looking at an ordinary birthchart. At a person, in other words. The idea of some intangible "entity" or "meta-personality" hovering bodilessly in the ethers between a man and a woman may be confusing. But **people**–you see them every day. You're accustomed to watching them, figuring them out. You have a lifetime of practice there. So start your interpretive work with the composite chart by trying to imagine that it represents a flesh-and-blood individual. Who is that person? What's his style? What are her secrets? Then apply all those insights to that bodiless "entity" that may have been befuddling you a moment before.

If the Fitzgeralds' composite chart were the birthchart of a person, what would that man or woman be like? Witty, sharp, charismatic, theatrical...yet somehow distant and unavailable. Those words simply translate into plain English the astrological ambiguities we've just analyzed in terms of their Sun-Moon square. And that translation moves us from a baffling world to daily life–a world where you have reservoirs of wisdom based on your own years of living among the human family.

Make that translation from astrological symbolism into every-day language. Then tap into your reservoir of wisdom. Do that, and you'll be a real astrologer, not just someone who's memorized a handful of odd words and Babylonian runes.

If the Fitzgeralds' composite chart were a person, one observa-tion about that individual leaps out: He or she would be awfully tough to get to know well. Pleasurable, light social contact would come quite readily. But real intimacy and knowledge of his or her inner workings would challenge the wiles of the most cunning psychologist.

The elusive quality of the Fitzgeralds' ambiguous "extraverted introvert" composite chart is confirmed by the words of their (temporarily) close friend Gerald Murphy: "I don't think they cared very much for parties...and I don't think they stayed at them very long...They usually had their own funny little plans–they'd be with you for a while and then they'd disappear and go on to some other place–and then you'd see them again somehow–they'd seek you out again."

The Fitzgeralds' deeper reality was buried in the labyrinthine underworld of the fourth house, behind their glittering first-house Geminian display. To achieve true intimacy with them was possible, but only if they themselves chose to open the doors. Scott, perhaps saying more than he knew, wrote: "There never was a good biography of a good novelist. There couldn't be. He is too many people if he's any good."

Consistent with this deduction, we detect astrological evidence that the Fitzgeralds' "meta-personality" might well have existed in a state of relative isolation from intimate human contact–or at least that such contact would arise only as a result of substantial efforts on their part. What is the evidence? In their seventh house, the traditional "house of marriage," we see a conjunction of Saturn and Uranus in Sagittarius. In the context of an individual birthchart, a traditional astrologer would say that Saturn ("the lord of solitude") in the house of marriage means loneliness and frustration in intimacy, while Uranus (independence; individuality) there signifies marital instability and erratic sexual behavior. In a composite chart the couple itself would experience that isolation and instability in its relations with other people–if we are to trust the fortune-teller.

A healthier, more accurate reading of the configuration would not be so fatalistic. There are higher possibilities, but reaching them requires determination. The fortune-teller's interpretation is real only if people are unwilling to make honest effort.

Couples, like individuals, usually benefit from the perspective and support that comes from friendship. Marriage is not always easy, but just watching another couple face their own dramas can help it along. We can learn from their mistakes, benefit by their realizations. This is especially true when our composite chart shows seventh-house planets, as did the Fitzgeralds'. They, as a couple, had soulmates. That is, the meta-personality of their marriage depended for its health and growth upon input from other people. Their seventh-house composite planets at once show the nature of the Fitzgeralds' soulmates and the lessons they needed to learn from them.

To form such supportive bonds the Fitzgeralds would have needed to develop self-control (Saturn at its best) and radical honesty (Uranus at its best). Loneliness and erratic, crazy behavior are just the shadows those planets cast. An evolutionary astrologer would suggest that the Fitzgeralds make an effort to sustain those relationships (Saturn) and to be themselves there (Uranus). None of this would be phrased as Scott and Zelda's "destiny." Rather, the creation and maintenance of those bonds would be portrayed as high challenge, spiritual discipline–and ultimately as a strategy for their psychological survival.

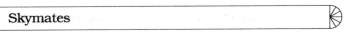

Did the Fitzgeralds succeed? Only partially. They did form a close bond with an expatriate American couple, Gerald and Sara Murphy, who were living in France. The Murphys were older than the Fitzgeralds, quieter, less flamboyant –and yet colorful. They had left a prosperous familial commercial empire, choosing instead to live abroad on a relatively modest income, studying art. They had Saturnine sobriety mixed with Uranian rebelliousness, and thus bore the mark foretold in the Fitzgeralds' composite chart.

At first the bond between the two couples was profound. In a letter to the Fitzgeralds written on the occasion of a temporary leave-taking, Gerald Murphy wrote: "Ultimately, I suppose, one must judge the degree of love for a person by the hush and the emptiness that descends upon the day after the departure...We four communicate by our presence...so that where we meet and when will never count. Currents race between us regardless: Scott will uncover for me values in Sara, just as Sara has known them in Zelda through her affection for Scott."

Those last lines especially emphasize the soulmate quality of the interaction between the Murphys and the Fitzgeralds. Through their mutual sharing, each couple helped the other to see itself more clearly, thereby promoting the intensification of self-aware-ness characteristic of this magical kind of human love.

Within a year the Fitzgeralds' crazed "mask" and its wild behavior had at least partly soured the bond. Drunken driving, violent quarreling, and endless competitiveness took their toll. Sensing the defensive quality of Scott and Zelda's histrionics, Sara Murphy wrote, "If you can't take friends largely and without suspicion–then they are not friends at all." And in reference to a situation in which Scott, drunk, threw a fig at one Princesse de Caraman-Chimay, a guest at a Murphy dinner party, she added, "We cannot–Gerald and I–at our age and stage in life be bothered with sophomoric situations like last night."

The Murphys' support, so critical to the stability and sanity of the Fitzgeralds' marriage, was thus squandered. With their solid Saturnine sense of responsibility and their simultaneously col-orful Uranian style of living, the Murphys held out an ideal to Scott and Zelda. Had they been able to learn the lesson their soulmates offered, the Fitzgeralds might have achieved the synthesis of their pyrotechnical lunar mask and their conservative solar core, thereby balancing the opposing forces that threatened to tear them apart.

That synthesis was the soulmate gift the Murphys offered the Fitzgeralds. Tragically they refused it.

Why? The question is fundamental. To answer it, we must return to the most elemental observations about the Fitzgeralds' composite chart. We must return to the Sun.

In their deepest solar self Scott and Zelda Fitzgerald were shaped by the requirements of Virgo and the fourth house. As we have seen, the maintenance of their vitality as a couple ultimately rested upon their ability to deal precisely, effectively, and competently (Virgo) with the dual fourth-house territories of personal psychology and simple home life. Should they fail, then that solar vitality would gradually erode, tossing them into a spiral of escalating self-doubt (Virgo shadow) and fourth-house problems of rootlessness and psychological instability.

That they took the second course is a matter of history. That the first course was open to them is the keystone of modern astrological theory.

As the solar core of the Fitzgeralds' marriage fizzled, they increasingly attempted to compensate for the resultant Virgoan insecurity by pumping up their first-house mask. It was that defensiveness that finally made sincerity with the Murphys–and everyone else–impossible. And with their mounting desperation, that walled-in tension began to resemble madness. When, for example, Scott flirted with dancer Isadora Duncan, Zelda wordlessly threw herself headfirst down a flight of stone steps. One night Scott allowed Zelda to challenge him to a series of dangerous high-dives from the Riviera cliffs into the sea. Both anecdotes reveal the self-destructiveness characteristic of Virgo when it fails to achieve the high standards it sets for itself.

The fourth house is a realm of unbridled subjectivity. It can be a source of creative inspiration. It can also represent a kind of psychic "black hole" into which the healthy adult personality can collapse. As the Fitzgeralds' marriage gradually succumbed to self-imposed strangulation, it is no accident that Scott and Zelda both fell into pathologically subjective fourth-house states, out of touch with outward reality: he, to alcoholic torpor; she, to schizophrenia.

Could they have done differently? Of course. That at least is the only legitimate astrological answer to the question. Slowing down a bit, giving themselves more privacy, establishing a home life–all were pieces of the puzzle. All would have helped establish an existential framework within which the Fitzgeralds might have undertaken the real fourth-house work: self-administered psychoanalysis. Their Venusian love for each other, had it been coupled with humility rather than humiliation, might have catalyzed a healing of the dark forces within each of them, the forces that instead drove Scott to the gin bottle and Zelda to the madhouse.

Ultimately, fourth house work is spiritual–that is, pertaining to deep consciousness. Zelda and Scott might have healed each other's haunted spirits. Instead they bought drinks for the drunkard, while taunting and dazzling the madwoman.

"Spiritual": the word immediately directs our attention to the one remaining planet in the Fitzgeralds' composite chart–Neptune. The planet of consciousness itself. The visionary–and the drunk. The mystic–and the madwoman. Where was it? In Gemini, on the cusp of the second house: the "house of money" and, more significantly, of self-confidence.

For Scott and Zelda to feel real faith in their union, they needed to make a high response to that Neptune. That is, they required some kind of spiritual, evolutionary perspective on their marriage. In other words, to the basic "self-administered psycho-analysis" suggested by their fourth-house Sun, they must add a hint of something higher, more self-transcendent.

And if they failed? Then they would seek to bolster confidence in their marriage through less wholesome Neptunian means, hyping themselves with Neptunian shadows, such as "glamor" and "whiskey courage," not to mention compulsive, unrealistic financial extravagance. Again, history records that here too the Fitzgeralds fell prey to the lower course. That does not diminish the reality of the higher one.

Could an evolutionary astrologer have saved Scott and Zelda Fitzgerald's marriage? It is tempting to react reflexively to that question and say "Of course not!"

Perhaps that's the correct answer. The giddy, self-flattering "high" of their early years was blissfully addictive, and like most addiction, it led inexorably to a painful crash. But were there seeds of wisdom in this man and woman, even amidst the glorious fantasy of their first years together? We cannot know. Were they bound inextricably to the nose-diving patterns of their biographies? Or was the equilibrium between insanity's gravity and love's uplifting touch so delicate that a featherweight would have tipped the scales of fate?

These questions are imponderable.

No astrologer need wrestle with them. Our work, in unraveling the message of a composite chart, is not to make pronouncements, be they baleful or full of hope. Our work is only to help, only to offer a gesture toward the higher road and to point an incisive finger at the Shadow in all its seductive guises. Beyond that, the couple itself must choose.

Maybe an astrologer could have helped Zelda and Scott. Maybe he or she, arriving at precisely the right instant, wielding the weight of a feather, could have upset the balance, planting seeds of peace and regeneration.

Again, we cannot know. But if astrology ever regains a place of honor among the allies of humankind, it will be because of individuals like you, reader, lying in bed wide-eyed late at night, struggling to find the words that might have made the difference.

Do such words exist? Not if we believe in ironhanded fate. But perhaps "fate" is an empty concept, only a lie, only a device we use to hide from a notion a thousand times more awesome: that the featherweight that truly tips the balance of our lives is not mechanical destiny but rather our own innate capacity to make choices.

Maybe Zelda and Scott Fitzgerald, even deep in their pain, given a little help and a little hope, could have wielded that feather. No matter how true or how false that statement might be, if you're the type of human being who's cut out to be a modern astrologer, you probably at least half believe it.

And for anyone who feels that holding out that kind of faith is like writing letters to Santa Claus, we quote a letter from Scott to Zelda. These words were written in 1934, in desolation, while she was in the asylum and he was trying– and failing–to ration himself to an ounce of gin per hour:

> *"The sadness of the past is with me always. The*
> *things that we have done together and the awful*
> *splits that have broken us into war survivals...stay*

like a sort of atmosphere around any house that I inhabit.   The good things and the first years together...will stay with me forever, and you should feel like I do that they can be renewed, if not in a new spring, then in a new summer. I love you my darling, darling."

CHAPTER ELEVEN

DÉTENTE: POLITICS
WITH THE COMPOSITE CHART

It's the year 2100. In terms of the tension between America and Russia, not much has changed. National defense claims larger and larger portions of each country's budget. Communication exists but could be improved. Arms talks accomplish little. The deadlock frustrates the politicians as much as the populace, but no one knows how to get out of the impasse.

Then one day, astronomers pick up signals from approaching extraterrestrials, ordering us to surrender...

If America and Russia didn't panic in such a situation, it would be hard to imagine something more likely to unite us, force us to work out our differences and introduce change and growth into our relationship.

Couples operate the same way. A dyad, a system with two parts, can easily become locked into polarization. "You say yes; I'll say no. You want a schedule; I want to be spontaneous. You want to sleep with the window shut; I want to sleep with it open." The tendency for partners to drift into that combat zone is powerful, and damaging if allowed to continue unchecked.

No need to wait for the spaceships to arrive. In synastry the third force is the logic of the relationship itself, represented by the composite chart. Ideally the composite chart helps cast a tie-breaking vote, assisting in the resolution of conflicts between two people. It functions as a mediating entity.

Sometimes the nature of that composite chart aligns itself with one or the other person, or with neither. A variety of different "political" situations arise, depending on the inclination of the composite chart. Maybe the "extraterrestrial force" backs one side. Maybe it terrorizes both parties, inciting a stampede out of the partnership, much as Orson Welles' radio broadcast of H. G. Wells' *War of the Worlds* provoked a panic-stricken exodus of listeners who believed that Martians really were invading the Earth. Let's examine a few of those political balances of power formed between two birthcharts and their composite chart. Few composite charts fall precisely into the following categories. They are intended only as general guidelines to help you organize your analysis.

Culture Shock

Vickie is a fourth-house Cancer with a Cancer Moon and Pisces rising. She's a reserved, gentle young woman who raises award-winning orchids. Much of her time is tranquilly spent in a fragrant greenhouse, coaxing incredible blooms from her plants. At an orchid show Vickie meets Nathan when their flowers tie for first prize. Nathan owns a greenhouse fifty miles away; he's a twelfth-house Capricorn with Pisces rising and a first-house Pisces Moon. These dreamy, introverted people are surprised and pleased when they strike up a friendship that quickly deepens into love. But their friends are flabbergasted when Vickie and Nathan take a safari down the Amazon together in search of rare orchid specimens. Six months ago, the prospect of even getting the shots needed for such a journey would have traumatized them. What happened?

Vickie and Nathan's composite chart shows the Sun and Moon both in Aries and the first house, with Aries rising. The logic of their relationship itself demands that they share adventurous experiences, face challenges, and enthusiastically engage themselves with life, as a couple. Fourth-house Cancer or twelfth-house Capricorn experiential food, which would sustain them as individuals, will starve them as a steady diet if they stay together.

But if Vickie forces herself to live in a gung-ho world that is completely alien to her, she will feel crazy, cut off from her fourth-house Cancer center–just as crazy as Nathan will feel if he bends over backward to live a lifestyle equally foreign to his twelfth-house Capricorn energy.

Their composite chart, wildly at odds with their birthcharts, shows that Vickie and Nathan are in **Culture Shock**. To maintain that kind of bond requires incredible adjustments from both partners. Can such a couple stay together? Certainly, if each person is willing to make those compromises, and if their lives are structured so that each person has enough time alone to be able to recharge. It's difficult to stay sane when cut off from the experiences symbolized by one's birthchart for too long.

Couples in Culture Shock need three kinds of experience, one for each partner and one for the couple itself. In our example, Vickie might take time alone in her greenhouse, Nathan on the road to orchid shows, and the two of them together on those Arian safaris. Each type of experience should be granted equal importance for the happiness of Vickie, Nathan, and their relationship.

If you and your mate are in Culture Shock, recognize that too much togetherness is not what you need. Be generous about allotting one another "space," autonomy, separate friends, hobbies, vacations, or apartments. But be sure to create an area in your lives where you participate together in the experiences indicated by the composite chart, or your bond will not be fed. Value the gift of Culture Shock: it can keep you from becoming too set in your ways.

The Fitzgeralds' composite chart, discussed in the previous chapter, is an example of Culture Shock. Scott was an eighth-house Libra with a third-house Taurus Moon, Capricorn rising, three planets in the fifth house, and Jupiter in the seventh. Despite a reticent Capricorn surface and an eighth-house Sun's liking for privacy, Scott's chart reveals a need for relationships and much communication with the outside world. Zelda was a twelfth-house Leo with Leo rising, and eleventh-house Cancer Moon, four other planets in the eleventh house of goals, the future, and association with like- minded others, and two planets in the fifth house. Her chart also demands a lot of human contact, in spite of the twelfth-house placement of her Sun. Their composite chart has a fourth-house Virgo Sun-Venus conjunction, Taurus rising, and a first-house Gemini Moon, with Mars and Pluto also in the first. As a couple they required a fourth-house Virgo "nest" to perfect their relationship, with a Taurus Ascendant adding to the need for calm, simple comforts, and regular routines. A home and a family in the country might have been a way to respond to this part of their composite, with frequent trips into the city to feed their composite Gemini Moon's need for experience. Perhaps they could have invited interesting friends to stay with them as another way to satisfy the Moon's requirement for the life of the mind. Perhaps they could have run a writer's colony. The composite chart's overall need for withdrawal was not so familiar to their birthcharts as the composite's first-house Gemini Moon's need for excitement. They fed the latter and weakened the heart of their relationship (fourth-house Virgo Sun-Venus conjunction), always a danger in Culture Shock.

The Feudal System

Will is a fifth-house Gemini with a Leo Moon and Aquarius rising. Linda is a Taurus with a Cancer Moon and Sagittarius rising. Their composite chart shows a fifth-house Gemini Sun, a Leo Moon, and an Aquarian Ascendant. In other words, their composite chart looks much like Will's birthchart. Since they've been together, Linda has become uneasy about how Will "always gets what he wants." Linda wants to move to the West Coast; Will wants to stay in the East. Will lands a great job in the town where they live, his mother in the next county contracts a chronic disease, and Linda's job offer out west falls through. They abandon all thoughts of moving west. Then Linda wants to rent an old house in quiet residential neighborhood north of town. Will promotes moving into a luxury condominium now and selling it in a few years. The house Linda that wants to rent is partially destroyed by a freak tornado; Will wins a condo in a radio contest.

Beginning to appreciate that Linda might feel uneasy? That can happen when the composite chart resembles one partner's chart much more than the other's. When does that occur? There are no hard and fast rules, but keep the following guidelines in mind. When two or more signs in the composite's primal triad are the same as those in one person's chart, regardless of whether the Sun, the Moon or the Ascendant occupy those signs, that constitutes a strong resemblance. If a stellium in a particular house in one partner's birthchart reappears in the same house in the composite chart, the two charts resemble each other, although not so much as in the first case. If an individual's chart and the composite both lack any planets in one of the elements, there is a certain, fainter correspondence between them. In general, the more that the composite chart reminds you of one of the couple's charts, the more configurations that they have in common, the more that they give you the same feeling, the greater the resemblance between the two.

Such a partnership works like the Feudal System. There is a concentration of power in favor of the individual whose chart the composite resembles, as if life unfairly, arbitrarily gives one person every right and privilege, leaving nothing for the other person. The experiences that one person needs are precisely those that the relationship requires, and events tend to occur in such a way that what happens in the couple is what the "sovereign" wants, and the "serf" feels powerless.

A relationship with a Feudal System composite can be very touchy. The serf can accuse the sovereign of deliberately tyrannical behavior. Sadly, there may be truth in that accusation. Feudal System sovereigns rarely start out with the intention of controlling the partnership. However, the composite chart, the logic of the entity itself, favors the sovereign, and it takes a very conscious person not to abuse that power. If you're the sovereign in such a couple, strive to become that conscious! Make every effort to consider your mate's point of view, to yield. Share your power. Such compromise creates positive outcomes: trust, openness, willing commitment and participation. Sovereigns can be benevolent when they recognize where their bread is buttered.

"Power corrupts, and absolute power corrupts absolutely," according to the proverb. But in the Feudal System composite, the sovereign does not have absolute power. The serf can always walk out. If you're the serf, remember that, but don't threaten it constantly, and don't give way to paranoia, subversion, and passive aggression. Assert yourself reasonably. Distinguish between the flow of events and your mate's premeditated actions.

Aim for a democracy. And if you're positive that your mate will persist in taking advantage of the composite, claiming a mile when circumstances give him or her an inch, recognize that you are not trapped in the Feudal System; you can always leave.

Edward VIII, almost a sovereign in real life, and Wallis Simpson had a composite chart that resembled Edward's more than hers. He was a fifth-house Cancer with Aquarius rising and a first-house Pisces Moon. She was a fifth-house Gemini with Aquarius rising and an eighth-house Libra Moon. Notice that they both have fifth-house Suns and Aquarius rising, so the potential for Democracy was increased, in spite of their composite fifth-house Cancer Sun, Aquarius rising (like Edward) and eleventh-house Sagittarian Moon. We would expect circumstances to favor Edward in their association. The circumstances of his royal birth, her common birth, and her divorce would have prevented their marriage if Edward (the sovereign!) had not chosen to abdicate.

Democracy

Christine has a fourth-house Scorpio Sun, a tenth-house Aries Moon, and Cancer rising. Sam has an eighth-house Taurus Sun, a ninth-house Gemini Moon, and Libra rising. Their composite shows an eleventh-house Cancer Sun, a ninth-house Taurus Moon, and Virgo rising. Christine's Cancer Ascendant is represented in the composite chart by the composite Sun in Cancer. Sam's Taurus Sun is represented by the composite's Taurus Moon, and the composite's ninth-house Moon echoes Sam's ninth-house Moon. The composite's Virgo Ascendant is reminiscent of Christine's tenth-house Moon–that is, both positions have something to do with meaningful work. Neither Christine's chart nor Sam's dominate this composite, and they both find common ground in it. We call this situation Democracy.

Democracy is easier to live with than either Culture Shock or the Feudal System. Its dangers, however, are identical to those of the other two patterns: components of each person's nature that are not supported in the composite chart may find that they have to struggle for recognition in the relationship. If that happens, Democracy can turn into the tyranny of the majority over the minority.

In our previous example, a composite chart with a peaceful Cancer/Taurus/Virgo blend doesn't contain much room for the expression of Christine's fiery Aries Moon, or Sam's Gemini Moon with its need for experience and stimulation. They must depend on their composite ninth-house Moon to pull them out of any rut that starts to form. The composite's Cancer Sun also has to carry the intensity of Christine's Scorpio Sun and Sam's eighth-house Sun, without becoming hypersensitive and shutting down risky but essential lines of communication.

If you're in a Democracy, enjoy and make good use of the points of harmony revealed by your composite chart, without disenfranchising parts of you not directly represented in the composite. If those qualities still find room for expression somewhere in your lives and in the relationship, they are less likely to behave like terrorists sniping at the government.

Paul Newman and Joanne Woodward are a striking illustration of Democracy. Their composite has a second-house Aquarian Moon and Capricorn rising. All three charts have Mercury in the first house.

Jimmy and Rosalynn Carter's composite chart shows a twelfth-house Virgo Sun-Venus conjunction, Libra rising, and a fifth-house Aquarian Moon-Jupiter conjunction. Each individual chart has a twelfth-house Sun, Jimmy's in Libra and Rosalynn's in Leo. Rosalynn has Virgo rising and Jimmy has Libra rising, and the composite's Moon-Jupiter conjunction echoes Rosalynn's ninth-house Moon.

These three patterns–Culture Shock, the Feudal System, and Democracy–are meant as guidelines to start you thinking about the possible patterns of relationship among individual birthcharts and the composites they form. Most situations probably resemble one pattern more than another, but few pure examples of any type exist. As you work with composites, you may well discover other patterns, too.

Regardless of what category the composite chart represents, we need to add one more dimension to our thinking in order to complete the picture. We must consider what aspects the composite's planets make to each individual's charts. See Chapter Eight if you think you need a refresher on interaspects.

Aspects Between the Composite and the Birthcharts

The composite chart describes the entity of the relationship itself. "Entity" is a synonym for "ghost," and ghosts typically haunt people; people seldom haunt ghosts. When you consider the aspects between the composite chart and the birthcharts, concentrate on the effect that the entity of the couple, symbolized by their composite chart, has on the individual birthcharts. Aspects made by the composite to the birthcharts describe that effect. Aspects made by the birthcharts to the composite are not dismissable, but greater weight should be assigned to the composite chart's connections to the birthcharts. The composite "entity" haunts the couple more than they haunt it.

Rule one: When analyzing aspects between the composite and the two birthcharts, pay more attention to the composite's effect on the birthcharts than vice versa.

Once you've absorbed Rule One, you can understand these interaspects as you would any other. The difference is that the entity of the couple solarizes Joe's Moon or Jan's Sun, rather than an individual's doing so. If Joe stays with Jan, he can expect that their life together will bring the lunar side of his character into prominence (solarization). Jan will experience the core of her identity (Sun) flooded with feelings and images (lunarization) by her association with Joe.

Should you draw an interaspect diagram for **all** of the composite chart's planets and their impact on each birthchart? That's up to you. The human brain can only handle so much data without turning into spaghetti. If the thought of laboring to calculate all those interaspects makes you wish you had never heard of astrology, don't do it. We suggest running your eyes over all three charts, keeping alert for interaspects made by the composite's primal triad (Sun, Moon, and Ascendant), Venus and Mars, at a minimum. The former is the heart of the composite chart, and the latter two planets say much about the couple's relating style as a couple. If you can deal with more information, take a look at interaspects made by the composite's Mercury and Saturn, which give clues about how each person experiences the level of communication in their partnership (composite Mercury) and the blockages they share or collude in (composite Saturn). Add more planets as you feel capable of understanding them without blowing your circuits.

Let's look at some examples. *The Changing Sky* describes Gauguin and Van Gogh's turbulent friendship, which did not improve Van Gogh's precarious mental state. Their composite Sun conjuncts Van Gogh's Saturn-Uranus conjunction, enhancing his sense of struggling against limits or being stymied in attempts at independence. Their composite Moon opposes Van Gogh's Pluto-Uranus conjunction, adding a lunar, emotional, irrational quality to Van Gogh's expression of these two outer planets. Pluto can feel like a voice saying "Your life is a joke," and Uranus can feel like a voice saying "To hell with everything; break away." Van Gogh had other responses available than those he made, but his friendship with Gauguin made those voices louder.

Simone de Beauvoir and Jean-Paul Sartre both have Scorpio rising; so does their composite chart. Their style (Ascendant) as a couple is much the same as their individual self-presentations (Ascendants). Their lifelong association required no adjustment of their masks (Ascendant). Comparison of these three charts yields many aspects made by the composite to each birthchart, indicating a proportionally great impact made by the relationship on both of their lives.

Rosalynn Carter didn't think she'd be able to make political speeches but rose to the occasion while campaigning with Jimmy. Their composite Sun conjuncts Rosalynn's Ascendant and her first-house Mars-Venus conjunction, bringing out the charming (Venus) warrior (Mars) in her mask. Their composite Mars falls on Rosalynn's third-house Saturn, challenging (Mars) the communicative (third house) blockage (Saturn) that she felt.

Pete Townshend and Roger Daltrey's composite Sun falls on Townshend's Venus-Mars conjunction, stimulating Townshend's creative (Venus) drive (Mars). Their composite Venus falls on Daltrey's Sun; the music they created together venusified Daltrey's retiring fourth-house Pisces nature, made it more attractive and noticeable. It also opposes Townshend's twelfth-house Moon, drawing on his lunar depths for their art.

Part Five

LIVING SYNASTRY

CHAPTER TWELVE

PUTTING IT ALL TOGETHER

Ever been confused by love? Ask a hundred people. You'll get ninety-nine positive responses and maybe one demurral from a Rambo-type with a bad case of testosterone poisoning. Getting along with another human being may be one of life's most rewarding experiences, but it can also push us toward our mental and emotional ragged edges. In the secret world of intimacy, common sense is half-suspended. Logic is bent, rules are changed. It's beautiful and perplexing.

In synastry, astrology offers us a metaphor for love. It offers a symbol. A streamlined representation of a phenomenon too complex for the mind to grasp any other way.

How do we benefit from using such a metaphor? By allowing it to simplify and schematize for us the essential dynamics of a particular partnership. What do we gain? Clarity. And what does that clarity cost? A high price. To gain clarity we must invariably sacrifice some of the truth. As we move further into the realm of symbols, we put increasing distance between ourselves and the immediate reality of living.

The astrologer's task–your task–is to find a point of balance. On one hand, we have life with its boundless spiderweb of infinitesimal details. On the other hand, we have astrology: a few dozen symbols trying to represent that spiderweb. Go too far in the direction of the symbols and your interpretations become either trivial ("Leos should never marry Scorpios") or so heady they become vacuous, disconnected from everyday experience ("Nine planets in Scorpio in your composite twelfth house? That means you two were Black Magicians in Lemuria in a former life together").

Go too far in the other direction, away from the symbols and back toward life, and what happens? Astrology's simplifying, clarifying diagram falls away, leaving you just as confused as you were before you bought the astrology book. Then the same old fights reemerge punctuated with new phrases..."your infuriatingly patriarchal, domineering Saturn"..."your smarmy, obsequious Pisces Moon"...

Balance is the answer. Take in as much complexity as you can, then stop. Find your own comfort zone. Astrology is flexible. Tailor it to your personal needs and mental strengths. Keep one eye on reality. Keep the other eye on all those interaspects and house transpositions. But never let the symbols overwhelm you. When you start to feel perplexed, back up. Flex astrology back toward simplicity, even if that means moving temporarily into crude generalizations. Then go forward again, adding the details and subtleties that make synastry come alive.

Let the symbols speak to your heart, in other words. And if your heart has trouble with four-syllable words, limit the symbols to three-syllable words for a while. How? Read on. That's what the rest of this chapter is about.

I'll Never Be Able to Figure All This Out

Right?

Unless you're the kind of person who can solve calculus problems in her head while reciting long Shakespearean passages in Swahili, you probably haven't remembered every detail in the preceding chapters, let alone figured out how to get them all working in concert. Synastry is complicated. It had better be! After all, it's trying to mirror human love.

He: intimacy-hungry with many eighth-house Libran planets. She: private and solitary, with Saturn a key player in her birthchart. His Moon sextile her Sun. Her Uranus conjunct his Venus in the fourth house. Composite Mars on their Aquarian

Ascendant.   Each of these factors and dozens more must be analyzed, understood, and fitted into the larger scheme. And you must accomplish that task without ever losing your sense of the big picture.

Who can succeed?   Maybe nobody. Our brains have limits. Perfect understanding of even a single birthchart is probably beyond us. In synastry we face two such birthcharts, plus their interactions. Top it off with a composite chart, and the mind boggles.

How You Can Succeed Anyway

There are two guidelines that guarantee success in synastry despite the density of the astrological information. One we've already briefly considered: whenever you start to get confused, simply retreat back to a simpler level of astrological analysis.

"Guideline Number One: Accept the fact that no human intelligence can successfully correlate all the details in a synastric interaction.   Proceed by starting with the simplest levels of analysis. Add layers until you feel mental strain. Then stop and work as deeply as you can with what you have."

In other words, don't push too hard. It doesn't work. There's no sense diverting so much energy into the purely analytical parts of your brain that you starve your heart and your intuition. That happens easily, and it makes for dried-out, pedantic astrology.

The second guideline, outlined precisely throughout the rest of this chapter, is to follow an orderly, step-by-step procedure in your analysis. Otherwise the resulting tidal wave of undigested astrological ideas will surely wash away your concentration, leaving you with one of those blank, slack-jawed stares you used to see on the faces of the kids in the back row of algebra class.

"Guideline Number Two: Plan your attack! Make an outline and stick to it. By absorbing specific, predefined interpretive strategies and tactics, you can rightly judge the order in which to ask yourself questions and you can put the answers into a coherent, comprehensible pattern."

A vivid overview of two Sun or Moon signs, profoundly understood and clearly presented, is vastly more helpful than a confused, disorderly gloss of buzz words describing dozens of more obscure interaspects. That realization is the core of the first guideline.   Throw in guideline number two–a systematic approach–and you'll likely discover that you've been underestimating your interpretive powers.

Staying on Top of the Symbols

A systematic approach: that's the key to staying on top of synastry's flood of information.   It's a lot like playing jazz. To succeed, you must learn to improvise within a structure. In jazz, that structure is a pattern of musical chords.   In synastry, it's a logical sequence of astrological questions. Each must be answered in the correct order.   Miss a step, and you'll blow a sour note for sure.

In the preceding chapters we've been looking at the astrology of intimacy from a theoretical perspective.   In the remainder of this chapter we leave the world of theory and enter the realm of everyday astrological practice.   With the knowledge of theory you've gained, you are like a budding jazz musician. You know your scales. You know what notes fit each chord. You can tap out complex rhythms. You have some mastery of your instrument. Now all you need is a melody! That is, a structure within which to play and thereby to explore and expand your skills.

Just as there are an infinite number of possible melodies, there are probably an infinite number of ways to organize an astrological analysis. In the pages that follow, we don't mean to exclude dogmatically other methods, and we certainly don't mean to stifle your own creativity. Our aim is only to offer a practical, effective interpretive system.   With a fair understanding of the details we've already covered, coupled with the following procedural outline, we guarantee that you'll be able to provide yourself and your friends with insightful comprehensible astrological interpretations. This, in other words, is our melody. Maybe later you'll compose your own.

The Grand Scheme

You've come this far, reading along, understanding most of what you've read, a little baffled by how it all works in practice. You have your own birthchart and the chart of a friend. You wonder how they fit together. How do you proceed?

Clear off a tabletop. Get out your collection of felt-tip pens. Put a bright light nearby. Turn on your telephone answering machine. And make a pot of tea.

Settle down. You'll be here awhile. Don't expect anything to happen quickly. You're going to have an exciting experience, but it won't be exciting in the shock-a-minute way that the latest Hollywood blockbuster is exciting. More like the excitement of watching the dawn unfold a perfect morning glory.

Your first step is to get all the mechanical work out of the way. Fill out your Synastry Worksheet (see Chapter Four). That means figure out all the interaspects and house transpositions. Next, if you haven't had a computer construct the composite chart in advance, set it up now (see Appendix). Don't worry about interpreting anything yet. Just become a human microchip for half an hour.

Now you're ready to begin to squeeze meaning out of that chaos of symbolism.

How? Start with:

"Guideline Number Three: Put aside the synastry worksheet. Put aside the composite chart. Look at the two birthcharts, one at a time."

Every human being is different. That's one of the reasons life–and astrology–is so fascinating. Since we're all different, each of us brings different needs and expectations into intimacy. Don't miss those differences! Use the birthchart to help you understand whom in particular you are discussing.

Miss this step and you'll fall into the insidious trap of imagining that what's obvious and real to you is equally obvious and real to everyone else. You might find it perfectly natural if your lover never wears anything but blue jeans and a sweatshirt. But let his or her political sentiments diverge one inch from your own and sparks fly. That's fine. Just don't let those personal predilections blind you to the fact that the world is full of honorable people who couldn't care less about their lovers' politics, but for whom stylish appearance is a critical ingredient in maintaining the electricity of a sexual bond.

Here's the procedure:

Pick one of the birthcharts. Start your analysis by looking at the "primal triad": the Sun-Moon-Ascendant blend. Use the formula we introduced in *The Inner Sky* (and reviewed in Chapter

Two of this book) to turn that blend into a single sentence based on fundamental archetypes. This person, for example, may be the Storyteller (Gemini Sun) with the soul of the Hermit (Capricorn Moon) wearing the mask of the Hypnotist (Scorpio Ascendant). Think about the sentence. Get a feel for it.

Add the house positions of the Sun and Moon. Where is this "Storyteller's" life happening? In the house of career? In the house of marriage?

Now mix in some planets. Anything in conjunction with one of those "primal triad" factors? Is Neptune, the planet of mysticism, fused with that Hermit's soul? Is Mars, the god of war, fused with that Hypnotist's mask? Are there many planets grouped in a single house or sign?

Pay particular attention to Venus and Mars. Why? Are they more important than other planets? Not really–it's just that they play pivotal roles in love and sexuality, so in synastry we accord them special attention.

Look at Venus. What sign does it occupy? That tells you what best fills this person with warm, romantic feelings. What does he or she need in a mate in order to maintain long-term interest in the bond? What are his or her perhaps-unconscious assumptions about the purpose of love? And how does this person go about radiating attractiveness?

Now consider Mars. What sign shapes its action in this birthchart? The red planet offers you insights into the more passionate dimensions of the individual's character. What fills her with desire? What turns him on? How does he or she go about actively pursuing the object of his or her fancies?

If you need a deeper review of Mars and Venus, go back and scan Chapter Five.

Next, check the "arc of intimacy," houses five through eight. (If you need a review of those houses, turn back to Chapter Six.) Are there any planets located there? If so, they are keys to this person's intimacy-puzzle. Does he or she face any lessons in the area of emotional spontaneity, love-play, or expressiveness? (Are there any planets in the fifth house, in other words?) What lessons do they teach? What resources do they offer? How can their energies be misapplied? Now move on to the sixth house: what about issues of responsibility and self-sacrifice, so essential to any kind of ongoing commitment? Planets in the seventh house? Here in the traditional "House of Marriage" you'll uncover portraits of specific soulmates whom that person is destined to meet–and vivid descriptions of the lessons he or she needs to learn if those bonds are to prove productive and harmonious. Finally, if there are any planets in the eighth house, you've revealed the formula for opening that man or woman to those half- incomprehensible, transformative sexual emotions we label "electricity" or "chemistry."

Head spinning?

If it is, then perhaps you've gone far enough. Maybe it's time to remember guideline number one: Don't strain yourself. You may have only scratched the surface of the birthchart, but you were scratching a vein of gold. You've learned a lot. You've gotten a sense of who the **person** is behind that chart, and that's enough to satisfy the minimal requirements of guideline number three.

Pour yourself another cup of tea. Take a breather. Do you have a feeling about that chart you've been investigating? Can you visualize the big picture? Are you resonating with that person the way you might still be resonating with a movie character as you walk out of the theater? Or with an old friend five minutes after you hang up from a coast-to-coast phone call? Is your body feeling that birthchart, in other words? If so, you're doing fine. If not, then back up. Start over again..." the storyteller with the soul of the hermit wearing the mask of the hypnotist"...let it sink in.

Why this emphasis upon subjective reactions? For one simple reason: as you move on to the next steps in your synastry analysis, you need temporarily to store all those ideas about the first birthchart. To keep them on ice for a while. No way to do that purely intellectually. There's too much information. As you move into the next phase of your interpretation, you run the risk of forgetting half of what you learned in phase one. But human consciousness can organize vast quantities of information for storage in the form of emotional impressions. That's basically how we remember people–and it's a good way to remember birthcharts too.

Maybe you're a more advanced astrologer, with more than an elementary knowledge of birthcharts. If so, then go further in your astrological analysis. Consider each planet, the aspects it forms, the house and sign it occupies. Guideline number one is not meant to be an endorsement of laziness, only a realistic recognition of limits. Push these limits! Go as far as you can in unraveling each chart. Just remember to assess yourself every now and then. Are you getting lost in details? Have you begun to lose the overview?

Whether you are capable of world-class birthchart interpretations or barely able to recall a few archetypes and key words for each sign, the process is essentially the same. Look at the birthchart. Learn what you can. Understand it. Feel it. And know your limits.

When you're done, put the first birthchart aside. Take another sip of tea. And repeat the entire process with the second birthchart.

At this point, if you've played your cards right, you've internalized the essential spirit of both birthcharts. If you're a beginner at astrology, such understanding might seem to be an elusive goal. Don't let that daunt you. Be persistent. Once you couldn't read a person's face. You didn't know **that** symbolism. Now, after a few years' experience, you can probably do a fair job of picking out the crazies and the energy-vampires at a glance. Astrology is the same. Give it a little time, and those hieroglyphics will communicate just as much to you as any zoned-out gaze or hungry leer.

With the two birthcharts unraveled individually, you are ready to proceed to the second major phase of your synastry analysis: watching them interact.

"Guideline Number Four: After you have absorbed the two birthcharts independently of each other, move on to consider the interaspects they form."

You spent a few minutes filling out your Synastry Worksheet. Now you're ready to reap the fruits of your labors. But look at it! There are dozens and dozens of interaspects. How will you ever soak up all that information? Once again, take refuge in guideline number one: you probably **won't** grasp each and every one of those interaspects, and that's okay. You don't really need to pay attention to all of them. If you can, that's wonderful and your synastry analysis will be deeper and more precise as a result. But if you can't absorb them all, you can still do useful, accurate interpretations. The trick lies in figuring out which of the interaspects are essential to your understanding of the partner-ship and which ones are merely fine-tuning.

Start with the interaspects formed by the Sun, the Moon, and the Ascendant. How does Jack's primal triad impact upon Jill's birthchart as a whole? Does his Sun form an aspect to her Venus? That is, does he solarize (emphasize; bring out) her Venusian qualities of attractiveness, affiliativeness, and warmth? Now consider the specific nature of the interaspect. Is it a square? That is, does that solarization occur through a tense, perhaps annoying process in which Jack applies friction to Jill's Venusian circuitry? Or is the aspect formed between his Sun and her Venus a harmonious trine? Then solarization occurs in a flowing way, with his identity (Sun) enhancing (trine) her qualities of natural grace and affection (Venus).

If you're fuzzy about the details of interaspect analysis, you may want to reread chapters Seven and Eight.

Similarly, Jack's Moon and Ascendant probably form interaspects with sensitive points in Jill's birthchart. Consider each primal triad interaspect, one at a time, until you've covered them all. Then reverse the process, considering how Jill's primal triad fits into Jack's planetary patterns.

Perhaps you feel comfortable with your understanding of those critical interaspects. Great! Now add more planets, paying particular attention to Venus and Mars and their aspects. Does Jill have a prominent Mercury? Then consider its interaspects carefully. Is her Neptune relatively obscure? In that case its interaspects won't be so important and you should give them lower priority. Keep going until you begin to feel that telltale strain.

Maybe you felt that strain as soon as you considered the first interaspect. Time for another cup of tea! Relax. Go slowly. Remember that gut-level understanding of a single interaspect is worth a lot more than skimming many of them superficially.

If you're straining, then your strategy is to reduce the number of interaspects with which you are working. But resist the temptation to eliminate the Moon or Ascendant from your considerations. A better way to narrow your field of inquiry is to tighten the orbs of the interaspects. Maybe Jack's Moon lies in twelve degrees of Cancer, squaring Jill's Mars in five degrees of

Libra. For that square to be perfect, Jill's Mars would of course have to lie in twelve degrees of Libra, exactly ninety degrees from Jack's Moon. As it is, the interaspect is seven degrees away from being precise–close enough to work, but not nearly as powerful as it would be if the orbs were narrower. By considering only interaspects within, say, two degrees of perfection, you drastically reduce the number of planetary relationships. More importantly, in narrowing your orbs, you systematically throw away your pennies before you throw away your nickels and dimes. You're left with only the truly pivotal interaspects.

Using stricter orbs, in all likelihood you'll be left with only a handful of primal triad interaspects. If even that handful is too much, limit your attention to those contacts involving the interaction of Jack's primal triad with Jill's primal triad. His Moon might square her Sun, for example. Those interaspects are really basic, and when you look at them, you're looking at bedrock. But the chances of there being more than three or four such relationships between two birthcharts are very slim. Analyze them carefully, and you've got the foundation for a stripped-down but incisive synastry interpretation.

Again, just as in the analysis of a single birthchart, your strategy is to avoid overburdening yourself. How do you know when you've crossed the line? Simple: your emotions turn off. You stop feeling the human reality behind those planetary geometries. When you experience astrology more like a vexing crossword puzzle and less like a rollicking, poignant novel, then it's time to simplify your analysis and reengage your heart.

Maybe you've gotten a feeling for every interaspect on the Synastry Worksheet. Maybe you've felt only a glimmer of understanding for three or four of them. Either way, the secret of success in synastry lies in customizing your approach to the symbols, making sure it fits your level of skill and experience. As long as you're not overextended, you're doing fine and you're ready to proceed to the next step in your analysis.

"Guideline Number Five: After absorbing the interaspects, move on to consider where the planets in the first chart would fall if placed in the houses of the second chart, and vice versa."

Where would Jack's planets lie if they were placed in Jill's birthchart? That is, which houses would they occupy? If Jack has Jupiter in 19 Scorpio, and Jill's ninth house begins in 15

Scorpio, then **his** Jupiter lies in **her** ninth house. What does that mean? In this case, he jovializes (expands; encourages) her ninth-house qualities of adventure and philosophy.

If the reasoning behind these house transpositions is unclear to you, please review Chapter Nine, "Your Planets, My Sky."

How do you work with house transpositions in practice? When you filled out your Synastry Worksheet, you made note of where each person's planets fell in the other's wheel of houses...didn't you? At least there was space for that information. We find it helpful to complete all rote computational work before beginning the more poetic process of interpretation. There's less mental gear shifting that way. If you haven't figured the house transpositions yet, then take time to do it right now. The process is easy. Start with Jack's Sun. Make a mental note of what sign and degree it occupies. Now glance at Jill's chart. In which house does that sign and degree fall? That's your answer. Continue the same way with Jill's planets. It sounds like a lot of effort, but with practice, figuring house transpositions occupies no more than two or three minutes.

If you're a visually oriented person, it can be helpful actually to draw both transpositional charts. Make a photocopy of Jack's birthchart. Then with a colored pen, write in Jill's planets, showing where they fall when placed in the framework of Jack's houses. Then do the same with Jill's chart and Jack's planets. What you have drawn is a pair of charts that graphically indicate exactly where and how each person stimulates experience and growth in the other one.

Ideally the astrologer would consider each house transposition separately and in detail. With some experience, that ideal is not hard to reach. The quantity of information available here is not so vast as what we uncover in the webwork of interaspects. Still, feel free to invoke guideline number one. You don't need to comprehend every house transposition in order to do effective interpretations. Even with only a few of them understood, you can have a solid grasp on this step in your synastry analysis. The trick lies in knowing which house transpositions are really essential to understand and which ones are secondary. If you start simplifying in a random way, you might mistakenly throw out the key that could unlock the secrets of the partnership.

Sun, Moon, and Ascendant–one again, these primal triad factors are critical. Novice or otherwise, begin your house transposition analysis there. Where does Jill's Sun lie in Jack's chart? Where, in other words, does she solarize his life? You can safely assume that the issues, experiences, and pitfalls of that existential arena will be pushed into great prominence in Jack's life so long as he remains close to Jill. Similarly, Jack's Sun falls in one of Jill's houses, solarizing that dimension of her experience.

The transpositions of the Moons are next on our list. Here the process is lunarization. Where does Jack introduce a deeper element of emotion, imagination, and creativity in Jill's life? Where does she most emphasize his subjective, psychological responses?

Jill's Ascendant impacts upon one of Jack's houses. Here she pushes the affairs of that part of his life into more active behavior, helping to shape their self-expressive style, often adding confidence and flair.   Her Ascendant may lie in his third house (communication). Maybe she encourages Jack to write or simply to speak more freely and comfortable. Maybe she helps him "find his voice." Jack of course ascendantalizes Jill in return, perhaps stimulating her eighth house through that transposition. Then, among other effects, he helps her express her sexuality in a more confident, colorful way.

Two Suns, two Moons, two Ascendants. Six house transpositions. If you've considered all of them and gotten an impression of how they operate, then you've fulfilled the minimal requirement in this phase of our synastry analysis. Maybe that's enough. Once again, monitor yourself for mental strain. If you're comfortable, try going a little further. We've emphasized the importance of avoiding overextension. Be just as wary of underextension! Maybe you can take your house transposition analysis a step further.

Which planet should come next? There is no rigid answer. The rule of thumb is that the more central a role a planet plays in the individual birthchart, the more important is its role in synastry. Jack's Mercury might be very powerful, lying in its own natural sign, Gemini, and ruling his Virgo Ascendant. Knowing that it falls in Jill's seventh house (intimacy; marriage) is a critical piece of information. On the other hand, Jill's Mercury might play only a bit part in her birthchart, lying unaspected in Taurus in the backwaters of her twelfth house. In any but the most detailed of synastry interpretations, its house transpositions might very well be ignored.

In general, Venus and Mars should receive attention. They're important in intimacy questions regardless of how obscure they might be in the individual birthchart.

Saturn, through its house transpositions and its interaspects, often gives a clue about areas of frustration in a partnership, especially areas where one partner feels overly controlled by the other one. More significantly, through the sign it occupies, Saturn illuminates the particular methods available for overcoming those problems.

If you're uncertain about the specific meanings of any of the planets, review Chapter Eight. The logic behind all the basic interaspect processes–saturnization, uranization, neptunification, and so on–is exactly the same in house transpositions. Just remember that the planet now impacts upon an entire house rather than another planet.

Pay special attention when more than one planet is transposed into a single house. Jill might, for example, transpose Mercury, Venus, Neptune, and her Sun into Jack's seventh house. While each planet has particular meaning, the message you need to receive loud and clear is that she's **bombing** his "House of Marriage." Then you add the subtleties by considering each planet's separate significance.

Time for Another Trip to the Teapot

You've covered a lot of ground. In step one, you got acquainted with the two individual birthcharts. In step two, you considered their interactions through a systematic analysis of their interaspects and house transpositions. Are you ready to proceed to step three? Not quite. You still haven't poured yourself that cup of tea.

Never forget that nothing else is so precious in astrological interpretation as a feeling for the big picture. A sense of the whole. And remember that there is a cunning little demon running around in your head who hates astrology and doesn't want it to work and would like nothing better than to ensnare you in a quagmire of details. He'll gladly grant you a profound under-standing of how Jack's Jupiter fits into Jill's twelfth house in a loose sextile to her Mercury–provided you pay the price of forgetting that their Ascendants are conjunct and their Suns form a square aspect. Or that he's conservative and bookish, while she's preparing for an assault on the town's jalapeño-pepper-eating crown.

That's why there is so much emphasis on the teapot in these instructions. It's up there with the ephemeris and the pocket calculator, high on the list of essential astrological tools. Every now and then you need to sit back and let the wholeness of what you are seeing wash over you. Relaxing over a cup of tea might help you do that. So might a shower or a blast of loud music. Whatever method you choose, make sure you use it. Especially now. At this juncture in our synastry outline, you're as busy as a starving lizard in a swarm of mosquitoes. Don't get so busy you lose perspective.

Take time out. Are you feeling the filigree structure of attractions and tensions between those charts? Are the two people becoming living characters in your mind, like Frodo Baggins and Gollum or Humphrey Bogart and Lauren Bacall? Do you sense patterns of friction and enhancement, of joined purposes and cross-purposes? Just as with two individual birthcharts, these questions do not revolve so much around precise understanding of separate astrological configurations. Rather they refer to primordial human feelings of wordless empathy with the two charts. If those feelings are there, then you're ready to advance to the next step. If not, then there's no point in building your towers any higher. The foundation is too shaky.

How did the foundation get that way? If it's shaky, then almost certainly you violated guideline number one, biting off more house transpositions and interaspects than you could chew–and digest. How do you fix it? Back up. Start over again, simplifying your approach. Astrology is half science, half art. If you've come this far without your heart fluttering a little, then science is the fat kid on the seesaw and the poor skinny artist in you is stuck in midair. Feed him!

Ready to go on? Then finish your tea, put aside the birthcharts and the Worksheet, and get out the composite chart.

"Guideline Number Six: With both birthcharts understood individually and with analysis of their interaspects and house transpositions completed, push that information aside temporarily and turn your attention to the composite chart."

You have two close friends, Terry and Suzanne. Both of them have big hearts–and loud mouths. Even though they have a lot in common, you've never thought of introducing them. It's not that you think they'd respond badly to each other, more that the quality of your bond with each one is so different that the meeting would be awkward. With Terry you really cut loose. One of the reasons you like her so much is that you can say anything that comes to mind. With her, your speech would embarrass a sailor, your opinions are more passionate, your stories longer. You enjoy that playful spontaneity and so does she. Trouble is, whenever you get together, half your friends consider leaving town. For many of them, the composite entity that you two create together is about as attractive as a wet Irish setter at a fancy French restaurant.

Suzanne, your second friend, is just as outspoken as Terry and every bit as outrageous. But your bond with her has an entirely different tone. With Suzanne your pattern is to hole up together for hours over coffee, talking seriously. You are counselors to each other. Spiritual advisers. You've known her for years and think of her as one of your dearest friends. But when you throw a party, the idea of inviting her never crosses your mind. That's not the way your friendship works. The entity that you and Suzanne compose together is reclusive, introverted, psychological, perhaps even misanthropic. Its character is completely different from Terry-and-you, despite the fact that there are pronounced parallels in the personalities of the two women.

If you can empathize with the principle behind this story–that the **whole** of a partnership is more complex than the **sum** of the personalities involved–then you are well on your way to grasping the meaning of the composite chart. Even though Terry and Suzanne have much in common, the chemistry that arises as you pair off with each of them is unique. The role of the composite chart is to describe that chemistry with great precision.

Composite charts do more than describe. They also prescribe. Just like individual birthcharts, they suggest certain kinds of experiential "vitamins" that help feed the partnership, bringing out the best of what it is, nourishing its development. They also warn of poisons to which the partnership is susceptible, those diets of beer and cotton candy that may tempt us but which lead only to starvation.

You and Terry, stuck on a desert island, might drive each other loony in less than a week. That kind of claustrophobic intimacy is your version of beer and cotton candy. With Suzanne, you might get along splendidly there. The entity you create with Terry thrives on brief doses of rambunctious contact. (Your composite chart shows the Sun and five planets in Sagittarius in the fifth house, with Leo rising: mud wrestling, not desert islands.) The entity you form with Suzanne prefers isolation and inwardness. For you, that Robinson Crusoe lifestyle is as healthy as carrot juice and green vegetables. When a ship appears on the horizon, you might both run and hide. (Together, you show a strong composite Saturn and concentrations of planets in houses four, eight, and twelve.)

If the reasoning behind any of these ideas is vague to you, before proceeding any further you might want to go back and review chapters Ten and Eleven.

Composite Charts in Practice

Begin your survey of the composite chart with a simple trick: Forget for a moment that it's a composite chart. Treat it like a birthchart. Pretend that it's an astrological description of an individual–a two-legged, air-breathing spiritual monkey like yourself. Build a picture in your head, imagining a person born with these motifs, then translate that picture into terms appropriate to composite charts. How? Simply by erasing that imaginary person's body! (Don't worry, he'll never know what hit him.)

After you've established an empathic link with the chart by thinking of it in familiar human terms, you've very nearly gone the distance. All that remains is to recognize that you're not really talking about a person, but rather a kind of invisible Casper the Friendly Ghost who hovers in the space between the two people whose charts you're unraveling and whispers in their ears.

Just as in the interpretation of a normal birthchart, when it comes to composites, you need to be wary of overextension. Better really to internalize only the primal triad than to frazzle your nervous system trying to figure out a witty one-liner for every planet and every aspect.

A few pages back, under guideline number three, we covered a set of procedures designed to help you quickly analyze individual birthcharts. In essence we presented a schematic way of customizing your interpretive strategy to fit your own personal level of astrological skill and confidence. Use that same approach with the composite chart. If anything, be even more conservative with your energy. What you're aiming for is only an impression. Just a feeling for the diet that best feeds old Casper, and an awareness of his special vulnerabilities.

Once you've gotten the sense of the composite chart...you guessed it: teatime. Put your feet up and take a few moments to consider the broad outlines of the situation you've uncovered. Don't make the mistake of rushing headlong into a fragmented analysis of astrological details. You'll miss the big picture that way.

How does the tone of the composite chart compare with the tones of the two individual birthcharts? Think in the broadest, simplest terms available. At this point you're not comparing specific configurations. Instead, you are comparing your general impressions of the three charts.

Is the composite chart extroverted and experience-oriented? Does it therefore have more in common with Jill's birthchart than with Jack's? Then the relationship between the two partners and the entity they create can be characterized as a **Feudal System**. That is, the composite chart sides with one partner over the other, leading to a potentially dangerous imbalance. For such a bond to remain healthy, the empowered partner must make a conscious effort to be generous and compassionate, insuring that his or her mate's needs are met. At the same time, the disempowered partner needs to be equally generous and compassionate, avoiding the posture of "victim," locked into blaming and criticizing the mate for "insensitivity" or "authoritarianism."

Perhaps the composite chart reflects elements of each person's character. It might, for example, support Jill's hunger for adventure in exotic places, while simultaneously underscoring Jack's need for many hours of private time with his lover each week. Then the politics among the two individuals and their composite personality can be described as **Democracy**. This is the easiest and most common of situations, but nothing astrological can be assumed to be automatically wonderful–or automatically dreadful. Everything depends ultimately upon choices people make within each planetary environment. The trick, in democracy, lies in the definition of appropriate spheres of influence for each partner. If Jill, in other words, has to wait for Jack to suggest a trip to Greece, she might wait a very long time. In the meantime, Jack-and-Jill could starve. As a couple they need that trip. Nurturing the adventuresome aspect of their relationship naturally falls in Jill's province. For the good of their partnership she needs to be granted considerable authority there. Similarly, Jack's nature is such that he is vastly more alert than Jill to the appearance of those subtle fissures and tensions that arise when the couple has been overextended socially and needs to cuddle up in bed for a day. When he shows up with a handful of murder mysteries, a bottle of champagne, and a bag of croissants, Jill needs to bow to his greater wisdom in this area and abandon her plans for volleyball that day.

There is a third possibility. Perhaps the composite chart introduces entirely alien concepts, foreign to the natures of both individuals. This situation we characterize as **Culture Shock**. Maybe, if left to their own devices, neither Jack nor Jill would ever put much energy into playing a role in their community. But their composite chart shows a triple conjunction of the Sun, Pluto, and Jupiter in the tenth house. If their bond is to survive happily, Jack-and-Jill must take some public stand. Perhaps they work together, sharing a career. Perhaps they become involved with the Greenpeace organization or with a local political campaign. The point is that their partnership thrives on a kind of input that neither of them needs as individuals. Astrology is a powerful ally in such a situation. Although the two lovers might successfully follow their instincts and find that common ground without astrological support, a glance at their composite chart might instantly bring those vague instincts into explicit awareness, saving them a lot of angst.

These three "political" situations–the Feudal System, Democracy, and Culture Shock–are of course schematic simplifications. Just head games. That's exactly why they are so helpful. Although no partnership is likely to fit any such scenario flawlessly, by organizing your thinking around one of these three models, you encourage the kind of broad, pattern-seeking analysis that's characteristic of effective astrology.

If you need a booster shot in the area of how composite charts and birthcharts come to terms with each other, we encourage you to review Chapter Eleven.

Whole-Brained Astrology

Imagine that Mae West, Miss Manners, and the Lone Ranger got stuck in an elevator together. What would happen? We don't know either, but like you, we could certainly speculate. Those personalities are vivid ones. All of us have a feeling for each one of them, a sense of their values, their styles, what makes them tick. We can't help but smile when we imagine the situation that trio would create–the possible alliances, the inevitable ruffled feathers, the misunderstandings, the truces.

Mae West. Miss Manners. The Masked Man. Something inside you has registered ten million minuscule details about each person and converted those details into a feeling. That's the form in which your psyche stores its impressions. When we say "Mae West" or "Miss Manners," those stored feelings are immediately invoked in you. Instantly the wholeness of the person is called up in your mind's eye. Similarly, if we mention the Lone Ranger, you first intuit a framework of emotions, a certain posture in life. Only later does your brain flesh out that framework with reminders about silver bullets, days of yesteryear, and a well-manicured Indian by the name of Tonto.

The juxtaposition of those three disparate characters in the incongruous circumstances of a stalled elevator probably made you smile. If so, great. The world can always use another smile. But the purpose behind our employing that humorous image is a serious one. We want to demonstrate that in reacting to that scenario, your brain accomplished something quite remarkable. In a few milliseconds it successfully correlated three complex and unrelated bodies of information and placed them in an alien context. It also instantly began generating models of all the possible outcomes of their interaction. And in its spare time, your brain took a moment to make an aesthetic response: it decided that there was something funny about this particular alignment of information.

What's more amazing, you didn't need to be Albert Einstein to get the joke. Almost anyone familiar with the basic mythology of our culture is capable of digesting that image and reacting to it.

When people lament that "astrology is too hard for them," what they're really saying is that their approach is wrong. They're trying to do something with their conscious intellects that really calls for the use of their entire brain. Walking is hard too–if you try to do it on your fingers.

"Guideline Number Seven: The astrological symbols serve only one purpose: to convey a body of information to the heart where it can be felt, interpreted, and returned to conscious awareness in the form of compassionate insight."

The heart, in other words, does most of the work. But you won't have to teach your heart anything new in order to have success with synastry. Why? Because your heart's already had many years of training. Every time it's loved or hated, laughed or cried, it's learned something about how to breathe life into the astrological symbols.

The successful astrologer does not bypass the intellect. To be whole-brained we have to use our intelligence as well as our emotions. That astrologer has done the homework, learning by rote all the details and procedures of this ancient technology. But that astrologer knows **why** he or she went to all that trouble. Once the language of astrology is absorbed, it can speak directly to the heart. Then the heart can work its magic, plugging astrology into a storehouse of wisdom and experience far too variegated for intellect to encompass. How? Exactly like the more familiar human processes by which we got to know Mae West, Miss Manners, and the Lone Ranger–by reading the signals of body language, facial gestures, and voice inflections. Except that now those inflections and gestures are planetary configurations.

Ultimately, what's the difference between "a suspicious glance" and "Mercury conjunct Saturn in Scorpio in the first house"?

Only that your brain has a lot more experience decoding and digesting suspicious glances.

Practice is the key. Practice and patience. Persistence too. Your heart has had time to learn body language. Astrology, although just as rich, is less familiar. You've got to stick with it awhile, giving the symbols time to mesh with your own inner vocabulary.

Begin teaching your whole brain to use astrological language by learning the technicalities, the ins and outs of astrology as a logical system. Then try to gather as much experience as you can. Press your friends to come up with their birthtimes. Set up their birthcharts. Those people are a gold mine for you. Since they're your friends, you already have an emotional reaction to them. Your heart already senses them, in other words. Now all you have to do is peer at them through the filters of their charts. That way you'll learn to associate the human feelings you already possess with astrological structures.

Another productive strategy is to study the birthcharts of well-known people. You may understand in an abstract way that the fifth house has something to do with pleasure–but when you discover that Marie Antoinette ("Let them eat cake!") had her Sun and Moon there, your understanding takes on a new dimension! You may also realize that the deepest fifth-house pleasures arise when we tap into our capacities for creative self-expression. But knowing that composer Maurice Ravel also had his Sun and Moon in that house gives that realization substance. See our list of "Suggestions for Further Reading" in the Appendix–several compendia of interesting birthcharts are included there.

Stick with it. Go slowly. Never be too embarrassed to retreat to simpler levels of astrological analysis. Don't be intimidated by the labyrinthine intellectual complexity of the system. Seven times out of ten, even a professional astrologer bases interpretations on a few simple, bedrock feelings about a birthchart.

Give astrology time, trust yourself, and before you know it, you'll find yourself getting misty over the way your lover's Venus makes that delicate trine to your weary Saturn, just as if he or she had sent you a love poem. When that happens, your heart has learned the most ancient language the earth has ever known. And you can call yourself an astrologer.

BORDER WARS

J. C. Eaglesmith is an American Indian, a holder of the Sacred Pipe, a veteran of the ordeal known as the Sun Dance. He is a former Marine who served in combat in Vietnam. He weighs maybe 250 pounds and most of it's muscle. He played professional football and looks it. In short, when it comes to "masculinity," he makes the average street-corner bullyboy look like your grandmother's knitting.

He stood before us at a conference not long ago, talking about "male" and "female" and what those words really mean. His eyes steady, his face impassive, he addressed us in a deep baritone. "I am half woman." A moment's pause, a hint of a smile, then: "My mother was one."

We all laughed. So did J. C. But what he said was true. Physically he is a man. But that just diagrams his plumbing. Once we recognize that a human being is far more than a mass of cells and bones, we enter the realm of mystery. And in that realm no one is so simple as a beard or a breast.

Humanity is realizing this, and it's knocking the stilts out from under a picture of the world that's held us in thrall for ten thousand years. "I am half woman." "I am half man." Those words represent a revolution just as profound as the discovery that the Earth is a sphere floating in the void.

Male and female. What do the words really signify? Apart from obvious physical differences, perhaps no one really knows. Women cry more than men. But why? Are women inherently more emotional or have they been trained that way? Men are more aggressive. Why? No one knows. Nature and nurture are inseparable. Each of us is an amalgam. What we are intrinsically blends seamlessly with what we have been taught to think we are.

Quagmires of social mythology surround us from birth. Winnowing the essential Self out of those quagmires is perhaps the core purpose of astrology. As we learn to decipher the birthchart, we recognize an individual's elemental nature and help free it from the deadening sinkholes of blind conformity and hero worship. That's how astrology works for individuals. Can it perform a similar winnowing on the scale of nations and societies? Can astrology help us clarify the difference between the mind of woman and the mind of man?

Traditional astrology books, written in times when people were dogmatically certain about sex roles, often contain differing interpretations of the same configurations depending on the person's gender. "In the chart of a man, Mars in Aquarius means..." The problem is that there's no way, looking at a birthchart, to discern whether that chart belongs to a woman or a man. They look the same. In their time, those Victorian astrologers may have been doing accurate work. But they may also have been mistaking whimsies of Victorian society for immutable laws of the universe.

The Moon with its sensitivity has traditionally been viewed as "feminine." The Sun with its charisma has been seen as "masculine." But even proper, blue-haired dowagers in the garden club respond to the Sun, while their huffing, puffing husbands down at the Moose Lodge know the touch of the Moon. No human being is immune to the energies of any of the planets. If you're alive, you're playing ping-pong with all ten of them

Does astrology, arguably the truest mirror in humanity's possession, suggest that there are no psychic or spiritual differences between men and women? Hard to say. Truth is, astrology's rather mum on the subject. But it certainly tells us loud and clear that, whatever those differences might be, we've spent a lot of years and a lot of lives overestimating and misdefining them. Every man has a Moon. Every woman has a

Sun. One of the darkest skeletons in astrology's closet is the fact that astrologers were not the first to point that out.

How come? Why weren't astrologers quicker to see the unnaturalness of parceling out parts of human consciousness according to gender? Nature versus nurture again. Those astrologers lived, as the rest of our ancestors did, in a world where women were encouraged to be creatures of the Moon– emotional, caring, timid, fond of hearth and home–while men were given the realm of the Sun: power, reason, character, adventure, accomplishment. Our forebears, astrologers included, swallowed that lie with gusto.

Perhaps there was a payoff. Perhaps this devil's bargain of dividing human consciousness into so-called "feminine" and "masculine" functions served a purpose. A radical feminist might argue that this schism was Man's way of disempowering Woman, keeping her dependent and weak. A radical "masculinist"–if there were any–might counter that Woman created the schism in order to shift an unfair, insufferable burden of practical responsibility to Man, thereby condemning him to eternally higher rates of suicide, alcoholism, and stress-related diseases. Meanwhile, the couch potatoes watching the debate on television might shrug and say, "That's just how God made us," then change the channel. And who knows? Maybe they're right.

Still...we have cryptic evidence in the sky. Sun and Moon shine down on all of us, whether we start the morning with shaving cream or a choice of skirts. And if there's anything to astrology, then Sun and Moon resonate somehow in every one of us–unless we collude in the ancient deception.

One point is sure–life is twice as easy if you only have to face half of it. Maybe **that's** the payoff. Maybe feminist rage and macho haughtiness are nothing but camouflage. Maybe it's laziness, not sexual politics, that lies at the bottom of the schism.

Men kill. Women cook. Men make war. Women make babies. It's an old story, but let's look at it in a different way. Imagine killing! Forget codes of honor, waving flags, the stirring lies old men tell young men. Just imagine killing. Destroying life. It's ugly, bloody. Especially with primitive weapons. Something visceral in us cries out against it. Yet warring and hunting have been with humanity since the beginning. And the responsibility for those processes fell to men. Why? Because men are bigger and stronger. And what did ancient man do with the pain that entered him when he killed? What did he do with the sickness in his stomach? What in other words did he do with his Moon? He denied it! The killer can have no Moon, not and still kill.

Man could not endure his Moon, so he thrust it upon Woman. Let her be the one to quake and cry and feel.

Woman, meanwhile, found herself pregnant. In a world where most children died in infancy, survival depended upon her ability to nurture. Imagine it! If you could go back in time to the caves of Lascaux or Altamira and look into such a woman's eyes, what would you see? An animal? No: you'd see depth and soul and intelligence. A human being. And she faced a task that would put tears in the eyes of the bravest man. In the cold light of impossibility and endless death, she had to hold that infant in her arms and try to keep the spark of life glowing. How could she bear it? Foolishly we might imagine that she hardened herself. But that idea doesn't stand up to scrutiny. If primitive woman hardened herself, then she'd fail as a nurturer. How can a hardened person return to the crying, dying child again and again? What would be the motivation?

Woman, no matter how bitterly difficult a life she endured, had to set aside her natural human selfishness and accept her lot as mother and healer. She needed, in other words, to set aside her Sun. Woman had to love, lest humanity die. But what about the part of her that was just plain angry at her circumstances? What about the part of her that wanted to lash out at something–anything–as a primal release of rebellion and frustration? What about the part of her that hated her children for confining her? What about the part of her that hated her children for dying? Down the drain. Down into the nightside of human awareness, into the Unconscious. The nurturer can have no Sun, not and still make the enormous self-sacrifice of nurturing.

Woman surrendered her Sun, thrust it upon Man. Let him be the one to have enough pride and illusions of glory to rage against nature's heavy hand.

Humankind has been civilized for about one half of one percent of its history. Our assumptions about "male" and "female" are vastly more archaic–so archaic, in fact, that when we began to record ideas and establish cultures, the notions of male ferocity and female domesticity were already ancient, lodged firmly in what Carl Jung would call the "collective unconscious." To our ancestors it must have seemed that those scripts had been ordained by the gods. At any rate, we soon began to enforce them as though the Lord of the Universe had appeared only yesterday, insisting that men mimic His Glorious Works while women made sure dinner was on the table.

That myth is dying. We who live today are witnessing the collapse of a sexual myth whose roots are more primeval than memory. The usefulness of the myth ended some time ago, back when men stopped spending most of their time hunting and fighting and when women began living long and comfortably enough to do more than struggle with babies. But the myth has survived anyway, on momentum, right up until this century.

Good riddance? Yes, probably, but let's not underestimate the depth of the change. There's a lot more going on here than women getting jobs and men being allowed to shed a tear. No one's going to ride off into the Sunset anytime soon, with justice done, the bad guys in stir, and the good guys back on the ranch. When men recover the Moon and women the Sun, the earth moves beneath our feet. Familiar ground shifts precipitously. Antediluvian energies, long fossilized, are released in a shattering detonation.

Anger pours out. Old, bitter anger, long repressed. The anger of our foremothers and forefathers who were nailed to the wall by those mythologies. The anger of the female William Shakespeare whose voice was never heard. The anger of every soldier who saw a fearful reflection of himself in the eyes of his enemy just before he brought down the weight of the bloody ax.

Now, as the sexual paradigms shift, we see that anger manifesting among women in the more vitriolic branches of feminism. We see it in blind hostility toward men, the idea that men are insensitive and brutish, incapable of love. On the male side, we see that same anger manifesting even more primitively in the rise of violent pornography, the exponential rise of rape, and the adolescent hoots that assail any woman who walks down the street.

Perhaps the anger is inevitable. But anger is a cheap lens. It distorts anything we observe, magnifying hurts, diminishing complexities. Let's use a better microscope. Compassion. Let's imagine for a moment that humanity has been doing the best it could. The primal Man who shut down his feeling Moon in the face of the overwhelming fear and blood and death of his rough existence–was he wrong? The primal Woman who sacrificed her solar creativity and individuality so that she could pour her life into insuring the survival of the next generation–was she in error? If they were wrong, then humanity owes its presence in the world to their mistakes.

The problem is that the system worked too well. Like a neurotic spender with a brand-new credit card, we got hooked. Man projected his lunar side onto Woman. She projected her solar side onto him. Gradually, what originated as a practical psychological adjustment was no longer necessary or appropriate.

Those gender projections made life easier. A man lost his job; no problem: his woman could experience all the insecurities and frustrations on his behalf while he set about the task of finding another job. A woman's car broke down; no problem: her man would strain to experience the logic and power of repairing it while she felt all those emotions of self-doubt and confusion that he was too busy to feel. The practical world, in other words, became a male preserve. But women were not left out. The other side of life–the world of feeling and nurturing–was theirs. Marriage in trouble? Woman would feel the problem and help Man talk about it. Did Man look a little wan and flushed? Woman would ask him if he had a fever and cajole him into caring for himself. Child need a kind word? Go ask mommy.

Today, many women are rediscovering the Sun. It heals them, makes them whole. They are finding their solar power, their self-reliance, their voice, their creativity, their ability to shape the myths and symbols of society.

Meanwhile, men are beginning to rediscover the Moon. They too are healed and made whole as they reabsorb their own lost lunar capacity to love, to ask for help, to cry, to feel, to nurture.

That's the good news.

The bad news is that both women and men are terribly out of practice with their Suns and Moons. They don't know quite what to do with them. As the reintegration takes place, there is a period of awkwardness. Like a blind man whose vision has been restored, the acquisition of these "new" solar and lunar functions causes both sexes to spend a while bumping into things.

Women, as they claim the authority and self-reliance of the Sun, run the risk of becoming icy and dictatorial–picking up solar diseases, in other words. Unlike men, they have no clear role models, no tradition, even a flawed one, for dealing with those excesses. Some go too far and begin to lose their Moons, mimicking the madness of men. Others, more cautious, don't go far enough, and experience frustration, low self-esteem, and resentment as they fall short of the solar ideals.

Men, meanwhile, have no traditions or mythologies to help them make peace with their lunar sides. They risk drowning in the mysticism and subjectivity of their new-found Moons, becoming narcissistic, overly attentive to their own issues, crippled by "sensitivity." That, or they find themselves so submerged in lunar emotions that their characters deteriorate. They lose that ancient kingpin of the masculine solar myth: their sense of honor. No longer can they maintain commitments, resist temptations, and fulfill responsibilities. Spooked by the Moon, they begin to lose their Suns.

And those are the people on the cutting edge, the ones who actually wrestling with reintegration!

Naturally, among those most frightened by the collapse of the ancient system, a backlash arises. *The Total Woman*– motherly, obedient, vacant–dances in the *zeitgeist.* *Rambo*– fearless, insensitive, efficient at the hunt–wrestles the archetypal enemy. But increasingly those figures seem empty and quaint, comically nostalgic.

As humanity reclaims its solar-lunar totality, it is torn between an ill-defined, uncreated future and a burned-out past. We're a bit like a timid kid in her first week at an out-of-state college. Tempted to go home again. But we can't. We've outgrown that possibility. Men are raising children, going into psychotherapy, exploring forbidden "feminine" emotional territories. Women are flying in space, entering government, making their presence felt in science, art, and athletics. We can't go back–and we're not sure where forward **is** or what it looks like.

Compassion again. That's our clear lens. Our microscope. A million years of habit is a formidable adversary. Just breaking free of that is a Herculean task–and an Amazonian one.

What about those who have broken the archaic chain? Who are no longer reciting lines from the ancient script? Certainly such individuals exist–but their journey is only half behind them. Ahead lies the problem of creating the solar-lunar future. How does that future look? That's not an easy question. The possibilities are multitudinous. Will the old gender patterns endure in some modified way? Will men and women reverse roles? Will people feel free to be distinctly solar or lunar depending on their personal predilections? Is the future unisex? Is it correct to assume that the "optimum human being" balances solar and lunar qualities evenly? If such balance is possible, does it follow inevitably that there would be no practical role divisions based on gender? What, if anything, do the words "feminine" and "masculine" ultimately mean–and how much do they have to do with one's physical anatomy?

Dogmatic answers to these questions abound. But dogmatism is the shadow insecurity casts. The deeper truth is that no one really knows the answers yet, and that frightens us. Humanity, as a species, is undergoing an identity crisis.

Can astrology help resolve that identity crisis? Yes and no. On the negative side, no birthchart can carry an astrologer beyond the limitations imposed by his or her own unchallenged prejudices and assumptions. Fatalistic astrologers look at charts and see inescapable fate. Depressed ones see impossibility. Psychological ones see psychology. Spiritual ones see evolving souls. Everything depends upon viewpoint, in other words, and no astrologer who is already certain of the meanings of femininity and masculinity is likely to see much more than the vindication of his or her convictions.

But astrology can make a positive contribution to the healing of the schism in the human soul. Not by giving us ultimate answers, prefabricated and predigested. Rather by helping us to find answers ourselves. Astrology is, above all, a language. Like any language, its elemental purpose is to implement communication. Astrology's advantage over other languages is that it is optimized for communication of psychological information. In other words, if you want to ask an electrician how to rewire your refrigerator, stick to English. But if you want to ask your husband or wife or lover about some hot-wired dimension of your partnership, the language of astrology is unparalleled. No other system of symbols can approach it for delicacy of nuance or laser-like penetration.

Humanity today is in dire need of such a language. We have most of the information we need. Sun and Moon, male and female–they've been around a long time. The trouble is that all our information is tied up in neat little boxes, separately. We need to mix it up, see how it settles out. We're dying for some conversation.

Conversation between men and women, perhaps spurred and sharpened by astrology, can be part of the solution. But we must recognize that the schism between the sexes is a symptom of a far deeper rift: the one that sundered individual human psyches a million years ago when men fled the Moon and women surrendered the Sun. The conversation, in other words, originates privately, in the shadowy recesses of every modern mind. And from there it proceeds into the world of intimacy.

Nor should the conversation stop there. The same rift that divides lunar female and solar male also splits the world into poets and rationalists, mystics and scientists, feelers and thinkers. Half-wits all. One half of human consciousness developed and emphasized; the other half banished to the shadows.

Rift or no, the planets spin above us impersonally, much as they did in the days of the Neanderthals. They pass through the same signs, make the same aspects, travel the same twelve houses. Midtown Manhattan or Olduvai Gorge, it makes no difference. Astrology, like death and food and love, is one of those human constants.

Or is it? Only partly so. The truth is that astrology can, at best, provide only half the picture. Astrological forces interact with something far less constant: human consciousness, with its endless creativity and changing social patterns. Astrology may remind us of the archetypal outlines of sanity and wholeness, but within that outline humanity writes its own lines.

Those who use astrological language today–especially those who practice synastry–must recognize the changing framework of ideas through which humanity perceives itself and makes sense of its sexuality. That's the other half of the picture. The planets may be constant, but men and women are not. Were a medieval astrologer to slip through a crack in time and try to establish a synastry practice in modern San Francisco, he'd be half crazy before he even figured out how to **talk** to people. He might know something about astrology in the abstract, but how to **apply** astrology to its primary task as a medium of communication in the modern era–of that, he would know nothing.

As our time-traveling astrologer got his bearings and began to practice synastry, one of his most shocking realizations would be our divorce rate. There was plenty of sex where he came from, both inside and outside marriage, but marriage itself was bedrock. Happy or otherwise, not much could shake it. Why? The answer lies with yet another seductive side effect of the sexual schism between Sun and Moon: it had a remarkably stabilizing effect upon marriage. An artificial dependency was created between men and women, one that went far beyond natural attraction. A woman simply could not survive alone; that at least was the myth. She could not support herself, protect herself, even think for herself. Similarly, a man on his own would fall–theoretically–into sickness, squalor, and moral turpitude. Who would see to his nutrition? Who would patch his socks? Who would prevent him from becoming an alcoholic? Sun cannot live without Moon. Moon cannot survive without Sun. As long as one sex cornered either market, marriage left the realm of choice and entered the realm of necessity.

By gender-dividing the skills that are necessary to the maintenance of life, our ancestors–and in many cases our parents–created a phony neediness between women and men. Any astrologer who accepts that same division today is as out of place as our medieval time-traveler. In the old view so many of the intimacy concerns that motivate modern people– concerns such as personal growth, sexual fulfillment, and keeping the magic alive–took a back seat to merely maximizing a couple's capacity to tolerate each other's presence. Strategic silences arose; lies were agreed upon; worlds were kept separate. In distance there was peace.

Stay together or die: that, in a nutshell, was the old formula.

Many "modern" astrology texts slavishly repeat those medieval principles, as if that formula still had widespread relevance. "Good" interaspects–trines and sextiles–are seen as "positive omens" for marriage. Why? Because they are quiet! Squares and oppositions are treated like bloody handwriting on the wall. How come? Because those aspects indicate a pressing need for communication! Sweet-tempered, oil-on-the-waters Venus had better shine brightly in the linkages between the birthcharts. Otherwise the couple plays a perilous game: they face their clashes squarely without bailing out into politeness and empty rituals of forgiveness– dangerous business if mere stability is our aim. And if solitary Saturn or confrontive Mars should rear their hideous heads in those birthcharts, then you'd better hope the bride knows a good lawyer.

Silliness. The first principle we must remember in recreating synastry for the modern era is that **people** are free. No astrological configuration guarantees failure or success, perpetual antagonism or endless orgasm. Personal commitment–a question of solar honor–and openness to personal growth–a question of lunar sensitivity–are the critical ingredients. Given enough of those qualities, any partnership can operate in a satisfactory way, regardless of how the birthcharts are configured.

The second principle to remember is that **conflict** can be a positive force. Back when the consequences of divorce were so dire, honest, soul-penetrating conflict became taboo. It was too dangerous to tolerate. Inevitably conflict still developed. But it was released indirectly and symbolically in peevishness and irrelevant arguments. Men would "get" women by patronizing them. Women would "get" men with moodiness and bitchiness. Solar weapons and lunar weapons. Such gambits release rage. But they never address the source of the rage. That source is left untouched, ready to explode anew whenever the ground trembles.

The majority of the people who come to us for astrological counsel today are women. The ratio is not as dramatic as it once was, maybe sixty/forty. But it's consistent. Most of the men whom we see come to us open-mindedly, but only after having been encouraged to make the appointment by a woman.

The pattern is no quirk. Doctors, psychotherapists, most people in helping professions–all report the same picture. Women are more willing to ask for help than are men. The nurturers, in other words, know how to nurture themselves as well as others. Even in a field such as astrology, which, because of its reputation, selects for a clientele that is more independent, iconoclastic, and plain curious than the norm, women outnumber men. An administrator at the New York Open Center, a teaching forum receptive to controversial subjects, put it bluntly. She said, "The New Age is female."

Why? What's happened to the men? Gone fishing. Gone hunting. Males, or least a significant proportion of them, are still hooked into the solar-dominated mythology that allows no room

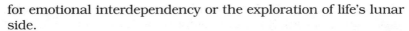

for emotional interdependency or the exploration of life's lunar side.

But as we've seen, the basis for that myth eroded long ago. It's been running on empty, running on momentum alone, for centuries. Men are breaking out of it, but not in such great numbers as women. The reason behind the pattern is extraordinarily simple. The reintegration of lunar and solar qualities is fundamentally a psychological change. The forces that propel it originate in the psyche, that is, in the subjective, lunar world. And who's been left in charge of that dimension of life? Women! Naturally they'd be the first to **feel** that something was fundamentally wrong with the way we were living. Thus, feminism precedes masculinism. Reason would predict it, and history bears it out. Woman precedes Man into the subjective realm, just as surely as Man has preceded Woman into the objective realm of space flight, and for similar reasons.

Is astrology "feminine"? In the archaic view of the word, yes— in that mental framework, anything that pertains to the inward, emotive side of life is "feminine." Poet Robert Bly, in his provocative essay "I Came Out of the Mother Naked," calls astrology "the great intellectual triumph of the Mother civilization." He postulates an era previous to the present patriarchal civilizations in which matriarchy held sway on earth. Astrology, with its "feminine" emphasis upon humanity's mutual interpenetration with nature, arose naturally in that intellectual climate— and was anathema to the later patriarchy with its emphasis upon objective conquest and control.

So the same tide that washes feminism into human consciousness also washes in an astrological renaissance, and a renaissance in other "feminine" arts, such as poetry, psychology, and mysticism.

Are men left out? That's a key question. Some women seek to exclude men from the renaissance, as if access to the Moon were limited to those with wide hips and hairless faces. Madness. Men, freed of the ancient schism, are creatures of Moon and Night just as much as women. Astrology—and "feminism"—work for everyone. Those men who fear them fear their own Moons. They are victims of the ancient lie. Those women who seek to possess it exclusively for their gender fall into the ancient solar disease of dominance, control, and obsession with territory. In recovering their Suns, they have succumbed to them. Either way, the real goal–the restoration of our lost wholeness–is missed.

Male or female, if you've read this book, you can call yourself a student of astrology. As such, you hold something precious. A blueprint for sanity. A link to the primordial feminine–and to the primordial masculine. Above all, you hold a language, a basis for communication. But not a language like English or Russian or French, with all their built-in assumptions about gender. In astrology there are no loaded words such as "mankind," "effeminate," or "ladylike." Nothing but the raw language of life, newborn and primitive. Try to keep it like that. Try to resist the reflexive tendency to look at astrology through the eyes of your culture. You can't resist that tendency entirely, of course. But make the effort. Astrology's great asset is its capacity to address what is natural in us, both as unique individuals and as human beings. If we allow the arbitrary values of our society to influence our view of the symbols too deeply, we've compromised astrology's objectivity and clarity.

Such compromise would be a loss under any circumstances, but that's especially so today. At this point in our history we need all the clarity we can muster. "Feminine" and "masculine," long separate, are converging. Along with them, other parallel convergences are taking place. In discovering quantum physics and Einsteinian relativity, humanity has set the stage for the convergence of science and mysticism. In creating the "global village" we are creating a convergence of Industrial and Third World cultures–another marriage of "masculine" and "feminine." With computer, cinema, and electronic musical instruments, we are developing art forms in which lunar imagination must converge with solar logic. Environmentalism reflects the same pattern: the lunar urge to nurture the earth is inextricably tied to solar ideals of scientific analysis and planning. The list is long. We live in an age of revolutions, all of which reflect perhaps the greatest single revolution humanity has ever known: the healing of the schism between Sun and Moon.

Astrologers–you and we–are in a unique position to promote that healing. With our precise language we can promote communication and reconciliation between the estranged parts of each individual.

Recognizing the diseases of our times, we astrologers can speak supportively to women regarding the "masculine" parts of their birthcharts. We can help them make peace with Mars and Uranus and the Sun, while inspiring them with new respect for their socially devalued lunar instincts.

We can speak gently, coaxingly to men about the Moon, Venus, and Neptune, encouraging them to nourish and strengthen those "feminine" dimensions of their own beings– without sacrificing their solar sense of initiative and honor.

If we remain true to the symbolism, reading it in innocence, wary of biases, we astrologers can use our craft to help ease people back into balance, into the pleasure and freedom of wholeness.

Marriage is perhaps the most perfect incubator for the reconciliation of Sun and Moon. But that reconciliation is a fiery, explosive process. Those who marry today, or who make any similar commitment, are on the front lines. With time-honored mythologies collapsing all around their ears, such individuals are left with little but their own creativity to rescue them. Old answers are exploding like so many skyrockets. New answers are not yet invented.

Synastry can help them. A man and a woman who dare to form a bond in the contemporary world are on humanity's cutting edge. If their experiment is to be successful, communication is essential, both within their own individualities and between them. To suggest that they couldn't succeed without astrology would be misleading; but to suggest that they can't succeed without dialogue is certain. Dialogue–communication–is the heart of reconciliation.

If you choose to practice synastry, trust the symbols. Begin by letting them guide you deeper into yourself. Whatever your gender, find your maleness, find your femaleness. Let the inner dialogue commence.

Then look up from the astrology books. Lift your eyes and face the source of it all: the sky. What do you see? Two great Lights. Sun and Moon. Mysterious. Enigmatic. But identical in their apparent size! Let those Lights be the same size in you too. Then you've tuned your instrument of perception, brought it into harmony with the message of the heavens. With your instrument tuned, with heart and mind open, you are ready to speak the healing language of synastry in this wondrous, uncertain age.

APPENDICES

HOW TO SET UP
A COMPOSITE CHART

If doing arithmetic is wedged in between Nuclear Holocaust and learning Chinese on your to-be-avoided list, then we suggest you skip ahead to the next section–"How to Avoid Setting Up a Composite Chart." Otherwise, read on. You'll be surprised at how easy it is.

Provided that you already have copies of the two birthcharts, setting up a composite chart doesn't require much equipment– just an ordinary birthchart blank, an atlas, and a Table of Houses (see the "Tools of the Trade" section, page 269, for a lead on the latter). If you don't have copies of the birthcharts, then please refer back to *The Inner Sky* for detailed instructions for calculating them–or look at the next section.

Composite charts are based on *midpoints*. Once you understand how to derive them, then the rest is a cinch. Say a planet lies in the beginning of Capricorn. Another planet lies at the end of Capricorn. Then their midpoint–the point halfway between them–is in the middle of Capricorn. That's the concept. The rest is just fine-tuning.

Frankie's Sun lies in fourteen degrees of Aries. Annette's Sun is in eight degrees of Virgo. What is their midpoint? Start by visualizing the wheel of signs. Your first step is to determine exactly how many degrees separate the two Suns. Immediately you'll notice that there are really two answers to that question depending on whether you travel the long way around the circle or the short way. In calculating midpoints, always consider the shorter, more acute angle. How many complete signs lie between Aries and Virgo? Look at the wheel—there's Taurus, Gemini, Cancer, Leo. Four signs. Each one is thirty degrees wide, so right away we see that a total of 120 degrees separate those two Suns, plus fragments of Aries and Virgo. How far is it from fourteen degrees of Aries to the end of the sign? Aries is thirty degrees wide, so that leaves sixteen degrees. And from the beginning of Virgo to eight degrees of Virgo? Eight more degrees. So, to know the full distance between those Suns, we must add sixteen degrees plus eight degrees to 120 degrees. That comes to 144 degrees.

What is the midpoint of Frankie's Sun and Annette's Sun? Half of 144 degrees is 72 degrees. Add seventy-two to the position of Frankie's Sun, and you've got your answer. (You could equally well subtract the same figure from the position of Annette's Sun, but addition is simpler.) How exactly do you add seventy-two degrees to Frankie's Sun? The easiest way is to break seventy-two down into signs and degrees. Remembering that each sign is thirty degrees wide, seventy-two degrees equals two full signs, plus twelve degrees. Frankie's Sun lies in fourteen degrees Aries. Two signs farther, we come to fourteen Gemini. (Again, look at the wheel if you're fuzzy about how to visualize the signs.) Twelve degrees farther, we arrive at twenty-six degrees of Gemini—and that's the answer. What you've just calculated is the position of Frankie's and Annette's *composite Sun*, which is simply the midpoint of their personal Suns.

If you understand the previous couple of paragraphs, you've grasped the mathematical tool that allows you to derive composite charts.

Here's the procedure:

1. Calculate the composite Midheaven–that is, the Midpoint of the Midheavens of the two birth-charts.

2. Enter the Table of Houses on the page associated with that composite Midheaven degree, and read out the cusps for the latitude of the place where the couple first met. That gives you the composite Ascendant and intervening house cusps.

3. Write those cusps on the birthchart blank.

4. Calculate the composite Sun, as we did in our example. Enter it on the birthchart blank in the appropriate house.

5. Repeat Step 4 with the Moon and each of the planets.

6. Calculate aspects and enter them on the aspect grid.

And that's your composite chart.

HOW TO AVOID CALCULATING A COMPOSITE CHART

Or any other kind of chart for that matter.

We have a computer that's programmed to do astrological calculations. We'll be happy to set up any kind of chart for you, from individual birthcharts up to and including composites. Write to us for a price list.

Our addresses are:

> Alpha Lyra Astrological Services
> P. O. Box 2345
> Chapel Hill, NC 27515-2345
>
> Astro Communications Services, Inc.
> P. O. Box 34487
> San Diego, CA 92163-4487
> 1-800-888-9983

If you're a more advanced astrologer and want computerized progressions, solar returns, or relocation charts, or if you're interested in personalized chart interpretations or tapes of astrological classes, drop us a note.

For the Synastry Worksheets mentioned in this book, query Alpha Lyra for prices.

SUGGESTIONS FOR
FURTHER READING

Tools of the Trade

The Concise Planetary Ephemeris for 1050-2000 (or *for 1900 to 1950*). Hieratic Publishing Company, 1977.

The American Ephemeris for the 20th Century–1900 to 2000 (Revised Fifth Edition). ACS Publications (available in both noon and midnight editions).

Dalton, Joseph G. *The Spherical Basis of Astrology*. Macoy, 1893 (Placidus Table of Houses).

The American Book of Tables. ACS Publications (Placidus Table of Houses).

The International Atlas: World Latitudes, Longitudes, and Time Changes (Revised Third Edition). ACS Publications, 1991.

The American Atlas: US Latitudes and Longitudes, Time Changes, and Time Zones (Expanded Fifth Edition). ACS Publications, 1990.

Also for keeping current, try:

The Association for Astrological Networking (AFAN) Newsletter.
8306 Wilshire Blvd., #537, Beverly Hills, CA 90211
Aspects: A Quarterly Astrological Magazine. P. O. Box 556,
Encino, CA 91426
The Astrological Journal. Bay Villa, Plymouth Rd., Totnes, Devon
TQ9 5PQ, England.
Astrotalk. Matrix Software, 315 Marion Ave., Big Rapids, MI
49307
Considerations. P. O. Box 491, Mount Kisco, NY 10549.
Geocosmic News: The National Council for Geocosmic Research
Newsletter. 78 Hubbard Ave., Stamford, CT 06905
Kosmos: The Quarterly Publication of ISAR. P. O. Box 38613, Los
Angeles, CA 90038.
The Mercury Hour. 3509 Waterlick Rd., C-7, Lynchburg, VA
24502
The Mutable Dilemma. 838 Fifth Ave., Los Angeles, CA 90005
Planet Watch. 319 West 18th St., New York, NY 10011.
Transit. 24 Birchington Ct., West End Lane, London NW6 4PB,
Great Britain.
*Welcome to Planet Earth: A Journal of the New Astrology in the
Contemporary World.* Great Bear Press, P. O. Box
5164, Eugene, OR 97405

Basic Books

Addey, John. *Harmonic Anthology.* Cambridge Circle, 1976.
Alexander, Roy. *The Astrology of Choice.* Weiser, 1983
Arroyo, Stephen. *Astrology, karma, and Transformation.* CRCS
Publications, 1978.
_____. *Astrology, Psychology, and the Four Elements.* CRCS
Publications, 1975.
_____. *The Practice and Profession of Astrology.* CRCS
Publications, 1984.
_____. *Relationships and Life-Cycles.* CRCS Publications,
1979.
Arroyo, Stephen, and Liz Greene. *The Jupiter-Saturn Conference
Lectures.* CRCS Publications, 1983.

Ashman, Bernie. *Astrological Games People Play.* ACS
        Publications, 1986.
Busteed, Tiffany, Wergin. *Phases of the Moon.* Shambala, 1974.
Carter, Charles E. O. *The Astrological Aspects.* Fowler, 1930.
_____. *The Principles of Astrology.* Theosophical, 1925.
Collin, Rodney. *The Theory of Celestial Influence.* Shambala,
        1984 (reissue).
_____. *Theory of Eternal Life.* Watkins, 1974 Shambala, 1984,
        (reprint).
Cunningham, Donna. *An Astrological Guide to Self-Awareness.*
        CRCS Publications, 1978.
_____. *Being a Lunar Type in a Solar World.* Weiser, 1982.
_____. *Healing Pluto Problems.* Weiser, 1986.
Davison, Ronald. *Astrology.* Arco, 1963.
_____. *Synastry: Understanding Human Relationships Through
        Astrology.* ASI, 1977.
_____. *The Technique of Prediction.* London: Fowler, 1955.
Devore, Nicholas. *Encyclopedia of Astrology.* Crown, 1967
Dobyns, Zipporah. *Expanding Astrology's Universe.* ACS
        Publications, 1983
Epstein, Alan. *Psychodynamics of Inconjunctions.* Weiser, 1984.
Erlewine, Michael and Margaret. *Astrophysical Directions.* Heart
        Center, 1977.
Erlewine, Michael. *Manual of Computer Programming for
        Astrologers.* AFA, 1980.
Forrest, Steven. *The Inner Sky.* ACS Publications, 1989.
_____. *The Changing Sky.* ACS Publications, 1989.
Freeman, Martin. *How to Interpret a Birthchart.* Aquarian, 1981.
Gauquelin, Michel. *Birthtimes.* Hill and Wang, 1983.
_____. *Cosmic Influences on Human Behavior.* ASI, 1974
        (statistical evidence supportive of astrology).
_____. *The Gauquelin Book of American Charts.* ACS Publications,
        1981.
_____. *Scientific Basis of Astrology.* Stein and Day, 1969.
Goodavage, Joseph F. *Write Your Own Horoscope.* World, 1968.
Green, Jeff. *Pluto, The Transformational Journey of the Soul.*
        Llewellyn, 1986.
Greene, Liz. *The Astrology of Fate.* Weiser, 1985.
_____. *The Outer Planets and Their Cycles.* CRCS Publications,
        1983.

_____. *Relating: An Astrological Guide to Living with Others on a Small Planet.* Weiser, 1977.

_____. *Saturn: A New Look at an Old Devil.* Weiser, 1976.

Greene, Liz and Howard Sasportas. *The Development of the Personality.* Weiser, 1987.

Hamaker-Zondag, Dr. Karen. *Analyzing Aspects.* Schors, 1987.

_____. *Astro-Psychology.* Schors, 1980.

_____. *Elements and Crosses as the Basis of the Horoscope.* Schors, 1984.

_____. *Houses and Personality Development.* Schors, 1986.

_____. *Planetary Symbolism in the Horoscope.* Schors, 1985.

Hand, Robert. *Essays on Astrology.* Para Research, 1982.

_____. *Horoscope Symbols.* Para Research, 1981.

_____. *Planets in Composite.* Para Research, 1975.

_____. *Planets in Transit.* Para Research, 1976.

_____. *Planets in Youth: Patterns of Early Development.* Para Research, 1977.

Jansky, Robert. *Astrology, Nutrition, and Health.* Para Research, 1977.

Jay, Delphine. *Practical Harmonics.* AFA, 1983.

Jones, Marc Edmund. *Guide to Horoscope Interpretation.* Theosophical, 1972.

_____. *How to Learn Astrology.* Doubleday, 1969

Leo, Alan. *The Art of Synthesis.* Fowler, 1968 (reissue).

Lewi, Grant. *Astrology for the Millions.* Bantam, 1940.

Lofthus, Myrna. *A Spiritual Approach to Astrology.* CRCS Publications, 1983.

Lundsted, Betty. *Astrological Insights Into Personality.* ACS Publications, 1980.

Marks, Tracy. *The Art of Chart Synthesis.* Sagittarius, 1979.

_____. *The Astrology of Self-Discovery.* CRCS Publications, 1985.

_____. *How to Handle Your T-Square.* Sagittarius, 1978.

_____. *Neptune: Illusion or Illumination.* Sagittarius, 1980.

_____. *Pluto: From Darkness Into Light.* Sagittarius, 1980.

_____. *Principles of Depth Astrology.* Sagittarius, 1980.

_____. *Transits: The Next Step in Our Becoming.* Sagittarius, 1980.

Meyer, Michael. *Handbook for the Humanistic Astrologer.* Anchor/Doubleday, 1974.

Oken, Alan. *Alan Oken's Complete Astrology.* Bantam, 1980.

Penfield, Marc. *An Astrological Who's Who.* Arcane, 1972 (a collection of several hundred birthcharts of well-known people).

_____. *Horoscopes of the Western Hemisphere.* ACS Publications, 1984.

Pottenger, Maritha. *Healing With the Horoscope: A Guide to Counseling.* ACS Publications, 1982.

_____. *Complete Horoscope Interpretation: Putting Together Your Planetary Profile.* ACS Publications, 1986.

Rodden, Lois. *Profiles of Women: A Collection of Astrological Biographies.* AFA, 1979.

Rosenblum, Bernard. *The Astrologer's Guide to Counseling.* CRCS Publications, 1983.

Rudhyar, Dane. *The Astrological Houses.* Doubleday, 1972.

_____. *Astrological Insights Into the Spiritual Life.* ASI, 1979.

_____. *An Astrological Mandala.* Random House, 1973.

_____. *An Astrological Study of Psychological Complexes and Emotional Problems.* Servire, Wassenaar, 1966.

_____. *The Astrology of Personality.* Doubleday, 1936.

_____. *The Lunation Cycle.* Shambala, 1971.

_____. *The Practice of Astrology.* Penguin, 1936

Ruperti, Alexander. *Cycles of Becoming.* CRCS Publications, 1978.

Sargent, Lois. *How to Handle Your Human Relations.* AFA, 1958.

Schulman, Martin. *Celestial Harmony: A Guide to Horoscope Interpretation.* Weiser, 1980.

_____. *The Moon's Nodes and Reincarnation.* Weiser, 1975.

Seymour-Smith, Martin. *The New Astrologer.* Macmillan, 1981.

Tierney, Bil. *Dynamics of Aspect Analysis.* CRCS Publications, 1983.

Toonder, Jan Gerhard, and John Anthony West. *The Case for Astrology.* Penguin, 1970.

Townley, John. *Astrological Cycles and the Life Crisis Periods.* Weiser, 1977.

Tyl, Noel. *Analysis and Prediction.* Llewellyn, 1974.

_____. *The Expanded Present.* Llewellyn, 1974.

_____. *Guide to the Principles and Practice of Astrology.* Llewellyn, 1979.

_____. *Holistic Astrology.* TAI, 1980
_____. *Integrated Transits.* Llewellyn, 1974.
_____. *Special Horoscope Dimensions: Success, Sex, and Illness.* Llewellyn, 1975.
Van Toen, Donna. *The Astrologer's Node Book.* Weiser, 1981.
_____. *The Mars Book: Its Role in Astrology.* Weiser, 1987.
Weingarten, Henry. *The Study of Astrology.* ASI 1969.

Sources of Astrological Books and Tapes

ACS Publications, Inc., P. O. Box 34487, San Diego, CA 92163-4487.
Astrology Book Club, Astro-Analytics Publications, 16440 Haynes St., Van Nuys, CA 91406-5719.
CRCS Publications, P. O. Box 20850, Reno NV 89515.
DeVorss and Co., P. O. Box 550, Marina Del Rey, CA 90291.
Pegasus Tapes, School of Astro-Psychological Studies, P. O. Box 419, Santa Ysabel, CA 92070.
Samuel Weiser, Inc., P. O. Box 612, York Beach, ME 03910.
Tape and Book Club Bulletin, RKM Publishing, P. O. Box 23042, Euclid, OH 44123.
Yes! Bookshop, 1035 31st St. N.W., Washington, DC 20007.

Books for Perspective

Bly, Robert. *Sleepers Joining Hands.* Harper and Row, 1973.
Bolen, Jean Shinoda. *Goddesses in Every Woman.* Harper and Row, 1984.
Brown, Norman O. *Love's Body.* Random House, 1966.
Cameron-Bandler, Leslie. *Solutions: Practical and Effective Antidotes for Sexual and Relationship Problems.* FuturePace, 1985.
Downing, Christine. *The Goddess: Mythological Images of the Feminine.* Crossroad, 1981.
Halpern, Howard M. *How to Break Your Addiction to a Person.* Bantam, 1982.
Jackson, Don, and William Lederer. *The Mirages of Marriage.* Norton, 1968.
Johnson, Robert. *We: Understanding the Psychology of Romantic Love.* Harper and Row, 1985.

Jung, Carl G. *Man and His Symbols.* Dell, 1964.

_____. *Psyche and Symbol.* Doubleday, 1958.

Jung, Emma. *Animus and Anima.* Spring Publications, Inc., 1981.

LeGuin, Ursula K. *The Left Hand of Darkness.* Ace, 1969

Neill, Merrily, and Joanne Tangedahl. *A New Blueprint for Marriage.* Coleman Graphics, 1981.

Norwood, Robin. *Women Who Love Too Much.* Pocket Books, 1985.

Peck, M. Scott. *The Road Less Traveled.* Simon and Schuster, 1978.

Raymo, Chet. *The Soul of the Night: An Astronomical Pilgrimage.* Prentice-Hall, 1985.

Shain, Merle. *When Lovers Are Friends.* Lippincott, 1978.

Wickes, Frances. *The Inner World of Childhood.* Appleton, 1927.

VENUS EPHEMERIS

Venus is within forty-eight degrees of your Sun, so look for Venus no more than two signs away from your Sun sign. If you were born on the day of a sign change, we advise getting your chart cast by a professional astrologer for an accurate Venus position.

Dates Venus enters the signs 1900 - 2000

1900				**1904**		Aug	29	Virgo
Jan	20	Pisces	Jan	05	Sagittarius	Sep	22	Libra
Feb	13	Aries	Jan	30	Capricorn	Oct	16	Scorpio
Mar	10	Taurus	Feb	24	Aquarius	Nov	09	Sagittarius
Apr	06	Gemini	Mar	19	Pisces	Dec	03	Capricorn
May	05	Cancer	Apr	13	Aries	Dec	27	Aquarius
Sep	08	Leo	May	07	Taurus	**1908**		
Oct	08	Virgo	Jun	01	Gemini	Jan	20	Pisces
Nov	03	Libra	Jun	25	Cancer	Feb	14	Aries
Nov	28	Scorpio	Jul	19	Leo	Mar	10	Taurus
Dec	23	Sagittarius	Aug	13	Virgo	Apr	05	Gemini
1901			Sep	06	Libra	May	05	Cancer
Jan	16	Capricorn	Sep	30	Scorpio	Sep	08	Leo
Feb	09	Aquarius	Oct	25	Sagittarius	Oct	08	Virgo
Mar	05	Pisces	Nov	18	Capricorn	Nov	03	Libra
Mar	29	Aries	Dec	13	Aquarius	Nov	28	Scorpio
Apr	22	Taurus	**1905**			Dec	22	Sagittarius
May	17	Gemini	Jan	07	Pisces	**1909**		
Jun	10	Cancer	Feb	03	Aries	Jan	15	Capricorn
Jul	05	Leo	Mar	06	Taurus	Feb	09	Aquarius
Jul	29	Virgo	May	09	Aries	Mar	05	Pisces
Aug	23	Libra	May	28	Taurus	Mar	29	Aries
Sep	17	Scorpio	Jul	08	Gemini	Apr	22	Taurus
Oct	12	Sagittarius	Aug	06	Cancer	May	16	Gemini
Nov	07	Capricorn	Sep	01	Leo	Jun	10	Cancer
Dec	05	Aquarius	Sep	27	Virgo	Jul	04	Leo
1902			Oct	21	Libra	Jul	29	Virgo
Jan	11	Pisces	Nov	14	Scorpio	Aug	23	Libra
Feb	06	Aquarius	Dec	08	Sagittarius	Sep	17	Scorpio
Apr	04	Pisces	**1906**			Oct	12	Sagittarius
May	07	Aries	Jan	01	Capricorn	Nov	07	Capricorn
Jun	03	Taurus	Jan	25	Aquarius	Dec	05	Aquarius
Jun	30	Gemini	Feb	18	Pisces	**1910**		
Jul	25	Cancer	Mar	14	Aries	Jan	15	Pisces
Aug	19	Leo	Apr	07	Taurus	Jan	29	Aquarius
Sep	13	Virgo	May	02	Gemini	Apr	05	Pisces
Oct	07	Libra	May	26	Cancer	May	07	Aries
Oct	31	Scorpio	Jun	20	Leo	Jun	03	Taurus
Nov	24	Sagittarius	Jul	16	Virgo	Jun	29	Gemini
Dec	18	Capricorn	Aug	11	Libra	Jul	25	Cancer
1903			Sep	07	Scorpio	Aug	19	Leo
Jan	11	Aquarius	Oct	09	Sagittarius	Sep	12	Virgo
Feb	04	Pisces	Dec	15	Scorpio	Oct	06	Libra
Feb	28	Aries	Dec	25	Sagittarius	Oct	30	Scorpio
Mar	24	Taurus	**1907**			Nov	23	Sagittarius
Apr	18	Gemini	Feb	06	Capricorn	Dec	17	Capricorn
May	13	Cancer	Mar	06	Aquarius	**1911**		
Jun	09	Leo	Apr	02	Pisces	Jan	10	Aquarius
Jul	07	Virgo	Apr	27	Aries	Feb	03	Pisces
Aug	17	Libra	May	22	Taurus	Feb	27	Aries
Sep	06	Virgo	Jun	16	Gemini	Mar	23	Taurus
Nov	08	Libra	Jul	11	Cancer	Apr	17	Gemini
Dec	09	Scorpio	Aug	04	Leo	May	13	Cancer

Dates Venus enters the signs 1900 - 2000

Jun	08	Leo
Jul	07	Virgo
Nov	09	Libra
Dec	09	Scorpio
1912		
Jan	04	Sagittarius
Jan	29	Capricorn
Feb	23	Aquarius
Mar	19	Pisces
Apr	12	Aries
May	07	Taurus
May	31	Gemini
Jun	25	Cancer
Jul	19	Leo
Aug	12	Virgo
Sep	06	Libra
Sep	30	Scorpio
Oct	24	Sagittarius
Nov	18	Capricorn
Dec	12	Aquarius
1913		
Jan	07	Pisces
Feb	02	Aries
Mar	06	Taurus
May	02	Aries
May	31	Taurus
Jul	08	Gemini
Aug	05	Cancer
Sep	01	Leo
Sep	26	Virgo
Oct	21	Libra
Nov	14	Scorpio
Dec	08	Sagittarius
1914		
Jan	01	Capricorn
Jan	25	Aquarius
Feb	18	Pisces
Mar	14	Aries
Apr	07	Taurus
May	01	Gemini
May	26	Cancer
Jun	20	Leo
Jul	15	Virgo
Aug	10	Libra
Sep	07	Scorpio
Oct	10	Sagittarius
Dec	05	Scorpio
Dec	30	Sagittarius
1915		
Feb	06	Capricorn
Mar	06	Aquarius
Apr	01	Pisces
Apr	27	Aries

May	22	Taurus
Jun	16	Gemini
Jul	10	Cancer
Aug	04	Leo
Aug	28	Virgo
Sep	21	Libra
Oct	15	Scorpio
Nov	08	Sagittarius
Dec	02	Capricorn
Dec	26	Aquarius
1916		
Jan	20	Pisces
Feb	13	Aries
Mar	09	Taurus
Apr	05	Gemini
May	05	Cancer
Sep	08	Leo
Oct	07	Virgo
Nov	03	Libra
Nov	27	Scorpio
Dec	22	Sagittarius
1917		
Jan	15	Capricorn
Feb	08	Aquarius
Mar	04	Pisces
Mar	28	Aries
Apr	21	Taurus
May	16	Gemini
Jun	09	Cancer
Jul	04	Leo
Jul	28	Virgo
Aug	22	Libra
Sep	16	Scorpio
Oct	11	Sagittarius
Nov	07	Capricorn
Dec	05	Aquarius
1918		
Apr	05	Pisces
May	06	Aries
Jun	03	Taurus
Jun	29	Gemini
Jul	24	Cancer
Aug	18	Leo
Sep	12	Virgo
Oct	06	Libra
Oct	30	Scorpio
Nov	23	Sagittarius
Dec	17	Capricorn
1919		
Jan	10	Aquarius
Feb	02	Pisces
Feb	27	Aries

Mar	23	Taurus
Apr	17	Gemini
May	12	Cancer
Jun	08	Leo
Jul	07	Virgo
Nov	09	Libra
Dec	09	Scorpio
1920		
Jan	04	Sagittarius
Jan	29	Capricorn
Feb	23	Aquarius
Mar	18	Pisces
Apr	12	Aries
May	06	Taurus
May	31	Gemini
Jun	24	Cancer
Jul	18	Leo
Aug	12	Virgo
Sep	05	Libra
Sep	29	Scorpio
Oct	24	Sagittarius
Nov	17	Capricorn
Dec	12	Aquarius
1921		
Jan	06	Pisces
Feb	02	Aries
Mar	07	Taurus
Apr	25	Aries
Jun	02	Taurus
Jul	08	Gemini
Aug	05	Cancer
Aug	31	Leo
Sep	26	Virgo
Oct	20	Libra
Nov	13	Scorpio
Dec	07	Sagittarius
Dec	31	Capricorn
1922		
Jan	24	Aquarius
Feb	17	Pisces
Mar	13	Aries
Apr	06	Taurus
May	01	Gemini
May	25	Cancer
Jun	19	Leo
Jul	15	Virgo
Aug	10	Libra
Sep	07	Scorpio
Oct	10	Sagittarius
Nov	28	Scorpio
1923		
Jan	02	Sagittarius

Dates Venus enters the signs 1900 - 2000

Feb	06	Capricorn		**1927**		Oct	12	Sagittarius
Mar	06	Aquarius	Jan	09	Aquarius	Nov	22	Scorpio
Apr	01	Pisces	Feb	02	Pisces		**1931**	
Apr	26	Aries	Feb	26	Aries	Jan	03	Sagittarius
May	21	Taurus	Mar	22	Taurus	Feb	06	Capricorn
Jun	15	Gemini	Apr	16	Gemini	Mar	05	Aquarius
Jul	10	Cancer	May	12	Cancer	Mar	31	Pisces
Aug	03	Leo	Jun	08	Leo	Apr	26	Aries
Aug	27	Virgo	Jul	07	Virgo	May	21	Taurus
Sep	21	Libra	Nov	09	Libra	Jun	14	Gemini
Oct	15	Scorpio	Dec	08	Scorpio	Jul	09	Cancer
Nov	08	Sagittarius		**1928**		Aug	03	Leo
Dec	02	Capricorn	Jan	04	Sagittarius	Aug	27	Virgo
Dec	26	Aquarius	Jan	29	Capricorn	Sep	20	Libra
	1924		Feb	22	Aquarius	Oct	14	Scorpio
Jan	19	Pisces	Mar	18	Pisces	Nov	07	Sagittarius
Feb	13	Aries	Apr	11	Aries	Dec	01	Capricorn
Mar	09	Taurus	May	06	Cancer	Dec	25	Aquarius
Apr	05	Gemini	May	30	Gemini		**1932**	
May	06	Cancer	Jun	23	Cancer	Jan	19	Pisces
Sep	08	Leo	Jul	18	Leo	Feb	12	Aries
Oct	07	Virgo	Aug	11	Virgo	Mar	09	Taurus
Nov	02	Libra	Sep	04	Libra	Apr	05	Gemini
Nov	27	Scorpio	Sep	29	Scorpio	May	06	Taurus
Dec	21	Sagittarius	Oct	23	Sagittarius	Jul	13	Gemini
	1925		Nov	17	Capricorn	Jul	28	Cancer
Jan	14	Capricorn	Dec	12	Aquarius	Sep	08	Leo
Feb	07	Aquarius		**1929**		Oct	07	Virgo
Mar	04	Pisces	Jan	06	Pisces	Nov	02	Libra
Mar	28	Aries	Feb	02	Aries	Nov	27	Scorpio
Apr	21	Taurus	Mar	08	Taurus	Dec	21	Sagittarius
May	15	Gemini	Apr	20	Aries		**1933**	
Jun	09	Cancer	Jun	03	Taurus	Jan	14	Capricorn
Jul	03	Leo	Jul	08	Gemini	Feb	07	Aquarius
Jul	28	Virgo	Aug	05	Cancer	Mar	03	Pisces
Aug	22	Libra	Aug	31	Leo	Mar	27	Aries
Sep	16	Scorpio	Sep	25	Virgo	Apr	20	Taurus
Oct	11	Sagittarius	Oct	20	Libra	May	15	Gemini
Nov	06	Capricorn	Nov	13	Scorpio	Jun	08	Cancer
Dec	05	Aquarius	Dec	07	Sagittarius	Jul	03	Leo
	1926		Dec	31	Capricorn	Jul	27	Virgo
Apr	06	Pisces		**1930**		Aug	21	Libra
May	06	Aries	Jan	24	Aquarius	Sep	15	Scorpio
Jun	02	Taurus	Feb	16	Pisces	Oct	11	Sagittarius
Jun	28	Gemini	Mar	12	Aries	Nov	06	Capricorn
Jul	24	Cancer	Apr	06	Taurus	Dec	05	Aquarius
Aug	18	Leo	Apr	30	Gemini		**1934**	
Sep	11	Virgo	May	25	Cancer	Apr	06	Pisces
Oct	05	Libra	Jun	19	Leo	May	06	Aries
Oct	29	Scorpio	Jul	14	Virgo	Jun	02	Taurus
Nov	22	Sagittarius	Aug	10	Libra	Jun	28	Gemini
Dec	16	Capricorn	Sep	07	Scorpio	Jul	23	Cancer

Dates Venus enters the signs 1900 - 2000

Aug	17	Leo	Apr	29	Gemini		**1942**	
Sep	11	Virgo	May	24	Cancer	Apr	06	Pisces
Oct	05	Libra	Jun	18	Leo	May	06	Aries
Oct	29	Scorpio	Jul	14	Virgo	Jun	02	Taurus
Nov	22	Sagittarius	Aug	09	Libra	Jun	27	Gemini
Dec	16	Capricorn	Sep	07	Scorpio	Jul	23	Cancer
	1935		Oct	13	Sagittarius	Aug	17	Leo
Jan	08	Aquarius	Nov	15	Scorpio	Sep	10	Virgo
Feb	01	Pisces		**1939**		Oct	04	Libra
Feb	26	Aries	Jan	04	Sagittarius	Oct	28	Scorpio
Mar	22	Taurus	Feb	06	Capricorn	Nov	21	Sagittarius
Apr	16	Gemini	Mar	05	Aquarius	Dec	15	Capricorn
May	11	Cancer	Mar	31	Pisces		**1943**	
Jun	07	Leo	Apr	25	Aries	Jan	08	Aquarius
Jul	07	Virgo	May	20	Taurus	Feb	01	Pisces
Nov	09	Libra	Jun	14	Gemini	Feb	25	Aries
Dec	08	Scorpio	Jul	09	Cancer	Mar	21	Taurus
	1936		Aug	02	Leo	Apr	15	Gemini
Jan	03	Sagittarius	Aug	26	Virgo	May	11	Cancer
Jan	28	Capricorn	Sep	20	Libra	Jun	07	Leo
Feb	22	Aquarius	Oct	14	Scorpio	Jul	07	Virgo
Mar	17	Pisces	Nov	07	Sagittarius	Nov	09	Libra
Apr	11	Aries	Dec	01	Capricorn	Dec	08	Scorpio
May	05	Taurus	Dec	25	Aquarius		**1944**	
May	29	Gemini		**1940**		Jan	03	Sagittarius
Jun	23	Cancer	Jan	18	Pisces	Jan	28	Capricorn
Jul	17	Leo	Feb	12	Aries	Feb	21	Aquarius
Aug	11	Virgo	Mar	08	Taurus	Mar	17	Pisces
Sep	04	Libra	Apr	04	Gemini	Apr	10	Aries
Sep	28	Scorpio	May	06	Cancer	May	04	Taurus
Oct	23	Sagittarius	Jul	05	Gemini	May	29	Gemini
Nov	16	Capricorn	Aug	01	Cancer	Jun	22	Cancer
Dec	11	Aquarius	Sep	08	Leo	Jul	17	Leo
	1937		Oct	06	Virgo	Aug	10	Virgo
Jan	06	Pisces	Nov	01	Libra	Sep	03	Libra
Feb	02	Aries	Nov	26	Scorpio	Sep	28	Scorpio
Mar	09	Taurus	Dec	20	Sagittarius	Oct	22	Sagittarius
Apr	14	Aries		**1941**		Nov	16	Capricorn
Jun	04	Taurus	Jan	13	Capricorn	Dec	11	Aquarius
Jul	07	Gemini	Feb	06	Aquarius		**1945**	
Aug	04	Cancer	Mar	02	Pisces	Jan	05	Pisces
Aug	31	Leo	Mar	27	Aries	Feb	02	Aries
Sep	25	Virgo	Apr	20	Taurus	Mar	11	Taurus
Oct	19	Libra	May	14	Gemini	Apr	07	Aries
Nov	12	Scorpio	Jun	07	Cancer	Jun	04	Taurus
Dec	06	Sagittarius	Jul	02	Leo	Jul	07	Gemini
Dec	30	Capricorn	Jul	27	Virgo	Aug	04	Cancer
	1938		Aug	21	Libra	Aug	30	Leo
Jan	23	Aquarius	Sep	15	Scorpio	Sep	24	Virgo
Feb	16	Pisces	Oct	10	Sagittarius	Oct	19	Libra
Mar	12	Aries	Nov	06	Capricorn	Nov	12	Scorpio
Apr	05	Taurus	Dec	05	Aquarius	Dec	06	Sagittarius

Dates Venus enters the signs 1900 - 2000

Dec	30	Capricorn
1946		
Jan	22	Aquarius
Feb	15	Pisces
Mar	11	Aries
Apr	05	Taurus
Apr	29	Gemini
May	24	Cancer
Jun	18	Leo
Jul	13	Virgo
Aug	09	Libra
Sep	07	Scorpio
Oct	16	Sagittarius
Nov	08	Scorpio
1947		
Jan	05	Sagittarius
Feb	06	Capricorn
Mar	05	Aquarius
Mar	30	Pisces
Apr	25	Aries
May	20	Taurus
Jun	13	Gemini
Jul	08	Cancer
Aug	02	Leo
Aug	26	Virgo
Sep	19	Libra
Oct	13	Scorpio
Nov	06	Sagittarius
Nov	30	Capricorn
Dec	24	Aquarius
1948		
Jan	18	Pisces
Feb	11	Aries
Mar	08	Taurus
Apr	04	Gemini
May	04	Cancer
Jun	29	Gemini
Aug	03	Cancer
Sep	08	Leo
Oct	06	Virgo
Nov	01	Libra
Nov	26	Scorpio
Dec	20	Sagittarius
1949		
Jan	13	Capricorn
Feb	06	Aquarius
Mar	02	Pisces
Mar	26	Aries
Apr	19	Taurus
May	14	Gemini
Jun	07	Cancer
Jul	01	Leo

Jul	26	Virgo
Aug	20	Libra
Sep	14	Scorpio
Oct	10	Sagittarius
Nov	06	Capricorn
Dec	06	Aquarius
1950		
Apr	06	Pisces
May	05	Aries
Jun	01	Taurus
Jun	27	Gemini
Jul	22	Cancer
Aug	16	Leo
Sep	10	Virgo
Oct	04	Libra
Oct	28	Scorpio
Nov	21	Sagittarius
Dec	14	Capricorn
1951		
Jan	07	Aquarius
Jan	31	Pisces
Feb	24	Aries
Mar	21	Taurus
Apr	15	Gemini
May	11	Cancer
Jun	07	Leo
Jul	08	Virgo
Nov	09	Libra
Dec	08	Scorpio
1952		
Jan	02	Sagittarius
Jan	27	Capricorn
Feb	21	Aquarius
Mar	16	Pisces
Apr	09	Aries
May	04	Taurus
May	28	Gemini
Jun	22	Cancer
Jul	16	Leo
Aug	09	Virgo
Sep	03	Libra
Sep	27	Scorpio
Oct	22	Sagittarius
Nov	15	Capricorn
Dec	10	Aquarius
1953		
Jan	05	Pisces
Feb	02	Aries
Mar	14	Taurus
Mar	31	Aries
Jun	05	Taurus
Jul	07	Gemini

Aug	04	Cancer
Aug	30	Leo
Sep	24	Virgo
Oct	18	Libra
Nov	11	Scorpio
Dec	05	Sagittarius
Dec	29	Capricorn
1954		
Jan	22	Aquarius
Feb	15	Pisces
Mar	11	Aries
Apr	04	Taurus
Apr	28	Gemini
May	23	Cancer
Jun	17	Leo
Jul	13	Virgo
Aug	09	Libra
Sep	06	Scorpio
Oct	23	Sagittarius
Oct	27	Scorpio
1955		
Jan	06	Sagittarius
Feb	06	Capricorn
Mar	04	Aquarius
Mar	30	Pisces
Apr	24	Aries
May	19	Taurus
Jun	13	Gemini
Jul	08	Cancer
Aug	01	Leo
Aug	25	Virgo
Sep	18	Libra
Oct	13	Scorpio
Nov	06	Sagittarius
Nov	30	Capricorn
Dec	24	Aquarius
1956		
Jan	17	Pisces
Feb	11	Aries
Mar	07	Taurus
Apr	04	Gemini
May	08	Cancer
Jun	23	Gemini
Aug	04	Cancer
Sep	08	Leo
Oct	06	Virgo
Oct	31	Libra
Nov	25	Scorpio
Dec	19	Sagittarius
1957		
Jan	12	Capricorn
Feb	05	Aquarius

Dates Venus enters the signs 1900 - 2000

Mar	01	Pisces
Mar	25	Aries
Apr	19	Taurus
May	13	Gemini
Jun	06	Cancer
Jul	01	Leo
Jul	26	Virgo
Aug	20	Libra
Sep	14	Scorpio
Oct	10	Sagittarius
Nov	05	Capricorn
Dec	06	Aquarius
1958		
Apr	06	Pisces
May	05	Aries
Jun	01	Taurus
Jun	26	Gemini
Jul	22	Cancer
Aug	16	Leo
Sep	09	Virgo
Oct	03	Libra
Oct	27	Scorpio
Nov	20	Sagittarius
Dec	14	Capricorn
1959		
Jan	07	Aquarius
Jan	31	Pisces
Feb	24	Aries
Mar	20	Taurus
Apr	14	Gemini
May	10	Cancer
Jun	06	Leo
Jul	08	Virgo
Sep	20	Leo
Sep	25	Virgo
Nov	09	Libra
Dec	07	Scorpio
1960		
Jan	02	Sagittarius
Jan	27	Capricorn
Feb	20	Aquarius
Mar	16	Pisces
Apr	09	Aries
May	03	Taurus
May	28	Gemini
Jun	21	Cancer
Jul	16	Leo
Aug	09	Virgo
Sep	02	Libra
Sep	27	Scorpio
Oct	21	Sagittarius
Nov	15	Capricorn

Dec	10	Aquarius
1961		
Jan	05	Pisces
Feb	02	Aries
Jun	05	Taurus
Jul	07	Gemini
Aug	03	Cancer
Aug	29	Leo
Sep	23	Virgo
Oct	18	Libra
Nov	11	Scorpio
Dec	05	Sagittarius
Dec	29	Capricorn
1962		
Jan	21	Aquarius
Feb	14	Pisces
Mar	10	Aries
Apr	03	Taurus
Apr	28	Gemini
May	23	Cancer
Jun	17	Leo
Jul	12	Virgo
Aug	08	Libra
Sep	07	Scorpio
1963		
Jan	06	Sagittarius
Feb	05	Capricorn
Mar	04	Aquarius
Mar	30	Pisces
Apr	24	Aries
May	19	Taurus
Jun	12	Gemini
Jul	07	Cancer
Jul	31	Leo
Aug	25	Virgo
Sep	18	Libra
Oct	12	Scorpio
Nov	05	Sagittarius
Nov	29	Capricorn
Dec	23	Aquarius
1964		
Jan	17	Pisces
Feb	10	Aries
Mar	07	Taurus
Apr	04	Gemini
May	09	Cancer
Jun	17	Gemini
Aug	05	Cancer
Sep	08	Leo
Oct	05	Virgo
Oct	31	Libra
Nov	25	Scorpio

Dec	19	Sagittarius
1965		
Jan	12	Capricorn
Feb	05	Aquarius
Mar	01	Pisces
Mar	25	Aries
Apr	18	Taurus
May	12	Gemini
Jun	06	Cancer
Jun	30	Leo
Jul	25	Virgo
Aug	19	Libra
Sep	13	Scorpio
Oct	09	Sagittarius
Nov	05	Capricorn
Dec	07	Aquarius
1966		
Feb	06	Capricorn
Feb	25	Aquarius
Apr	06	Pisces
May	05	Aries
May	31	Taurus
Jun	26	Gemini
Jul	21	Cancer
Aug	15	Leo
Sep	08	Virgo
Oct	03	Libra
Oct	27	Scorpio
Nov	20	Sagittarius
Dec	13	Capricorn
1967		
Jan	06	Aquarius
Jan	30	Pisces
Feb	23	Aries
Mar	20	Taurus
Apr	14	Gemini
May	10	Cancer
Dec	06	Leo
Jul	08	Virgo
Sep	09	Leo
Oct	01	Virgo
Nov	09	Libra
Dec	07	Scorpio
1968		
Jan	01	Sagittarius
Jan	26	Capricorn
Feb	20	Aquarius
Mar	15	Pisces
Apr	08	Aries
May	03	Taurus
May	27	Gemini
Jun	21	Cancer

Dates Venus enters the signs 1900 - 2000

Jul	15	Leo	Jun	11	Gemini	Feb	19	Aquarius
Aug	08	Virgo	Aug	06	Cancer	Mar	15	Pisces
Sep	02	Libra	Sep	07	Leo	Apr	08	Aries
Sep	26	Scorpio	Oct	05	Virgo	May	02	Taurus
Oct	21	Sagittarius	Oct	30	Libra	May	27	Gemini
Nov	14	Capricorn	Nov	24	Scorpio	Jun	20	Cancer
Dec	09	Aquarius	Dec	18	Sagittarius	Jul	14	Leo
	1969			**1973**		Aug	08	Virgo
Jan	04	Pisces	Jan	11	Capricorn	Sep	01	Libra
Feb	02	Aries	Feb	04	Aquarius	Sep	26	Scorpio
Jun	06	Taurus	Feb	28	Pisces	Oct	20	Sagittarius
Jul	06	Gemini	Mar	24	Aries	Nov	14	Capricorn
Aug	03	Cancer	Apr	18	Taurus	Dec	09	Aquarius
Aug	29	Leo	May	12	Gemini		**1977**	
Sep	23	Virgo	Jun	05	Cancer	Jan	04	Pisces
Oct	17	Libra	Jun	30	Leo	Feb	02	Aries
Nov	10	Scorpio	Jul	25	Virgo	Jun	06	Taurus
Dec	04	Sagittarius	Aug	19	Libra	Jul	06	Gemini
Dec	28	Capricorn	Sep	13	Scorpio	Aug	02	Cancer
	1970		Oct	09	Sagittarius	Aug	28	Leo
Jan	21	Aquarius	Nov	05	Capricorn	Sep	22	Virgo
Feb	14	Pisces	Dec	07	Aquarius	Oct	17	Libra
Mar	10	Aries		**1974**		Nov	10	Scorpio
Apr	03	Taurus	Jan	29	Capricorn	Dec	04	Sagittarius
Apr	27	Gemini	Feb	28	Aquarius	Dec	27	Capricorn
May	22	Cancer	Apr	06	Pisces		**1978**	
Jun	16	Leo	May	04	Aries	Jan	20	Aquarius
Jul	12	Virgo	May	31	Taurus	Feb	13	Pisces
Aug	08	Libra	Jun	25	Gemini	Mar	09	Aries
Sep	07	Scorpio	Jul	21	Cancer	Apr	02	Taurus
	1971		Aug	14	Leo	Apr	27	Gemini
Jan	07	Sagittarius	Sep	08	Virgo	May	22	Cancer
Feb	05	Capricorn	Oct	02	Libra	Jun	16	Leo
Mar	04	Aquarius	Oct	26	Scorpio	Jul	12	Virgo
Mar	29	Pisces	Nov	19	Sagittarius	Aug	08	Libra
Apr	23	Aries	Dec	13	Capricorn	Sep	07	Scorpio
May	18	Taurus		**1975**			**1979**	
Jun	12	Gemini	Jan	06	Aquarius	Jan	07	Sagittarius
Jul	06	Cancer	Jan	30	Pisces	Feb	05	Capricorn
Jul	31	Leo	Feb	23	Aries	Mar	03	Aquarius
Aug	24	Virgo	Mar	19	Taurus	Mar	29	Pisces
Sep	17	Libra	Apr	13	Gemini	Apr	23	Aries
Oct	11	Scorpio	May	09	Cancer	May	18	Taurus
Nov	05	Sagittarius	Jun	06	Leo	Jun	11	Gemini
Nov	29	Capricorn	Jul	09	Virgo	Jul	06	Cancer
Dec	23	Aquarius	Sep	02	Leo	Jul	30	Leo
	1972		Oct	04	Virgo	Aug	24	Virgo
Jan	16	Pisces	Nov	09	Libra	Sep	17	Libra
Feb	10	Aries	Dec	07	Scorpio	Oct	11	Scorpio
Mar	07	Taurus		**1976**		Nov	04	Sagittarius
Apr	03	Gemini	Jan	01	Sagittarius	Nov	28	Capricorn
May	10	Cancer	Jan	26	Capricorn	Dec	22	Aquarius

Dates Venus enters the signs 1900 - 2000

1980		
Jan	16	Pisces
Feb	09	Aries
Mar	06	Taurus
Apr	03	Gemini
May	12	Cancer
Jun	05	Gemini
Aug	06	Cancer
Sep	07	Leo
Oct	04	Virgo
Oct	30	Libra
Nov	24	Scorpio
Dec	18	Sagittarius
1981		
Jan	11	Capricorn
Feb	04	Aquarius
Feb	28	Pisces
Mar	24	Aries
Apr	17	Taurus
May	11	Gemini
Jun	05	Cancer
Jun	29	Leo
Jul	24	Virgo
Aug	18	Libra
Sep	12	Scorpio
Oct	09	Sagittarius
Nov	05	Capricorn
Dec	08	Aquarius
1982		
Jan	23	Capricorn
Mar	02	Aquarius
Apr	06	Pisces
May	04	Aries
May	30	Taurus
Jun	25	Gemini
Jul	20	Cancer
Aug	14	Leo
Sep	07	Virgo
Oct	02	Libra
Oct	26	Scorpio
Nov	18	Sagittarius
Dec	12	Capricorn
1983		
Jan	05	Aquarius
Jan	29	Pisces
Feb	22	Aries
Mar	19	Taurus
Apr	13	Gemini
May	09	Cancer
Jun	06	Leo
Jul	10	Virgo
Aug	27	Leo

Oct	05	Virgo
Nov	09	Libra
Dec	06	Scorpio
1984		
Jan	01	Sagittarius
Jan	25	Capricorn
Feb	19	Aquarius
Mar	14	Pisces
Apr	07	Aries
May	02	Taurus
May	26	Gemini
Jun	20	Cancer
Jul	14	Leo
Aug	07	Virgo
Sep	01	Libra
Sep	25	Scorpio
Oct	20	Sagittarius
Nov	13	Capricorn
Dec	09	Aquarius
1985		
Jan	04	Pisces
Feb	02	Aries
Jun	06	Taurus
Jul	06	Gemini
Aug	02	Cancer
Aug	28	Leo
Sep	22	Virgo
Oct	16	Libra
Nov	09	Scorpio
Dec	03	Sagittarius
Dec	27	Capricorn
1986		
Jan	20	Aquarius
Feb	13	Pisces
Mar	09	Aries
Apr	02	Taurus
Apr	26	Gemini
May	21	Cancer
Jun	15	Leo
Jul	11	Virgo
Aug	07	Libra
Sep	07	Scorpio
1987		
Jan	07	Sagittarius
Feb	05	Capricorn
Mar	03	Aquarius
Mar	28	Pisces
Apr	22	Aries
May	17	Taurus
Jun	11	Gemini
Jul	05	Cancer
Jul	30	Leo

Aug	23	Virgo
Sep	16	Libra
Oct	10	Scorpio
Nov	03	Sagittarius
Nov	28	Capricorn
Dec	22	Aquarius
1988		
Jan	15	Pisces
Feb	09	Aries
Mar	06	Taurus
Apr	03	Gemini
May	17	Cancer
May	27	Gemini
Aug	06	Cancer
Sep	07	Leo
Oct	04	Virgo
Oct	29	Libra
Nov	23	Scorpio
Dec	17	Sagittarius
1989		
Jan	10	Capricorn
Feb	03	Aquarius
Feb	27	Pisces
Mar	23	Aries
Apr	16	Taurus
May	11	Gemini
Jun	04	Cancer
Jun	29	Leo
Jul	24	Virgo
Aug	18	Libra
Sep	12	Scorpio
Oct	08	Sagittarius
Nov	05	Capricorn
Dec	10	Aquarius
1990		
Jan	16	Capricorn
Mar	03	Aquarius
Apr	06	Pisces
May	04	Aries
May	30	Taurus
Jun	25	Gemini
Jul	20	Cancer
Aug	13	Leo
Sep	07	Virgo
Oct	01	Libra
Oct	25	Scorpio
Nov	18	Sagittarius
Dec	12	Capricorn
1991		
Jan	05	Aquarius
Jan	29	Pisces
Feb	22	Aries

Dates Venus enters the signs 1900 - 2000

Mar	18	Taurus	Jun	15	Leo	Nov	05	Capricorn
Apr	13	Gemini	Jul	11	Virgo	Dec	12	Aquarius
May	09	Cancer	Aug	07	Libra			**1998**
Jun	06	Leo	Sep	07	Scorpio	Jan	09	Capricorn
Jul	11	Virgo			**1995**	Mar	04	Aquarius
Aug	21	Leo	Jan	07	Sagittarius	Apr	06	Pisces
Oct	06	Virgo	Feb	04	Capricorn	May	03	Aries
Nov	09	Libra	Mar	02	Aquarius	May	29	Taurus
Dec	06	Scorpio	Mar	28	Pisces	Jun	24	Gemini
Dec	31	Sagittarius	Apr	22	Aries	Jul	19	Cancer
		1992	May	16	Taurus	Aug	13	Leo
Jan	25	Capricorn	Jun	10	Gemini	Sep	06	Virgo
Feb	18	Aquarius	Jul	05	Cancer	Sep	30	Libra
Mar	13	Pisces	Jul	29	Leo	Oct	24	Scorpio
Apr	07	Aries	Aug	23	Virgo	Nov	17	Sagittarius
May	01	Taurus	Sep	16	Libra	Dec	11	Capricorn
May	26	Gemini	Oct	10	Scorpio			**1999**
Jun	19	Cancer	Nov	03	Sagittarius	Jan	04	Aquarius
Jul	13	Leo	Nov	27	Capricorn	Jan	28	Pisces
Aug	07	Virgo	Dec	21	Aquarius	Feb	21	Aries
Aug	31	Libra			**1996**	Mar	18	Taurus
Sep	25	Scorpio	Jan	15	Pisces	Apr	12	Gemini
Oct	19	Sagittarius	Feb	09	Aries	May	08	Cancer
Nov	13	Capricorn	Mar	06	Taurus	Jun	05	Leo
Dec	08	Aquarius	Apr	03	Gemini	Jul	12	Virgo
		1993	Aug	07	Cancer	Aug	15	Leo
Jan	03	Pisces	Sep	07	Leo	Oct	07	Virgo
Feb	02	Aries	Oct	04	Virgo	Nov	09	Libra
Jun	06	Taurus	Oct	29	Libra	Dec	05	Scorpio
Jul	06	Gemini	Nov	23	Scorpio	Dec	31	Sagittarius
Aug	01	Cancer	Dec	17	Sagittarius			**2000**
Aug	27	Leo			**1997**	Jan	24	Capricorn
Sep	21	Virgo	Jan	10	Capricorn	Feb	18	Aquarius
Oct	16	Libra	Feb	03	Aquarius	Mar	13	Pisces
Nov	09	Scorpio	Feb	27	Pisces	Apr	06	Aries
Dec	02	Sagittarius	Mar	23	Aries	May	01	Taurus
Dec	26	Capricorn	Apr	16	Taurus	May	25	Gemini
		1994	May	10	Gemini	Jun	18	Cancer
Jan	19	Aquarius	Jun	04	Cancer	Jul	13	Leo
Feb	12	Pisces	Jun	28	Leo	Aug	06	Virgo
Mar	08	Aries	Jul	23	Virgo	Aug	31	Libra
Apr	01	Taurus	Aug	17	Libra	Sep	24	Scorpio
Apr	26	Gemini	Sep	12	Scorpio	Oct	19	Sagittarius
May	21	Cancer	Oct	08	Sagittarius	Nov	13	Capricorn
						Dec	08	Aquarius

APPENDIX FIVE

MARS EPHEMERIS

If you were born on a day when Mars changed signs, get your chart cast by a professional astrologer for an accurate Mars placement.

Dates Mars enters the signs 1900 - 2000

1900		
Jan	21	Aquarius
Feb	28	Pisces
Apr	08	Aries
May	17	Taurus
Jun	27	Gemini
Aug	10	Cancer
Sep	26	Leo
Nov	23	Virgo
1901		
Mar	01	Leo
May	11	Virgo
Jul	13	Libra
Aug	31	Scorpio
Oct	14	Sagittarius
Nov	24	Capricorn
1902		
Jan	01	Aquarius
Feb	08	Pisces
Mar	19	Aries
Apr	27	Taurus
Jun	07	Gemini
Jul	20	Cancer
Sep	04	Leo
Oct	23	Virgo
Dec	20	Libra
1903		
Apr	19	Virgo
May	30	Libra
Aug	06	Scorpio
Sep	22	Sagittarius
Nov	03	Capricorn
Dec	12	Aquarius
1904		
Jan	19	Pisces
Feb	27	Aries
Apr	06	Taurus
May	18	Gemini
Jun	30	Cancer
Aug	15	Leo
Oct	01	Virgo
Nov	20	Libra
1905		
Jan	13	Scorpio
Aug	21	Sagittarius
Oct	08	Capricorn
Nov	18	Aquarius
Dec	27	Pisces
1906		
Feb	04	Aries
Mar	17	Taurus
Apr	28	Gemini
Jun	11	Cancer
Jul	27	Leo

Sep	12	Virgo
Oct	30	Libra
Dec	17	Scorpio
1907		
Feb	05	Sagittarius
Apr	01	Capricorn
Oct	13	Aquarius
Nov	29	Pisces
1908		
Jan	11	Aries
Feb	23	Taurus
Apr	07	Gemini
May	22	Cancer
Jul	08	Leo
Aug	24	Virgo
Oct	10	Libra
Nov	25	Scorpio
1909		
Jan	10	Sagittarius
Feb	24	Capricorn
Apr	09	Aquarius
May	25	Pisces
Jul	21	Aries
Sep	26	Pisces
Nov	20	Aries
1910		
Jan	23	Taurus
Mar	14	Gemini
May	01	Cancer
Jun	19	Leo
Aug	06	Virgo
Sep	22	Libra
Nov	06	Scorpio
Dec	20	Sagittarius
1911		
Jan	31	Capricorn
Mar	14	Aquarius
Apr	23	Pisces
Jun	02	Aries
Jul	15	Taurus
Sep	05	Gemini
Nov	30	Taurus
1912		
Jan	30	Gemini
Apr	05	Cancer
May	28	Leo
Jul	17	Virgo
Sep	02	Libra
Oct	18	Scorpio
Nov	30	Sagittarius
1913		
Jan	10	Capricorn
Feb	19	Aquarius
Mar	30	Pisces

May	08	Aries
Jun	17	Taurus
Jul	29	Gemini
Sep	15	Cancer
1914		
May	01	Leo
Jun	26	Virgo
Aug	14	Libra
Sep	29	Scorpio
Nov	11	Sagittarius
Dec	22	Capricorn
1915		
Jan	30	Aquarius
Mar	09	Pisces
Apr	16	Aries
May	26	Taurus
Jul	06	Gemini
Aug	19	Cancer
Oct	07	Leo
1916		
May	28	Virgo
Jul	23	Libra
Sep	08	Scorpio
Oct	22	Sagittarius
Dec	01	Capricorn
1917		
Jan	09	Aquarius
Feb	16	Pisces
Mar	26	Aries
May	04	Taurus
Jun	14	Gemini
Jul	28	Cancer
Sep	12	Leo
Nov	02	Virgo
1918		
Jan	11	Libra
Feb	25	Virgo
Jun	23	Libra
Aug	17	Scorpio
Oct	01	Sagittarius
Nov	11	Capricorn
Dec	20	Aquarius
1919		
Jan	27	Pisces
Mar	06	Aries
Apr	15	Taurus
May	26	Gemini
Jul	08	Cancer
Aug	23	Leo
Oct	10	Virgo
Nov	30	Libra
1920		
Jan	31	Scorpio
Apr	23	Libra

Dates Mars enters the signs 1900 - 2000

Jul	10	Scorpio
Sep	04	Sagittarius
Oct	18	Capricorn
Nov	27	Aquarius
1921		
Jan	05	Pisces
Feb	13	Aries
Mar	25	Taurus
May	06	Gemini
Jun	18	Cancer
Aug	03	Leo
Sep	19	Virgo
Nov	06	Libra
Dec	26	Scorpio
1922		
Feb	18	Sagittarius
Sep	13	Capricorn
Oct	30	Aquarius
Dec	11	Pisces
1923		
Jan	21	Aries
Mar	04	Taurus
Apr	16	Gemini
May	30	Cancer
Jul	16	Leo
Sep	01	Virgo
Oct	18	Libra
Dec	04	Scorpio
1924		
Jan	19	Sagittarius
Mar	06	Capricorn
Apr	24	Aquarius
Jun	24	Pisces
Aug	24	Aquarius
Oct	19	Pisces
Dec	19	Aries
1925		
Feb	05	Taurus
Mar	24	Gemini
May	09	Cancer
Jun	26	Leo
Aug	12	Virgo
Sep	28	Libra
Nov	13	Scorpio
Dec	28	Sagittarius
1926		
Feb	09	Capricorn
Mar	23	Aquarius
May	03	Pisces
Jun	15	Aries
Aug	01	Taurus
1927		
Feb	22	Gemini
Apr	17	Cancer

Jun	06	Leo
Jul	25	Virgo
Sep	10	Libra
Oct	26	Scorpio
Dec	08	Sagittarius
1928		
Jan	19	Capricorn
Feb	28	Aquarius
Apr	07	Pisces
May	16	Aries
Jun	26	Taurus
Aug	09	Gemini
Oct	03	Taurus
Dec	20	Gemini
1929		
Mar	10	Cancer
May	13	Leo
Jul	04	Virgo
Aug	21	Libra
Oct	06	Scorpio
Nov	18	Sagittarius
Dec	29	Capricorn
1930		
Feb	06	Aquarius
Mar	17	Pisces
Apr	24	Aries
Jun	03	Taurus
Jul	14	Gemini
Aug	28	Cancer
Oct	20	Leo
1931		
Feb	16	Cancer
Mar	30	Leo
Jun	10	Virgo
Aug	01	Libra
Sep	17	Scorpio
Oct	30	Sagittarius
Dec	10	Capricorn
1932		
Jan	18	Aquarius
Feb	25	Pisces
Apr	03	Aries
May	12	Taurus
Jun	22	Gemini
Aug	04	Cancer
Sep	20	Leo
Nov	13	Virgo
1933		
Jul	06	Libra
Aug	26	Scorpio
Oct	09	Sagittarius
Nov	19	Capricorn
Dec	28	Aquarius

1934		
Feb	04	Pisces
Mar	14	Aries
Apr	22	Taurus
Jun	02	Gemini
Jul	15	Cancer
Aug	30	Leo
Oct	18	Virgo
Dec	11	Libra
1935		
Jul	29	Scorpio
Sep	16	Sagittarius
Oct	28	Capricorn
Dec	07	Aquarius
1936		
Jan	14	Pisces
Feb	22	Aries
Apr	01	Taurus
May	13	Gemini
Jun	25	Cancer
Aug	10	Leo
Sep	26	Virgo
Nov	14	Libra
1937		
Jan	05	Scorpio
Mar	13	Sagittarius
May	14	Scorpio
Aug	08	Sagittarius
Sep	30	Capricorn
Nov	11	Aquarius
Dec	21	Pisces
1938		
Jan	30	Aries
Mar	12	Taurus
Apr	23	Gemini
Jun	07	Cancer
Jul	22	Leo
Sep	07	Virgo
Oct	25	Libra
Dec	11	Scorpio
1939		
Jan	29	Sagittarius
Mar	21	Capricorn
May	25	Aquarius
Jul	21	Capricorn
Sep	24	Aquarius
Nov	19	Pisces
1940		
Jan	04	Aries
Feb	17	Taurus
Apr	01	Gemini
May	17	Cancer
Jul	03	Leo
Aug	19	Virgo

Dates Mars enters the signs 1900 - 2000

Oct	05	Libra
Nov	20	Scorpio
		1941
Jan	04	Sagittarius
Feb	17	Capricorn
Apr	02	Aquarius
May	16	Pisces
Jul	02	Aries
		1942
Jan	11	Taurus
Mar	07	Gemini
Apr	26	Cancer
Jun	14	Leo
Aug	01	Virgo
Sep	17	Libra
Nov	01	Scorpio
Dec	15	Sagittarius
		1943
Jan	26	Capricorn
Mar	08	Aquarius
Apr	17	Pisces
May	27	Aries
Jul	07	Taurus
Aug	23	Gemini
		1944
Mar	28	Cancer
May	22	Leo
Jul	12	Virgo
Aug	29	Libra
Oct	13	Scorpio
Nov	25	Sagittarius
		1945
Jan	05	Capricorn
Feb	14	Aquarius
Mar	25	Pisces
May	02	Aries
Jun	11	Taurus
Jul	23	Gemini
Sep	07	Cancer
Nov	11	Leo
Dec	26	Cancer
		1946
Apr	22	Leo
Jun	20	Virgo
Aug	09	Libra
Sep	24	Scorpio
Nov	06	Sagittarius
Dec	17	Capricorn
		1947
Jan	25	Aquarius
Mar	04	Pisces
Apr	11	Aries
May	21	Taurus
Jul	01	Gemini

Aug	13	Cancer
Oct	01	Leo
Dec	01	Virgo
		1948
Feb	12	Leo
May	18	Virgo
Jul	17	Libra
Sep	03	Scorpio
Oct	17	Sagittarius
Nov	26	Capricorn
		1949
Jan	04	Aquarius
Feb	11	Pisces
Mar	21	Aries
Apr	30	Taurus
Jun	10	Gemini
Jul	23	Cancer
Sep	07	Leo
Oct	27	Virgo
Dec	26	Libra
		1950
Mar	28	Virgo
Jun	11	Libra
Aug	10	Scorpio
Sep	25	Sagittarius
Nov	06	Capricorn
Dec	15	Aquarius
		1951
Jan	22	Pisces
Mar	01	Aries
Apr	10	Taurus
May	21	Gemini
Jul	03	Cancer
Aug	18	Leo
Oct	05	Virgo
Nov	24	Libra
		1952
Jan	20	Scorpio
Aug	27	Sagittarius
Oct	12	Capricorn
Nov	21	Aquarius
Dec	30	Pisces
		1953
Feb	08	Aries
Mar	20	Taurus
May	01	Gemini
Jun	14	Cancer
Jul	29	Leo
Sep	14	Virgo
Nov	01	Libra
Dec	20	Scorpio
		1954
Feb	09	Sagittarius
Apr	12	Capricorn

Jul	03	Sagittarius
Aug	24	Capricorn
Oct	21	Aquarius
Dec	04	Pisces
		1955
Jan	15	Aries
Feb	26	Taurus
Apr	10	Gemini
May	26	Cancer
Jul	11	Leo
Aug	27	Virgo
Oct	13	Libra
Nov	29	Scorpio
		1956
Jan	14	Sagittarius
Feb	28	Capricorn
Apr	14	Aquarius
Jun	03	Pisces
Dec	06	Aries
		1957
Jan	28	Taurus
Mar	17	Gemini
May	04	Cancer
Jun	21	Leo
Aug	08	Virgo
Sep	24	Libra
Nov	08	Scorpio
Dec	23	Sagittarius
		1958
Feb	03	Capricorn
Mar	17	Aquarius
Apr	27	Pisces
Jun	07	Aries
Jul	21	Taurus
Sep	21	Gemini
Oct	29	Taurus
		1959
Feb	10	Gemini
Apr	10	Cancer
Jun	01	Leo
Jul	20	Virgo
Sep	05	Libra
Oct	21	Scorpio
Dec	03	Sagittarius
		1960
Jan	14	Capricorn
Feb	23	Aquarius
Apr	02	Pisces
May	11	Aries
Jun	20	Taurus
Aug	02	Gemini
Sep	21	Cancer
		1961
Feb	05	Gemini

Dates Mars enters the signs 1900 - 2000

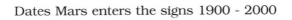

Feb	07	Cancer
May	06	Leo
Jun	28	Virgo
Aug	17	Libra
Oct	01	Scorpio
Nov	13	Sagittarius
Dec	24	Capricorn
1962		
Feb	01	Aquarius
Mar	12	Pisces
Apr	19	Aries
May	28	Taurus
Jul	09	Gemini
Aug	22	Cancer
Oct	11	Leo
1963		
Jun	03	Virgo
Jul	27	Libra
Sep	12	Scorpio
Oct	25	Sagittarius
Dec	05	Capricorn
1964		
Jan	13	Aquarius
Feb	20	Pisces
Mar	29	Aries
May	07	Taurus
Jun	17	Gemini
Jul	30	Cancer
Sep	15	Leo
Nov	06	Virgo
1965		
Jun	29	Libra
Aug	20	Scorpio
Oct	04	Sagittarius
Nov	14	Capricorn
Dec	23	Aquarius
1966		
Jan	30	Pisces
Mar	09	Aries
Apr	17	Taurus
May	28	Gemini
Jul	11	Cancer
Aug	25	Leo
Oct	12	Virgo
Dec	04	Libra
1967		
Feb	12	Scorpio
Mar	31	Libra
Jul	19	Scorpio
Sep	10	Sagittarius
Oct	23	Capricorn
Dec	01	Aquarius

1968		
Jan	09	Pisces
Feb	17	Aries
Mar	27	Taurus
May	08	Gemini
Jun	21	Cancer
Aug	05	Leo
Sep	21	Virgo
Nov	09	Libra
Dec	29	Scorpio
1969		
Feb	25	Sagittarius
Sep	21	Capricorn
Nov	04	Aquarius
Dec	15	Pisces
1970		
Jan	24	Aries
Mar	07	Taurus
Apr	18	Gemini
Jun	02	Cancer
Jul	18	Leo
Sep	03	Virgo
Oct	20	Libra
Dec	06	Scorpio
1971		
Jan	23	Sagittarius
Mar	12	Capricorn
May	03	Aquarius
Nov	06	Pisces
Dec	26	Aries
1972		
Feb	10	Taurus
Mar	27	Gemini
May	12	Cancer
Jun	28	Leo
Aug	15	Virgo
Sep	30	Libra
Nov	15	Scorpio
Dec	30	Sagittarius
1973		
Feb	12	Capricorn
Mar	26	Aquarius
May	08	Pisces
Jun	20	Aries
Aug	12	Taurus
Oct	29	Aries
Dec	24	Taurus
1974		
Feb	27	Gemini
Apr	20	Cancer
Jun	09	Leo
Jul	27	Virgo

Sep	12	Libra
Oct	28	Scorpio
Dec	10	Sagittarius
1975		
Jan	21	Capricorn
Mar	03	Aquarius
Apr	11	Pisces
May	21	Aries
Jul	01	Taurus
Aug	14	Gemini
Oct	17	Cancer
Nov	25	Gemini
1976		
Mar	18	Cancer
May	16	Leo
Jul	06	Virgo
Aug	24	Libra
Oct	08	Scorpio
Nov	20	Sagittarius
1977		
Jan	01	Capricorn
Feb	09	Aquarius
Mar	20	Pisces
Apr	27	Aries
Jun	06	Taurus
Jul	17	Gemini
Sep	01	Cancer
Oct	26	Leo
1978		
Jan	26	Cancer
Apr	10	Leo
Jun	14	Virgo
Aug	04	Libra
Sep	19	Scorpio
Nov	02	Sagittarius
Dec	12	Capricorn
1979		
Jan	20	Aquarius
Feb	27	Pisces
Apr	07	Aries
May	16	Taurus
Jun	26	Gemini
Aug	08	Cancer
Sep	24	Leo
Nov	19	Virgo
1980		
Mar	11	Leo
May	04	Virgo
Jul	10	Libra
Aug	29	Scorpio
Oct	12	Sagittarius
Nov	22	Capricorn
Dec	30	Aquarius

Dates Mars enters the signs 1900 - 2000

1981			**1988**			Jul	03	Gemini
Feb	06	Pisces	Jan	08	Sagittarius	Aug	16	Cancer
Mar	17	Aries	Feb	22	Capricorn	Oct	04	Leo
Apr	25	Taurus	Apr	06	Aquarius	Dec	12	Virgo
Jun	05	Gemini	May	22	Pisces	**1995**		
Jul	18	Cancer	Jul	13	Aries	Jan	22	Leo
Sep	02	Leo	Oct	23	Pisces	May	25	Virgo
Oct	21	Virgo	Nov	01	Aries	Jul	21	Libra
Dec	16	Libra	**1989**			Sep	07	Scorpio
1982			Jan	19	Taurus	Oct	20	Sagittarius
Aug	03	Scorpio	Mar	11	Gemini	Nov	30	Capricorn
Sep	20	Sagittarius	Apr	29	Cancer	**1996**		
Oct	31	Capricorn	Jun	16	Leo	Jan	08	Aquarius
Dec	10	Aquarius	Aug	03	Virgo	Feb	15	Pisces
1983			Sep	19	Libra	Mar	24	Aries
Jan	17	Pisces	Nov	04	Scorpio	May	02	Taurus
Feb	25	Aries	Dec	18	Sagittarius	Jun	12	Gemini
Apr	05	Taurus	**1990**			Jul	25	Cancer
May	16	Gemini	Jan	29	Capricorn	Sep	09	Leo
Jun	29	Cancer	Mar	11	Aquarius	Oct	30	Virgo
Aug	13	Leo	Apr	20	Pisces	**1997**		
Sep	30	Virgo	May	31	Aries	Jan	03	Libra
Nov	18	Libra	Jul	12	Taurus	Mar	08	Virgo
1984			Aug	31	Gemini	Jun	19	Libra
Jan	11	Scorpio	Dec	14	Taurus	Aug	14	Scorpio
Aug	17	Sagittarius	**1991**			Sep	28	Sagittarius
Oct	05	Capricorn	Jan	21	Gemini	Nov	09	Capricorn
Nov	15	Aquarius	Apr	03	Cancer	Dec	18	Aquarius
Dec	25	Pisces	May	26	Leo	**1998**		
1985			Jul	15	Virgo	Jan	25	Pisces
Feb	02	Aries	Sep	01	Libra	Mar	04	Aries
Mar	15	Taurus	Oct	16	Scorpio	Apr	13	Taurus
Apr	26	Gemini	Nov	29	Sagittarius	May	24	Gemini
Jun	09	Cancer	**1992**			Jul	06	Cancer
Jul	25	Leo	Jan	09	Capricorn	Aug	20	Leo
Sep	10	Virgo	Feb	18	Aquarius	Oct	07	Virgo
Oct	27	Libra	Mar	28	Pisces	Nov	27	Libra
Dec	14	Scorpio	May	05	Aries	**1999**		
1986			Jun	14	Taurus	Jan	26	Scorpio
Feb	02	Sagittarius	Jul	26	Gemini	May	05	Libra
Mar	28	Capricorn	Sep	12	Cancer	Jul	05	Scorpio
Oct	09	Aquarius	**1993**			Sep	02	Sagittarius
Nov	26	Pisces	Apr	27	Leo	Oct	17	Capricorn
1987			Jun	23	Virgo	Nov	26	Aquarius
Jan	08	Aries	Aug	12	Libra	**2000**		
Feb	20	Taurus	Sep	27	Scorpio	Jan	04	Pisces
Apr	05	Gemini	Nov	09	Sagittarius	Feb	12	Aries
May	21	Cancer	Dec	20	Capricorn	Mar	23	Taurus
Jul	06	Leo	**1994**			May	03	Gemini
Aug	22	Virgo	Jan	28	Aquarius	Jun	16	Cancer
Oct	08	Libra	Mar	07	Pisces	Aug	01	Leo
Nov	24	Scorpio	Apr	14	Aries	Sep	17	Virgo
			May	23	Taurus	Nov	04	Libra
						Dec	23	Scorpio

GLOSSARY

Air

One of the four elements, air symbolizes alertness, clarity of perception, and intelligence.

Angle

Cusp of the first, fourth, seventh, or tenth houses: either end of the horizon or meridian.

The Arc of Intimacy

Houses five, six, seven, and eight, whose planets and signs represent lessons in falling in love and play (5), responsibility (6), trust and commitment (7) and sexual and psychological intimacy and passion (8).

Ascendant

The eastern horizon or the sign rising there; the first house as a whole.

Ascendantalization

An interaspect made by the Ascendant of one chart to any point on another chart, symbolizing the process of stylization or caricaturization of the affected point.

Aspect

One of several critical geometrical angles formed between planets or between planets and angles.

Aspect Grid

Schematic graph representing all the aspects of a particular birthchart.

Astrological Nadir

See Nadir.

Birthchart

A map of the heavens as seen at the date and time of a person's birth, from the viewpoint of his or her birthplace.

Cardinal

One of the three modes of signs. Active, initiatory, and determinative, the cardinal signs are Aries, Cancer, Libra, and Capricorn.

Composite Chart   A synthetic chart that symbolizes the spirit of a particular human partnership, based on the midpoints of the individual birthcharts.

Conjunction   An aspect characterized by a 0-degree separation between two planets, symbolizing the process of fusion or collision. See Orb.

Culture Shock   A type of composite chart that is very different from either person's birthchart, indicating that they both need to make major adjustments to stay in the relationship.

Cusp   The beginning of a house. Actually a fuzzy zone extending about a degree and a half on either side of the precise beginning of a house.

Democracy   A type of composite chart that contains elements reminiscent of both partners, indicating it should be easy for each to have a voice in the union.

Descendant   The Western horizon, or the sign on it; the seventh house as a whole.

Direct   Normal motion of a planet forward through the signs. See Retrograde; Stationary.

Earth   One of the four elements; earth symbolizes patience, practicality, realism, and stability.

Ecliptic

The apparent path of the Sun, Moon, and planets against the stars; the zodiac.

Element

Fire, earth, air, or water. One of four fundamental psychic processes or orientations of consciousness.

Ephemeris

A book listing the positions of the planets each day at a certain time over a long period.

Feudal System

A type of composite chart that resembles one partner's chart more than the other's, indicating that circumstances seem to grant more "power" to the person whose chart the composite chart resembles.

Fire

One of the four elements; fire symbolizes the development of will.

Fixed

One of the three modes of signs. Stability, strength of purpose, stubbornness. The fixed signs are Taurus, Leo, Scorpio, and Aquarius.

Glyph

Any of the written symbols in astrology, used as a kind of shorthand.

Hemisphere

There are four hemispheres in any birthchart: above and below the local horizon, and east and west of the meridian.

Horizon

The horizontal axis of a birthchart connecting the Ascendant and the Descendant.

House	Any of twelve divisions of space above or below the local horizon; the basic "arenas" or "terrains" of life that the mind enters and experiences.
Interaspect	An aspect made by a planet or point in one person's birthchart to a planet or point in another person's birthchart.
Jovialization	An interaspect made by one person's Jupiter to any point on another's birthchart, symbolizing the uplifting and expansion or the flattering and overextension of the affected point.
Lunarization	An interaspect made by one person's Moon to any point on another person's chart, symbolizing the processes of sensitizing and inspiring or of emotionally upsetting the affected point.
Martialization	An interaspect made by one person's Mars to any point on another's chart. Martialization emboldens, arouses, frightens, or enrages the affected point.
Mercurialization	An interaspect formed by the Mercury of one person to any point on another person's chart, symbolizing the intellectual stimulation or confusion of the affected point.
Meridian	The vertical axis of the birthchart; the line connecting the Midheaven and the Nadir.
Midheaven	The highest zodiacal point above the horizon; the approximate position of the sun at noon; the cusp of the tenth house; the tenth house as a whole.

Minor aspects   Aspects other than the conjunction, sextile, square, trine, and opposition.

Minute of Arc   One sixtieth of a degree, often simply called a minute.

Mode   One of the three expressions of sign energy: cardinal, fixed, and mutable.

Mutable   One of the three modes of signs. Changeable, responsive, flowing, the mutable signs are Gemini, Virgo, Sagittarius, and Pisces.

Nadir   The zodiacal point farthest below the local horizon; the approximate position of the sun at midnight; the cusp of the fourth house or the fourth house as a whole.

Neptunification   An interaspect made by the Neptune of one person to any point on another's chart, symbolizing the inspiration and enchantment, or the dissipation and deception, of the affected point.

Opposition   An aspect characterized by a 180-degree separation between two planets, symbolizing the process of polarization or tension. See Orb.

Orb   The limits of tolerance within which an aspect is considered functional. Variable and subjective, but usually taken to be about seven degrees.

Planet   Any celestial body that moves through the zodiac in a predictable way. Astrologically, the term includes the Sun and Moon.

Plutonification   An interaspect made by one person's Pluto to any point on another's chart, symbolizing the penetration and transpersonalization or the corruption and domination of the affected point.

Primal Triad   The Sun, Moon and Ascendant taken together as the "skeleton" of the individuality.

Progressions   Any of a number of synthetic predictive techniques in which planets are made to move through the birthchart at varying rates.

Retrograde   Planetary condition characterized by an apparent "backward" motion through the sky. See Direct.

Rulership   A particularly strong affinity between a planet and a sign, allowing a clear expression of both.

Saturnization   An interaspect formed by one person's Saturn to any point on another's birthchart, symbolizing the crystallization and confrontation, or frustration and control, of the affected point.

Sextile   An aspect characterized by a 60-degree separation between two planets, symbolizing the process of excitation. See Orb.

Sidereal Time   An astronomically precise time used in setting up birthcharts.

Sign   One of the twelve basic divisions of the zodiac; a phase in the orbital relationship of the earth and the Sun; a fundamental psychological process.

Singleton
Any planet placed alone in a hemisphere.

Solarization
An interaspect made by one person's Sun to any point on another person's chart, symbolizing the process of revitalization or domination of the affected point.

Solstice
The day of the year when the night is longest (the winter solstice) or shortest (the summer solstice).

Square
An aspect characterized by a separation of 90 degrees between two planets, symbolizing the process of friction. See Orb.

Station
A planet is said to be "making a station" when it is stationary.

Stationary
A planet is stationary when it appears to be standing motionless relative to the zodiac, about to turn retrograde or direct.

Stationary Direct
Stationary and about to turn direct.

Stationary Retrograde
Stationary and about to turn retrograde.

Stellium
Any clustering of three or more planets in a single sign or house.

Synastry
The astrology of human relationships. Also, an astrological counseling session during which the principles of synastry are used.

Table of Houses   A book based on complex calculations in spherical trigonometry that shows the location of house cusps at various sidereal times and latitudes.

Transits   The actual, physical motion of the planets through the sky and therefore around the trigger points of the birthchart.

Transpose   To place, artificially, the planets of one person in the houses of another.

Transpositional chart   A birthchart with the transposed planets of another person drawn into or outside of the first person's houses.

Trine   An aspect characterized by a separation of 120 degrees between two planets, symbolizing the process of harmonization. See Orb.

Uranization   An interaspect made by one person's Uranus to any point on another's chart, symbolizing the individualization or disruption of the affected point.

Venusification   An interaspect made by one person's Venus to any point on another person's chart, symbolizing the increased attractiveness or manipulation of the affected point.

Water   One of the four elements; water symbolizes subjectivity, emotion, depth, and the ability to love.

Zodiac   The apparent path of the Sun, Moon, and planets around the earth; the twelve signs.

INDEX

Boldface type indicates major discussions of a topic.